BLOODSTAIN
The vanishing of Peter Falconio

Richard Shears

NEW
HOLLAND

This edition first published in 2005 by New Holland Publishers (UK) Ltd
London • Cape Town • Sydney • Auckland
www.newhollandpublishers.com

Garfield House, 86–88 Edgware Road, London W2 2EA, United Kingdom
80 McKenzie Street Cape Town 8001 South Africa
14 Aquatic Drive Frenchs Forest NSW 2086 Australia
218 Lake Road Northcote Auckland New Zealand

First published in Australia in 2005 by
New Holland Publishers (Australia) Pty Ltd

10 9 8 7 6 5 4 3 2 1

ISBN 1 74110 322 3

Publisher: Fiona Schultz
Editor: Jacqueline Blanchard
Designer: Karl Roper
Production: Linda Bottari
Printed in UK by Athenaeum Press Ltd, Tyne & Wear

Cover photographs: top courtesy of AAP; bottom courtesy of Richard Shears

About the Author

Richard Shears is the Australia-based senior foreign correspondent for London's *Daily Mail* newspaper. The award-winning writer is the author of more than 20 non-fiction books, which include the best-selling *Azaria*, surrounding the mysterious case of Lindy Chamberlain's baby; and *Highway to Nowhere*, a chilling account of the murders by serial killer Ivan Milat.

His other books have covered such varied titles as *The Rainbow Warrior Affair*, which delivered a detailed analysis of the sinking of the Greenpeace ship by French agents; and *Devi The Bandit Queen*, the thrilling story of a rape victim who wrought bloody revenge on her abusers.

Writing for the *Daily Mail*, Shears has covered wars in Ireland, Cyprus, East Timor, Afghanistan and Iraq, and was nominated for awards for his first-person accounts of the rescue of British soldiers trapped on a mountain in Borneo and the race to save lone yachtsman Tony Bullimore.

'The voice of the brother's blood crieth unto me from the ground.'

— *Genesis 4:10*

Contents

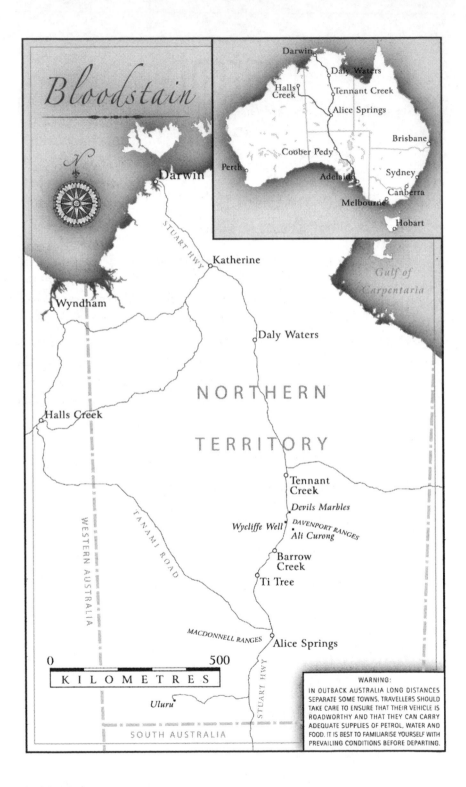

The Stuart Highway linking Adelaide and Darwin is a 3000 kilometre, two-lane stretch of unbroken bitumen. It cuts through the Australian heart, traversing desert that in prehistoric times was a vast inland lake where dinosaurs roamed and the first inhabitants started hunting at least 40 000 years ago. Heading north, the road passes through the town of Coober Pedy, where the temperature is so high—50° Celsius in summer—that people live in houses built underground.

Golden spinifex grass, mulga trees and saltbush line the roadside, sprawling east and west across the parched landscape. Towering anthills and rocky outcrops rise up through the stunted vegetation. There are scorpions, deadly taipan snakes, thick, sticky spiders' webs and, along the edges of the highway, the rotting carcasses of road kill—kangaroos, cattle and dingo. In places the tarred surface is smeared with animal blood, pieces of fur and bone dragged for hundreds of metres by huge road trains, long-distance trucks with up to three trailers that traverse the inland roads. These drivers travel alone, snatching naps in lay-bys and grabbing meals in isolated roadhouses.

And always, the sun beats down relentlessly during the summer months and while there is some seasonal relief from the heat the winter nights are bitterly cold. Whatever the weather, travellers are advised to drive by day, the exception being those road trains that thunder through at night, unable to stop quickly for anything in their way. At night truck drivers have the highway virtually to themselves, radios or CDs switched on for company, the monotony broken by the sometime crackle of the CB radio bursting into life as another driver calls in to break the boredom of his own journey, miles ahead or far behind. For these men there is no-one else to talk to at night.

Yet even these experienced men of the road agree on one thing: the Stuart Highway is not a place to be lost, alone, or in any kind of trouble.

'Crime scenes that involve bloodshed often contain a wealth of information in the form of bloodstains. The pattern, size, shape and the location of such stains may be very useful in the reconstruction of the events that occurred.'

— *Forensic consultants Dr William G Eckert and Stuart James*

Prologue

Bloodstain

Ena Rex sensed rain was on the way, blowing in on the south-easter that was whipping up red dust outside the house. She and the women were sitting cross-legged on the ground playing cards, but she knew they'd have to move inside soon because the cold was biting and the winter sun was no help.

She laid down a card knowing she wasn't going to win this hand. She saw the police four-wheel drive pulling up outside with Gwen Brown at the wheel.

'Come on Ena, get some more clothes on,' the policewoman called. 'You, me, Dudley, Joe, we got to go now. You'd better go to the toilet—long drive.'

Ena stared at the policewoman. Gwen was one of the tribal people but she was also an officer and had a duty to keep the place in order. What does she want me for? Ena wondered. She hadn't done anything wrong. Quiet Sunday afternoon, too. Nothing happening round here.

Doing as she was told, Ena wrapped herself in a blue woollen cardigan and climbed into the police truck. They drove around to Ronald Brown's place. Like all the other houses in the Ali Curung community north of Alice Springs, it was built of breeze blocks, with a concrete verandah and a corrugated iron roof. Gwen had to bang hard on the door to wake Ronald up. There were no studies today for his mechanical engineering course, so he was having a bit of a sleep. He came to the door blinking in the glare of the mid-afternoon winter sun, a tall man wearing a black donkey jacket.

Ronald didn't ask any questions when Gwen told him to get in the truck. He assumed his help was wanted, that was all. He was 44, but he knew the others would all be older and, out of respect, he took one of the rear seats.

Next, Gwen stopped by for old Joe Bird, one of the Warrabri tribal elders. He was wearing his tall grease-stained hat and chopping up a roo carcass for his mob of dogs, who were watching him from the mattresses scattered outside the house. His dogs spent every day snapping at flies and waiting for a feed, watching Joe drink his grog from a white plastic container. He never forgot his dogs, no matter how much grog he drank or who stopped by.

Joe didn't ask any questions either, but he shot Ena a look as he climbed into the police truck. Something big was going on, no doubt about that.

Gwen picked up Gerard Driver next. He was a pretty good tracker, too. He got in the back with Ronald. None of these Aboriginal people was used much by the police these days but the old trackers like Gerard could talk of earlier times when they were called out to look for people missing in the scrub or hunt down stock rustlers. Their tracking skills had been drummed into them from an early age, evolving from an ancient lore, their senses as honed as in their youth.

Finally, after driving around the community for a while, watching out for the dogs and kids who ran out onto the dusty road, and calling out at the houses he might be visiting, Gwen found Dudley Hines. He emerged from the dark interior of a building near a big water tank, jamming his trademark white hat on his head.

'Got youse all at last,' said Gwen, not looking at her passengers as she started down the 30 kilometre straight to the Stuart Highway. Driving into the sun, she pulled the visor down and accelerated to 70 kilometres per hour, which was fast enough on the narrow strip of bitumen.

It wasn't until she had turned south on the highway, away from Wycliff Well where tourists called in at the local store to hear legendary stories of strange lights in the sky and flying saucers, that she told them why they were needed.

'There's a white fella gone missing. He may be shot, but they can't find him. They want us to have a look around.'

Gwen told them that the night before there had been some kind of hold up. The Alice Springs detectives would tell them more when they got there.

Joe Bird was surprised. Long time since he'd worked on a man-hunt, although this sounded more like they were looking for a victim, not a suspect. The Northern Territory Police had been using trackers since the force was established in 1870 but with all the breakthroughs in imaging technology and DNA there hadn't been a great need for bush skills to help break a case. The police nowadays reckoned they could work things out pretty much for themselves. They must be in a bit of a fix now then, he thought.

In the back of the truck, Ronald Brown gazed out at the spinifex grass and saltbush flashing by. The desert stretched east and west for more than 900 kilometres in each direction, the land rising occasionally in ridges and escarpments. Far to the east were the rounded shapes of the MacDonnell Ranges and in the the south were the Davenport Ranges. Only his people could live on their wits without shelter out here where summer temperatures rose to more than 50° Celsius and where the temperature on these winter nights could drop below zero. White fellas who were lost or running away from something bad in their lives had tried to survive out here, but unless they'd grown up in the central Australian wilderness, had a weapon to catch their food and a sense of where water lay, they were usually dead within days. It was the last frontier.

Ronald Brown was thinking ahead. He was remembering what his father George had taught him and the tricks his old man had learned after years with the police in Tennant Creek looking for fugitives and bodies: *you've got to be there first or you're buggered.* He hoped the detectives from Alice Springs realised that.

Gwen accelerated to 140 kilometres per hour, and everyone prayed they weren't going to be confronted with a roo out looking for an early feed or a stray bullock. But it wasn't a surprise she was hurrying. It was already 3.30 pm and they wouldn't have much time before the sun went down.

Dudley Hines was having thoughts of his own. Related to Jimmy Hines, a famous tracker from Ti Tree, Dudley had already noted the sky's deepening blue, the darkening of the bushes as they began to fall into shadow, and wondered why they hadn't all been called out earlier. Didn't make sense to call them at the end of the day.

Joe Bird, as the oldest, was thinking about how they'd do it. Depending on what the coppers told them, they'd probably arrange a single-file line search, walking one behind the other in the same footsteps. This way, if the first in line missed something the second might spot a clue. They would be careful not to kill the ground or stomp out any clues, either. That was the way they'd done it for centuries.

They saw the police cars when they were a good kilometre away, parked on both sides of the long stretch of bitumen, late sunlight catching the vehicles' chrome. The usual stream of tourist traffic, never heavy anyway, was thinning as the day wore on.

'You people wait here,' said Gwen, pulling to a stop and jumping out of the vehicle to talk to one of the plain-clothes officers. The trackers sitting in the van peered out at the scene. They watched the policemen, several in blue coveralls, trudging haphazardly through the grass and pushing little markers into the earth. The Aborigines didn't have to say anything to know what each other was thinking: this didn't look good at all. The coppers were stomping over everything.

Gwen beckoned the group out of the vehicle and they listened as one of the officers pointed into the roadside scrub. 'The woman was in those bushes over there,' he said. 'We've found a couple of her bootprints. And here's the blood.'

They walked a few metres along the road to be shown a dark patch of blood on the roadside. At its widest point it stretched for half a metre and appeared to have run from the bitumen towards the edge of the road, dribbling over the white line that divided the hard surface from the loose gravel. It looked like someone had flung a heap of dirt over it.

Ronald concentrated on the bloodstain for a long time. He couldn't put his finger on it but something wasn't right. Then Gwen distracted him.

'We've got to find the man. That fellow that's missing, they think this is his blood. But he's not anywhere around here. They've looked through the grass and the bush and they can't find him.'

Old Joe was staring at the bush, age-weary but sharp-eyed. He scanned the winter grass, so dry and white, thirsty for the big rains that he knew were months away. Joe Bird could just look at a landscape and sense what was out of place. Some who had seen him and other trackers at work had even said it was a paranormal gift. Without seeing an animal or any of its tracks, Joe could say if a roo was resting a mile away. That was a gift all right, they all agreed.

'They want to show us the kombi they were travelling in,' said Gwen. 'They found it in the bush up the road. If you see anything, report it to me. Report everything to me.'

Some 300 metres back up the highway someone had parked an orange and white Volkswagen kombivan 30 metres off the main road on a faint track. If you looked hard enough, it could be seen from the road. Yellow police tape with bold black letters reading 'Crime Scene Do Not Enter' had been draped around some trees, protecting the site and any clues it might yield.

'The woman's okay now,' Gwen said 'but they don't know what's happened to the fella, if he's dead or injured or what. They reckon it was a hold up. They don't know if he's here somewhere or if he's been taken away. There's only the woman left.'

The policewoman told them she had been asked to go up shortly in a chopper. The police wanted her to look for clues from the air in case the missing man was lying somewhere a few kilometres out. The trackers split up, remaining silent over their disappointment about the contamination of the scene. Ronald could see where the shoes and boots of the policemen had trodden everywhere. Still, he'd do his best. Get a look at their shoes, find out where they had walked, and look for anything foreign. Work it out as best he could.

The aboriginals knew exactly what to do—remain keen-eyed, patient and logical. Let the earth and the trees speak to you. Ronald dropped to his hands and knees on the faint track leading to the kombi, looking for the Volkswagen's tyre marks. In places its tread would have to be well defined; in other parts it would be almost indistinguishable due to the ground's winter hardness. He could see where the VW had been driven by the way the kombi had rolled over the grass. Grass was always bent in the direction of travel and stones were pressed deeper into the ground.

He knew that everything around him should be able to tell him which way the driver had walked after leaving the vehicle. Blades of grass, perhaps a crushed ant or a leaf could yield a clue. A good bush tracker could even find signs from the activities of insects that were busy by day and those that came out at night.

Ronald's eyes were also scanning the ground for something more obvious—like a footprint.

It didn't take long. Within minutes he found a clue. Across one of the wheel tracks he discovered two tiny furrows. Some time after the van had been driven into the scrub a bush cockroach, active after dark, had scuttled across the imprint of tyre marks. But this only confirmed what he had already been told—the vehicle had been driven there the night before.

His father had taught him that a blade pushed over at dawn will be almost upright again by dusk, but there will almost always be a tell-tale crease near its base. If he found the grass standing with that crease at the base he would know that someone had walked by here many hours ago. But what he found was chaos. The policemen's boots had trampled over the grass in all directions.

You've got to be there first.

Around the parked kombi the ground was too hard to find any shoe imprints. Whoever had left the vehicle parked in this position and walked away had kept clear of the softer earth, which defined the track.

Ronald called to one of the officers, although he wasn't supposed to be dealing directly with them. He wanted to know if any of the missing man's blood was in or on the Volkswagen. No, none that they had been able to find. He considered it unlikely then, that he'd find any blood in the grass. But it was worth a look. He'd need only a few specks and that would be the start of a trail that could lead to the missing man—alive or dead.

Exasperated, Ronald found nothing; no blood in the red earth, no stains on any of the undergrowth, although it might have been rubbed out by the searchers who had tramped around earlier that day. He knew that Dudley, Old Joe and the others, scouring the ground on the highway, would be working just like him, dissecting every small detail and checking boot marks so they could eliminate evidence left by the police. They would all be listening, too, for a tell-tale hum—the flies that always swarmed around a carcass within hours of death. He looked up. If there *was* a body anywhere around here birds of prey would be circling too. But there were no eagles or crows. It seemed to Ronald that the missing man wasn't anywhere around this area.

Time was running out. The shadows were lengthening and the sky was turning pink as the sun dropped towards the horizon. He could see the clouds starting to gather. The helicopter ferrying Gwen suddenly roared into sight. It hovered over Ronald for a moment before flying east.

He joined the others near the roadside blood. Ena was shivering, arms wrapped across her chest. 'We can't find him,' she said. 'The police have been everywhere and messed up any tracks. They said it had to be done, that they had to walk all around looking for the man. They called us in too late.'

The police told Ena that the man and woman from the kombi had been attacked by a stranger who had a dog. The girl had escaped and the stranger had come looking for her with the dog but he hadn't found her in the dark. Ena was good with animals. So was old Joe. But they couldn't smell dog anywhere. No droppings, no stink of urine, no pawprints; but the coppers would have walked over them anyway.

Ronald thought again about the blood. There were no splashes near that large bloodstain to suggest that someone who had been shot had stumbled or been dragged away. There were a few tiny spots of blood on the small roadside stones, but it looked to him as if they had dropped from a shovel or something similar that had been used to scoop up gravel to cover the bigger pool. There should have been more signs that an injured or dead man had tried to move. Or been moved.

Old Joe ambled over. It was getting colder and like Ena, he was shivering. 'Can't find anybody's tracks,' he said. 'They want us to find if this other fella who shot him left footprints but we can't find anything.'

Each tracker had thoroughly investigated the road's edge, their keen eyes seeking out a tyre track or any other clue that might have shown what had happened the night before. They could find nothing, apart from the police footprints leading chaotically in all directions. And the footprint of a woman, which the police had identified earlier as belonging to the survivor.

A police officer led Ronald across to where the woman had said she had hidden from her attacker. The police had tramped all over this area, too. He looked for the place where the victim was supposed to have flattened herself under a bush to hide.

'Are you sure this is where she was?' he asked the officer.

'As sure as we can be,' the detective responded.

The tracker pursed his lips and rolled his head from side to side. There must be something wrong, he thought. They've shown me the wrong place. She couldn't have been here.

'This grass hasn't been disturbed', he told the detective.

The detective just stared at him.

X

It was dark when the trackers were dropped back at the Ali Curung community. Dogs howled and barked as Gwen stopped outside Ena's place. Ena had been enjoying the warmth inside the truck and the cold hit her as she stepped out. A few drops of rain fell on her face. 'Knew this was coming,' she said to Gwen.

The policewoman dropped off Ronald last. 'We couldn't help much,' he said. 'We knew as soon as we saw it down there that they'd messed it up. They'd walked all over the place.'

'That's okay,' said Gwen. 'They thought the fellow who was shot might be lying out there somewhere and they ran about everywhere. You can't blame them for that. I've got to put a report into the Super anyway. They might need you to give evidence,' she told him. 'Depends how this turns out.'

Ronald Brown walked across the courtyard, his giant frame just visible in the dark. He was tired and cold. It had been a strange day and he wondered what it had really accomplished. Could he have done more?

And then it hit him. *The blood.* He had never come across anything like it in all his years of hunting and shooting. For days after a kill, whether it was summer or winter, blood on the ground like that always attracted the ants. Swarms of them. There were no ants on the roadside today. Covered in earth or not, there should have been ants all over it. Now why was that?

Chapter 1

Out of the night

'Jesus Christ!' Vince Millar jammed his foot on the brake pedal and hauled on the wheel. With a hiss of brakes and burning rubber, the huge truck veered across the road.

'What the fuck?' growled Rod Adams, suddenly jolting awake in the passenger seat. He blinked sleepily through the windscreen. The road train's headlights pierced the darkness of the highway, adding an eerie whiteness to the roadside scrub. It was 1.45 am, in the early hours of Sunday 15 July 2001.

His mate, who always drove barefoot, was scrabbling around the cab looking for his thongs, the nightmare vision of seconds before flashing through his mind. Vince Millar was used to the long haul from Darwin to Adelaide, a monotonous two-day journey. He knew exactly what to do when a roo bounded across the truck's path—you just kept going. The five-tonne road train had reinforced bullbars and experience had taught him that when you were driving at 120 kilometres per hour you were always going to win. There would be no hope of stopping in time anyway—any attempt to swing the ass of the truck around and you'd be in God's or the Devil's hands. But this time ... Oh Jesus!

A figure had burst out of the night, out of the trees—a woman. It was just a flash—a vision, hands held up high, as if praying. Then, as the truck thundered by, she'd vanished.

Vince jumped down from the cab, fumbling nervously to switch on his torch. He didn't even notice the cold. He was more concerned about the horrible mess he might find under one of the three trailers. He was dead certain she'd gone under the truck.

Or had he imagined the whole bloody thing? In the dead of night you often saw shapes moving across the landscape. He knew that it was always his imagination playing tricks. All the drivers spoke of them—spooks that danced around the desert.

He hoped to God she'd seen how long his rig was—40 metres. If she thought it was a single truck that had no trailers, and had kept running out into the road, well, there wouldn't be much of her left.

Millar's breath steamed into the torch beam as he hunched over and searched under the first trailer. As he flashed the light around he could feel the heat of the tyres next to his face. She'd be mangled if she was under there.

Nothing.

He moved to the second trailer, again sweeping the beam around the far wheels and along the axles.

Nothing.

Then, above the sound of the engine he heard a shriek. It turned the hair on his neck.

'Help! Help me, please!'

It was dark, a quarter moon shedding only a weak light across the land-scape, but in the trailer's parking lights he could make her out as she came running along the road. A dark-haired woman in a light coloured T-shirt. She didn't stop running until she came right into his arms and almost knocked the torch from his hand.

There was black stuff around her neck, like tape, and her wrists were tied together. Adams stuck his head out of the window.

'You all right back there, Vince? What the fuck's going on?'

'We got some sheila out here all bloody tied up,' Millar called back. 'Want to come and give us a hand?'

The woman was distraught. 'Thank you, thank you for stopping,' she cried.

Millar now saw that the black tape that was around the lower part of her mouth was also around her throat.

'We were held up,' she cried. 'My boyfriend's missing. Please, please, we've got to look for him. I can't find him. I can't find my car.'

Jumping from the cab, Adams, a trained paramedic, recognised what an emotional mess she was in. She was almost hysterical. A physical mess, too, with all that tape around her neck and hands. Maybe she'd been raped. These things happened out here in the middle of nowhere. The truckies helped her into the cab and Adams used a knife to cut away the tape. Then he used a pair of wire cutters to snip through what he saw were plastic zip ties binding her wrists. The ties had been shaped into a crude pair of handcuffs and tied so tight that they were biting into her flesh.

As soon as she was free, the woman dropped her head onto Adams' shoulder, trembling. 'Please don't leave me. Please let me stay with you.' She started sobbing and cried out, 'I want my mum. I want my mum.' Adams, who had left his own family behind years ago to hit the highways of Australia, was suddenly overcome with emotion. He wanted to cry with her. Then she composed herself.

'Please, we've got to find Pete! I think he's been hurt.' She started rambling about how she and her boyfriend had been held up and he had now disappeared.

'Don't worry, we'll find him,' said Millar, hearing the nervousness in his own voice. He still wasn't sure what had happened.

The two men unhooked the trailers and turned the cab around to search the area where the woman said she and her boyfriend had been attacked. There was no other traffic around, which wasn't unusual for the Stuart Highway at close to 2 am.

They drove back a few hundred metres. Slowly. The woman was drawing in deep breaths, peering out through the windscreen, staring hard through the side windows. There was no sign of anyone out there at all.

In the strong headlights, a dark patch at the side of the road was clearly visible. It was about where she said she and her boyfriend had stopped their Volkswagen. But where was the Volkswagen, Millar wondered?

All three jumped out of the cab. Once on the road the two men could see what the dark patch was—a thin scattering of dirt.

'He came up beside us,' the woman said. 'He indicated there was something wrong with our exhaust. He said there were sparks coming out. Pete got out and then I heard a bang. Then this man was pointing a gun at my head.'

At the mention of a gun, the truckies froze.

'He tied me up, then dragged me into his car,' she went on. 'I managed to get away. But I think Pete's been shot. I heard the bang.'

The men stared at each other.

'What the bloody hell are we doing driving around the bush looking for a man with a gun?' cried Millar.

He turned to the woman. 'Sorry love, but we're going. The police will find your bloke.'

The men knew they weren't far from the small hotel at Barrow Creek, just five or ten minutes down the road. They'd wake them up and get help from there. After hitching the trailers on, they headed down the highway. Despite the warmth of the cab, the woman was trembling uncontrollably, repeating that she was worried about Pete and that he must be back there somewhere.

Any concerns the truckies had that the Barrow Creek Hotel would be in darkness were soon dispelled. There were cars, four-wheel drives and trucks outside, all the lights were on and they could hear music. It sounded like a party was in full swing.

Millar and Adams helped their distraught passenger into the small bar, where a group of drinkers turned to stare in astonishment at the bruised and bloodied woman dressed in just a pale green T-shirt, shorts and walking boots on a bitter night like this. They were holding an 'upside down' New Year's Eve party to celebrate the middle of winter and this was the last thing they expected. The barmaid went to get the owners.

Publican Helen Jones, who ran the hotel with her partner Les Pilton, had already gone to bed. She threw some clothes on and came out to the bar where the woman had been given a stool in front of an electric fire. Someone had already made the woman a cup of tea.

She was still shaking, her face streaked with dirt and tears. Adams was bathing the scratches on her knees and elbows, dressing them with ointment from the rig's medical chest. Millar returned from using the phone, cursing the police in Alice Springs who had hung up on him. 'I can't believe this. They think I'm a hoax caller. I'm going to try them again and they'd better listen this time.'

Helen Jones sat beside the young woman and asked her what happened. She listened as the woman said her name was Joanne Lees. She was from the UK. Helen, originally from Ireland, could pick the woman's north country accent. She was on a backpacking holiday with her boyfriend, Peter Falconio, and they'd been driving north from Alice Springs. A stranger had caught up with their kombivan. He had gestured that something was wrong with the back of their Volkswagen. Pete had not wanted to stop but then decided to pull over.

It was not easy to follow Joanne Lees' story—it was broken by despairing weeping about what might have happened to her boyfriend. She continued to say how much she missed her parents and her brother.

Les Pilton, whose 75-year-old pub was known to locals as the Pilton Hilton, joined the group of people standing around the Englishwoman. He was finding this hard to take in. He had a reputation for being quite the raconteur, regaling his customers with all manner of tales, spiced with humour. He often repeated the story of Tommy Roberts, the so-called Mayor of Barrow Creek, who dropped by in 1952, saying he was just 'passing through', but stayed on for 34 years, his ashes now lying behind a stone at the Telegraph Station. Yes, Les could tell all kinds of stories about characters like that, but he had a feeling that nothing was going to match the events that were being played out this night.

X

Millar had another go at calling the police in Alice Springs with more success. Sergeant Geoff Sullivan came on the line. 'Listen, mate, there's this girl here at Barrow Creek, her boyfriend's been shot, she thinks, and there's a gunman on the loose,' said Millar. 'You better get up here,' he added.

'This sounds pretty bizarre to me,' said Sullivan. 'Is this fair dinkum?'

'Mate,' the truck driver replied, 'this is as true as it gets.'

Sullivan hesitated, testing the words in his mind before announcing 'We're on the way.' He grabbed his service revolver and drew a pump-action shotgun from the locked cupboard. If there was a gunman on the loose he wasn't taking any chances. Then, with two other officers, he jumped into a pursuit car and sped up the highway.

Helen and Les suggested to Joanne she should lie down for a while. She reluctantly accepted the offer, but half an hour later, wrapped in a blanket, she was up again and pacing the bar, which had now emptied. As they waited for the police to arrive, the couple were able to piece together the Englishwoman's ordeal.

Although it was dark, she had been able to see into the cab of the vehicle that had drawn up beside them because the driver had switched the interior light on. She had urged Falconio not to stop but her boyfriend decided to pull over. The stranger's white van pulled in behind them and moments after Falconio got out she could hear the two of them talking at the rear of the Volkswagen. Then Falconio came to the side door and asked her to slide into the driver's seat and rev the engine so he could check the exhaust. As she was doing this she heard a bang. She supposed it was a backfire—but then the stranger had appeared at the door, a man with a big moustache, long dark hair, and wearing a baseball cap. He had a revolver, which he pushed into her face as he flung the door open.

As he tried to tie her hands behind her back, she struggled with him, kicking out and scratching, but he managed to get a sack over her head and bind her wrists. He tried to tie her feet with tape but he wasn't successful. As she continued to struggle, he dragged her into the front of his vehicle, and that was when the sack came off her head. She found herself in the front seat of the gunman's vehicle, a red-haired dog beside her. The stranger slammed the door on her and wandered away into the darkness.

While Helen and Les listened, Joanne told how she managed to scramble over the front seats and into the back tray of the man's ute. She rolled and crawled through the interior before dropping out the back of the tray and onto the road. Then, although there was tape loosely bound around her ankles, she managed to stumble into the roadside bushes, fearing the stranger would chase after her as she made her escape. She crashed to the ground in a clump of bushes and lay there in terror, hearing the sound of her heart pounding.

A few moments later she heard him looking for her. In the glow of a torch he carried, she could see his dog sniffing around. The man came so close to her at times she was terrified he would hear the thumping of her heart. She didn't know how long he looked, but she heard vehicles coming and going. She was unable to tell if he had driven off or not.

Helen and Pilton listened in silence as she relayed her ordeal, the bar clock indicating the lateness of the hour. Joanne told them that finally, after what seemed like an eternity, she decided to take a chance on raising the alarm when she heard a juggernaut coming down the highway. She knew it couldn't be the gunman's smaller vehicle.

'Oh God!' she suddenly cried, putting her hands to her face as she recalled the incident. 'This might be the last time I'll ever see Pete alive.'

Helen put her arms around the weeping woman and comforted her as best she could. She and Pilton realised that what they had heard was about as much as she was going to be able to tell them—especially as Sergeant Sullivan had just arrived with his colleagues. More detectives and other uniformed police were on the way, the officer announced. It was now close to 4 am, nearly two hours after Millar and Adams had picked up Joanne from the highway and some eight hours since Joanne Lees has last seen her boyfriend, Pete, alive.

Sullivan and his colleagues questioned Joanne Lees for two hours, asking her to go over her terrifying story. Armed police, meanwhile, were being called in from Alice Springs to set up roadblocks. They were asked to target anyone with a white ute. Not that they expected to find many vehicles out on the road at this time of night, but they needed to seal off all routes in any case.

'Go over it one more time,' Sergeant Sullivan requested. 'Describe this fellow.' She said she would never forget his face. This time, Joanne described him in more detail. She said he had a Mexican-style moustache, dark, shoulder-length hair, and he wore a black baseball cap with some kind of motif on the front. He was driving a white ute—some kind of four-wheel drive—she guessed, with a canvas cover over the back. He spoke with an Australian accent.

Dawn was breaking as she tried to recall other details of the vehicle. Suddenly, one of the police officers ran into the back room where she was relaying her story. 'There's a bloke looking like that who's just pulled up outside for fuel,' he said excitedly. 'Same description, same van. It's got to be him!'

The other officers stared at one another in astonishment. Could they really be that lucky?

Chapter 2

Suspects

Chris Malouf had nowhere he could really call home. A broken marriage, his kids off somewhere with his ex-wife, he'd been travelling through the outback for years, picking up work wherever he could.

Malouf was a carpenter by trade, but any kind of job would do him. He slept where he stopped, in camp sites, at the roadside and sometimes in men's shelters. In his mid-40s, he was a drifter, his white Toyota four-wheel drive ute taking him to sheep and cattle stations, to towns where leathery-faced men drank heavily into the night and where Aboriginal people sat on street corners watching the trucks roll through. He earned enough casual pay for fuel and tucker to take him to the next town or farm.

He'd travelled up from South Australia and was heading for Katherine and then Broome, on the north-coast of Western Australia, where he intended to do a spot of fishing. He drove into Alice Springs on the morning of Saturday 14 July 2001 and decided to spend that night further north of town.

When Chris Malouf drove into the Barrow Creek Hotel at first light the following morning for fuel, he suddenly found himself surrounded by police with guns trained on him. They grabbed his arms and cuffed him.

'Hey, what's going on?' he yelled. 'What have I done?'

Then he saw a woman being led out of the bar. A dark-haired woman with her eyes closed tight.

'Okay Joanne,' he heard one of the officers say to her. 'Do it. Feel his head first.'

With her eyes still shut, she ran her hands over Malouf's hair and down over his face, feeling his shoulders and his clothes. Malouf was terrified. What the hell was going on? Then the police took her to his van. She was asked to run her hands over the front seats and around the interior of the cab. His whole world was in there. *Shit.*

After feeling around the back of the vehicle, where he had tools, a bed roll, sleeping bag, a dog leash, old newspapers and a collection of bits and pieces that an odds-and-ends man like him thought might be useful for something sometime, she was led back inside. Her eyes were still shut.

They kept Malouf waiting for 15 minutes or so before unlocking his handcuffs and telling him he could go. As he filled up with fuel, his hands shaking from the ordeal, he asked what all that had been about. The best he could find out was that the girl had been held up at gunpoint during the night and the police were still looking for the assailant—and Chris Malouf answered the man's description. Her head had been covered for a time as she'd struggled with him, so they'd asked her to 'feel him out' with her eyes shut. There could be features she might recognise more by feel than sight, such as his long hair.

'Well, it wasn't me,' Malouf stressed. 'I made camp back down the road and I've just got up.' He started the motor and hit the highway, heading north. All he wanted to do was be left alone anyway.

Inside the hotel Joanne told Helen and Les that she should call her mother, Jennifer, and stepfather, Vincent James, in England. She also wanted to ring the Falconio family. Although she could not have guessed the extent of publicity her ordeal was about to generate, she did not want either family to hear about Peter Falconio's disappearance from the media first. But before she was allowed to make any calls, the police asked her to go over her account once again. And they wanted her to hand over her clothes.

She gave them her light-green coloured top with the stick-on slogan 'Try Hugs not Drugs', and her shorts, so the garments could be examined for

DNA. It was possible her attacker had left some trace as he struggled with her. Helen Jones loaned her a T-shirt and trousers, and after a shower she felt refreshed enough to continue answering questions. The police interviews took up the entire day and Joanne never made the call to warn her family or Pete's about what had happened.

X

Out on the highway, as the outback slowly woke up, traffic was being stopped and the drivers and passengers carefully checked before being allowed to move on. Armed police watched the proceedings as each vehicle was examined. But the greatest amount of activity was taking place around the area where the patch of dirt lay. For under it, detectives and forensic officers were quite sure, was blood. No-one would bet against it not being human, and it would only be a matter of time before it could be ascertained if it was Peter Falconio's.

As the sun rose higher, its rays struck something white among the pale green leaves of the mulga trees, just north of where Joanne had said the incident had taken place, 30 metres from the highway. Nature had uncovered the couple's Volkswagen.

Police carried out a quick search in case Falconio was lying injured or dead in the vehicle or nearby, then finding nothing, sealed off the surrounding area to prevent further contamination of the scene. But much of the damage had now already been done when they trampled through the undergrowth in their search for the missing Englishman.

By mid-afternoon, as the Aboriginal trackers in the Ali Curung community were being picked up by their local police officer to help with the investigation, news of the attack was spreading around the world. Early media reports spoke of a 'mad gunman' who was believed to have shot dead an English tourist and who was on the run in the outback, as heavily armed police hunted him throughout the Northern Territory. To add to the enormous media interest, Falconio's 'beautiful, raven-haired girlfriend', whose name had not yet been publicly revealed, had heard the roar of the gun that had killed her boyfriend but had managed to escape from her attacker. It was a story all right.

Police Commander Bob Fields, a sandy-haired veteran of 30 years in outback posts, asked motorists to be on their guard but also to keep their eyes out for the gunman. Further interviews with Joanne were giving them a more refined description of her attacker: he was between 40 and 45 years of age with dark, straight hair that was streaked with grey and fell down to the shoulders. He had a long, thin face, a droopy grey moustache with corners tapering down below his mouth and he had heavy bags under his eyes. He was of medium build, had a deep voice and an Australian accent. He was travelling with a red heeler dog.

The man's ute, according to the description given by Joanne, was a white four-wheel drive with bucket seats. It had a tray on the back with a canvas-covered roof and sides, and a clear open space at its rear. Joanne did not recall any obstacles in her way as she struggled towards the back exit to make her getaway.

'Do not approach him,' Commander Fields warned the public, using words that spread panic among tourists. 'He is armed and dangerous. Delay your trips. Don't travel at night. The fact that someone armed and dangerous is out there is of great concern to us and it should also be of great concern to the public.'

Throughout Sunday 15 July police reinforcements grew. Every available officer was called in. Leave for days ahead was cancelled. Wearing flak jackets and armed with sophisticated weapons, uniformed police officers and members of the crack Territory Response Group spread out at key points along the highway. Police were stopping cars as far north as Katherine, 1600 kilometres away, and at Kulgera, 320 kilometres distant on the South Australian border. Roadblocks were also set up in the east at Avon Downs, 645 kilometres away near the Queensland border. South of Katherine police were on guard at Top Springs. It was a vast area and there were thousands of places a fugitive could hide. Police knew that if the gunman had bush skills he would be even harder to find.

In the hope that the attacker's vehicle would be seen from the air, perhaps hidden between boulders or in shrubbery not visible from any track, police flew across hundreds of kilometres in eight separate aircraft. The authorities believed he had to be out there somewhere—unless he was in a cave or had cleverly concealed his vehicle under shrubbery, he would surely be found.

X

Chris Malouf was stopped by police at gunpoint five more times as he travelled north toward Katherine. Travellers stared at him. Desperately he scrawled a message in the dust on the side of his vehicle—*It wasn't me.* But still the police stopped him and the whispers continued. When he reached the town of Katherine he decided enough was enough and dropped in to see lawyers in the Northern Territory legal aid office to ask for their protection from police harassment.

Rumours were spreading faster than the police could move. The Volkswagen, it was being said around Alice Springs, was spattered with blood. A spent cartridge had been found. Police had found footprints and soon they would have a profile of the killer; an arrest was imminent. In fact, the only truth to the rumours was that they had found footprints in the bush. Just two—and they were both from Joanne's boots.

By mid-afternoon on Sunday, media inquiries were pouring into the Alice Springs police station and it was Commander Fields who took on the task of fending them off. 'Forensic tests are continuing,' he announced. 'We hope to have more information soon.'

As for the welfare of Peter Falconio, he was less optimistic. 'My fear is that some terrible fate has befallen him,' he said. 'I don't want to sound callous but all indications seem to show that something terrible happened to him.' Fields could confidently say that now. Early tests had confirmed that it was human blood under the dirt on the roadside.

Had Falconio's girlfriend been raped? Journalists wanted to know. Was Joanne Lees robbed? Had the English couple upset someone? Could it have been a revenge attack?

'There is no motive to this crime yet,' said Fields, answering yet another call. 'But I'm firmly convinced no action on the part of either of these victims caused this incident. We are on the horns of a dilemma. We are also very concerned about the safety of the public.'

Commander Fields thought of his colleague, Sergeant Glen Huitson, who was shot dead two years earlier by a lone gunman at a roadblock near Darwin. He realised just how vulnerable people could be on a major route like the Stuart Highway, cutting as it did through vast areas of wilderness. He knew he had to assume the gunman was capable of anything. Every word the police officer uttered carried a dire warning.

'We must look at this in the worst possible light,' he said. 'A person who has committed acts like those we are dealing with now may have no compunction in committing a similar act if the opportunity presented itself.'

After the first day of questioning Joanne Lees was exhausted. The police had wanted to know every fine detail. Where she and Falconio had travelled, who they had met, where they had stopped for the night. Throughout the questioning, Helen Jones remained at her side, bringing her tea and sandwiches, comforting her again and again whenever she broke down.

'You are so kind, Helen,' said Joanne during a break away from the police. 'You won't leave me, will you? Please, just stay with me.'

Commander Fields studied the reports that were coming from his detectives. He was filled with admiration. What that woman had endured would have certainly tested him. How she had gotten out of her predicament was beyond him. Her escape, he considered, was ... well, it was almost miraculous. How the gunman, with his red heeler dog, as she had described it, had failed to find her he didn't know. Perhaps he'd never know the answer to that. It was 11.30 pm before Joanne was finally permitted to retire to one of the pub's guestrooms. There had been no news of her boyfriend.

X

But news of Joanne's ordeal was beginning to spread rapidly around Australia. As the Australian and South East Asian correspondent for London's *Daily Mail*, my ears pricked up when I heard the first radio reports from my home in Sydney. Stories involving British people were always of interest to my newspaper and this was beginning to look like the kind of tale that would catch the eye of readers fascinated by Australia's wide outback and the dangers many perceived it to hold. Details were scant, however. An un-named British woman had escaped from an attacker on a lonely road and her boyfriend was missing. By that Sunday evening I had enough details from police, local journalists and photographers to write a dramatic story of the woman's ordeal—and I prepared to fly to Alice Springs to hear the full version from the lips of the heroine tourist, as she was already being described.

Chapter 3
Looking for clues

On Monday 16 July it was raining—a rare event in central Australia in July. It wasn't going to help the search for clues at the scene. At 8 am, Joanne was ready to be taken the 280 kilometres to Alice Springs but the questions were far from over.

For another woman who arrived in Alice Springs later that day the questions were just beginning. Carmen Eckhoff, a stocky blonde woman, was the Northern Territory's leading forensic scientist, working from a floor based in the old police headquarters building in Darwin. Over the 14 years she had been attached to the police force she had carried out thousands of analyses involving DNA profiles and blood splash examinations. She had given evidence in courts in Western Australia, Queensland and the Northern Territory. Now she was being warned by police in Alice Springs that the Falconio disappearance was a baffling case because initial examinations of the scene and the British couple's kombi had provided no clues.

On her arrival in the popular tourist town, Eckhoff was given a briefing, although she had learned something of the incident from the media. She was taken to the crime scene examination unit at the rear of Alice Springs police headquarters where the Volkswagen had by now been brought.

Sergeant Neil Hayes, a fingerprint expert, was already working on the vehicle and she waited while he completed his dusting. Then Alice Springs crime scene investigator Ian Spilsbury, who had already taken fingerprint samples from Joanne and the truck drivers who picked her up, showed Eckhoff areas of the van that might have blood smears—the rear bumper, the tow bar and the front wheel arch on the driver's side. She opened her kit and brought out a container of orthotolidine, a solution that shows up the presence of blood—human or animal.

The stains on the van were indeed blood. But it wasn't human, possibly blood from road kill that had splashed up onto the van at an earlier time. Dressed in gloves and a gown to guard against leaving any trace of her own presence, Eckhoff examined the inside of the vehicle. It was clean and tidy and nothing appeared to be out of place. Sergeant Hayes and Senior Constable Bill Towers made a photographic and video record as she carried out her examination.

Inside the kombi the detectives found the normal items that might be found in a backpacker van, including photographs of the couple taken at various places during their travels. Smiling, they peered out through the rear of the van in a photo taken by a friend. Another photograph showed them sitting together on the top of Uluru (Ayers Rock) and there was also a photo of them grinning at the camera in what looked like a pub. In the van were cameras, keys, compact discs, and a plastic bag containing sewing materials. Attached to the front shelf was a bulldog clip holding petrol receipts. In a front shelf the scientist found something that would be useful—Falconio's Ventolin asthma spray. Eckhoff would be able to get a control sample of his DNA, enabling her to eliminate him from whatever samples could be gleaned from the van and its contents, Miss Lees' clothing and the crime scene at Barrow Creek. Just to be sure, she also took swabs from soft drink cans and bottles found in the Volkswagen.

A few hours later, Eckhoff travelled north to Barrow Creek with Sergeant Hayes and Senior Constable Towers. It was 10.30 pm and the night was wet and bitterly cold. The scientist wished she'd brought warmer, more protective clothing with her, but as far as testing the area for blood was concerned this work was best done in darkness. Once again she prepared a luminol solution, aware that if there was a reaction in the area that she sprayed it would glow a luminous blue colour in the dark—it might still not be blood: metal products and bleach would also produce a result.

Ignoring the biting cold and the rain, Eckhoff aimed the luminol spray at the dark patch at the roadside. Almost immediately, blue light glowed like tiny stars through the soil, confirming what initial tests had shown, that the scattered soil was covering blood. Eckhoff then sprayed around areas at the roadside near the stain that the police had designated with markers in case there had been any spattering. There was a glow on some small stones, but she and the other officers decided these had been scattered about when the soil had been shovelled up from the roadside to cover the bloodstain. There was no other tell-tale glow. Blood had certainly been spilled at the roadside in that large pool and there were those explainable spots on the stones, but there was not a drop to be found anywhere else.

Finding a spatter or a spray of blood near the main pool would have indicated to Eckhoff that a gun had been used, or it could suggest that a body had been moved after the initial flow of blood. There was so much that could be learned from a bloodstain—the position of a body when the blood flowed, any movements after bloodshed, the type of weapon used, the point of impact, perhaps the direction the impact came from.

Spots of blood around the stain on the highway at Barrow Creek could suggest spattering at the time a bullet entered Falconio's body, or might indicate he had been moved even if the main flow of blood from his body had stopped. Forensic scientists will often argue over aspects of particular cases, but ballistic experts tend to agree that if someone is hit by a bullet— referred to as an HVIS, or high velocity impact spatter—there will be specks of blood around the main flow. And if someone is moved shortly after being shot there is usually a dripping pattern made by specks dropping onto the main pool.

There was nothing like that around the area that Eckhoff examined, though; nothing at all. Just that one patch of blood on the bitumen and the run-off towards the gravel at the roadside.

Long-serving homicide officers will tell you that crime scenes where blood is spilled are always messy; there's always a speck, a drop, a splash, somewhere away from the place of impact where weapon or bullet hit flesh and blood. But no matter how carefully Eckhoff searched, her equipment showed up nothing aside from the main bloodstain. No signs that someone was injured and tried to get help, no signs that someone had tried to move a dead body. It was not her job, however, to ask how a murderer had been able to pick up his victim so cleanly and vanish into the darkness with him.

Arc lights and torches illuminated the blackness of the outback night as Senior Constable Tim Sandry led Carmen Eckhoff up a track to the place where the Volkswagen had been found the day after the attack. Markers placed by the police designated the path taken by the vehicle, although she could tell by the squashed-down grasses where it had been driven. She sprayed luminol around the area in case blood had been spilled here, but once more there was no reaction to the chemical.

Eckhoff was confident that despite the rain the luminol spray would pick up a reaction to blood. There had been numerous cases around the world where murderers had attempted to wash away bloodstains but the chemical had still revealed where blood had flowed. Time was to reveal that the blood on the road at Barrow Creek would remain like an indelible stain for more than a year, remaining as a marker to a major incident despite blazing sun and lashing rain.

It was 12.30 am when Eckhoff left the scene, the only positive result being that the dark roadside patch was blood. She was shaking with cold as she got back in the police car for the journey back to Alice Springs.

Continuing her investigations the following morning, Eckhoff was shocked to see a police officer touch the steering wheel of the van without gloves when she was brought back to the crime scene examination unit. He was told in no uncertain terms that he had contaminated what could be vital evidence, although, given that police had tramped all over the scene at Barrow Creek, this was not the first time it had happened.

Eckhoff took swabs from parts of the steering wheel that the officer had not touched, then sprayed orthotolidine on the gear stick, seats and the accelerator, brake and clutch pedals. She also sprayed the van's rear curtains, a towel, clothing and shoes. All tests turned out to be negative. Sticky tape was used on the seats to lift any traces of skin, clothing and other particles that might be invisible to the naked eye, but which could be magnified under a microscope and provide vital clues if they were left by the stranger.

The ashtray contained a few butts. These were placed in a small plastic bag for later examination in the laboratory. In all, Eckhoff was to test 380 items for blood and other genetic material. Somewhere among these samples, she was convinced, was the key to Peter Falconio's disappearance. It was just a matter of time. Just how much time was anyone's guess.

Although she had obtained Falconio's DNA from the asthma reliever, which she would use as a control sample to eliminate him from other pieces of evidence collected, she also decided to ask members of the missing man's family to supply their DNA. Eckhoff and other officers then estimated the volume of blood making up the stain on the road. It was about half a litre, perhaps a little more, but certainly not enough to have rendered Falconio unconscious from loss of blood alone. On average, blood volume accounts for eight per cent of total body weight—five to six litres of blood for men and four to five litres for women. For someone to die from irreversible shock from blood loss, he or she would need to lose 40 per cent. To be incapacitated, too weak to move or even lapsing into unconsciousness, a person would need to lose one and a half litres.

X

By the night of Monday 16 July, Joanne Lees had undergone another 12 hours of questioning in Alice Springs, where she was asked to go over every fine detail again. She also helped detectives put together an identikit picture of her attacker, in which a computerised image is built up from various facial characteristics. The image showed the dark piercing eyes of her assailant, with black hair down to his shoulders and a Mexican-style moustache drooping down to just below his bottom lip. The poster was soon rushed around the country.

In the far-away north of England, Joanne's mother Jennifer and her mother's second husband, Vincent James, had already guessed that it was their daughter and Peter Falconio who were the British backpackers at the centre of the outback drama. They watched their local TV news from their home in Huddersfield with growing discomfort, for although no names had been mentioned, they knew Joanne and Peter were in the Alice Springs area and were heading north in a Volkswagen campervan.

Vincent immediately rang the Falconio family to express his concerns and then drove to the Huddersfield police station. The duty officer contacted the British consulate in Australia—and Vincent's worst fears were confirmed.

Peter Falconio's older brother Paul and his father Luciano also drove around to their local police station in Hepworth where the identities of the couple were also confirmed. They couldn't believe what was happening. Paul had spoken to his brother by phone on Friday, the day before the incident. Peter and Joanne were then in Alice Springs and said they were having the time of their lives. They were planning to continue driving north.

Shocked at learning Peter was now missing in such grim circumstances, father and son returned home to sit by the telephone and wait for news. 'Why Peter?' was a question the family asked repeatedly. 'Of all the tourists that travel around Australia, why our Peter?'

'I'll tell you why,' said Joan Falconio, who at that point had not been appraised of the full circumstances. She believed her son had stopped the Volkswagen to help a motorist in distress. 'It's because he always helps people. Stopping to help this man would be just typical of him. We all know he's the kindest boy in the world and he'd help anyone in trouble.'

X

Back in Australia the Stuart Highway emptied. Tourists heeded police advice to stay off the road while the gunman was still at large. While many decided to remain in towns such as Tennant Creek, Alice Springs and Katherine, those who found themselves miles from any large community formed convoys, believing there was safety in numbers. In caravan parks at night, people clustered together and took turns to watch for any strangers. Fear was in the air for hundreds of kilometres, fuelled by constant police warnings for people to stay in their cars and not to stop for anyone or anything. Families planning touring holidays to popular sites like Uluru and the Devil's Marbles cancelled their plans. In isolated communities residents locked their doors and windows and said they weren't going anywhere until the gunman was caught.

Commander Fields said nothing to minimise the spreading terror. He finally revealed that he was convinced Peter Falconio would not be found alive.

'I don't think things could look any blacker,' he said in a public announcement. He warned the gunman could strike again. 'The nature of the crime is such that we may have a person who is not thinking particularly rationally. It is not unknown for such a person to then become involved in another incident in a short space of time.'

He also believed the gunman could have, by that Monday, eluded police roadblocks. 'He was driving a four-wheel drive vehicle, and as you know, that allows you to go a lot of places conventional vehicles cannot. Unfortunately, this means he could go around roadblocks and he could go up and down tracks people don't normally bother going down in conventional vehicles.'

He sighed as he looked at a map of the Northern Territory that was pinned to the wall in his office. 'It's like looking for a needle in a haystack. And you don't get haystacks much bigger than the Territory.'

Paul Falconio and his father began making arrangements to fly to Australia. Joanne's stepfather also made hurried plans but first he had to get a passport. As all three men were packing, they managed to speak by phone to Joanne who gave them brief details of her ordeal. She tried to assure them that the police were using all their resources to find her boyfriend.

With many hours of questioning over—at least for the time being—police drove Joanne from the police station to a safe house in Alice Springs, where the media could not find her. She told detectives that she did not want to be interviewed and was insistent that she would not be appearing before any TV cameras to make a plea for help. This surprised a number of the police officers, who had found in the past that the loved ones of missing persons were anxious to receive as much publicity as they could get.

Travelling with Joanne to the secret address was Helen Jones, who had arranged for her partner Les to run the Barrow Creek Hotel on his own for as long as was necessary. 'I'll be with Joanne until she's through this,' she told him. 'She needs someone to be with her all the time. She's very vulnerable, very frightened.'

Journalists continued to implore police to let Joanne tell them her story in her own words, for what they had learned so far was full of gaps. Details of the horror she had been through had been sewn together piecemeal in the newspapers, on radio and TV from what reporters could glean from Les Pilton and Helen, the truck drivers who had picked her up and the police. If Joanne was prepared to go before the cameras and tell her story, journalists argued, what she had to say would have great impact and the public's awareness would be heightened. It would all help to keep people watching out for a man answering the gunman's description.

But while it was argued that the police and Joanne needed all possible help, there was to be no early public appearance by the woman at the centre of a story that was making headlines on both sides of the world. Commander Fields said she was still being questioned. The reality was that behind the scenes police were imploring her to go before the TV cameras and she constantly refused.

Meanwhile, Luciano Falconio and his son Paul had wasted no time. They flew into Australia on Wednesday 18 July and headed directly to Alice Springs where they were reunited with Joanne. The three hugged and cried at the private house she had been provided with and there she blurted out her story of that Saturday night.

At the request of Carmen Eckhoff, police asked father and son to provide a DNA sample. A swab was taken from their mouths so it could be compared with the make-up of the roadside blood, a small amount of which had been scraped up by Eckhoff. Now back in Darwin, her initial tests had told her what she suspected but the swabs from Luciano and Paul Falconio confirmed her belief; the roadside blood was Peter's, far beyond any doubt.

Father and son soon agreed to do what Joanne had refused to do and appeared at a press conference to make a composed appeal to all Australians to watch out for the gunman, who would be able to tell them where Pete was if the stranger could be caught. Luciano, a small, burly man with thick grey hair, sat with clenched hands in a room set aside for the brief conference and said he still held out hope that his boy was alive.

'I would not have come all this way if I did not believe that,' he said, his Italian accent strong. 'I have to hope that he is alive.'

Apart from her objections about appearing before the cameras, Joanne had a good reason for not attending the brief press conference. She was on her way back to Barrow Creek in a police car, having agreed to assist police with a re-enactment. It was decided not to put her through the ordeal of putting a bag over her head—a policewoman would play the role of Joanne, while a male officer pretended to be the gunman who had pulled up behind them. The couple's Volkswagen was used for the re-enactment and police had found a white ute similar to the description given by Joanne—not a difficult discovery, for many outback vehicles from the outside looked just like it.

The policewoman had her hands tied behind her back and then Joanne followed behind her as the officer stumbled into the bush. Joanne showed her where she had hidden as the gunman had searched for her. Whether the re-enactment, which was videotaped, had jogged Joanne's memory and provided police with additional information, they weren't going to reveal to the public.

Back in Alice Springs, Commander Max Pope, who had taken over from Bob Fields to deal with the growing press numbers, was revealing a few more details. After Joanne had been forced into the cabin of the gunman's ute, she sat there for a short time, bound hand and foot with a gag around her mouth and a bag over her head. The gunman had left her there for a moment, perhaps to check on Falconio's body—and in that time Joanne had somehow managed to slide through a gap behind the seats and drop into the rear of the ute.

From there, Commander Pope explained, choosing his words slowly and carefully, she had managed to escape through the open rear of the ute, at the same time removing the bag from her head and loosening her leg bonds. This appeared to be at odds with the description Joanne had given earlier to Helen Jones and Les Pilton. Earlier she had told the hotel owners that it was a sack, not a bag, that had been thrust over her head and that it had come off as she struggled with the stranger.

Even so, Pope repeated what many other police officers had been saying for most of that first week, 'She is one very lucky and courageous woman.'

What was lacking, and which would be helpful if the public were to identify the gunman, were detailed sketches of the perpetrator's ute, both inside and outside. The problem was that the regular police artist was on leave, so David Stagg, a teacher at the Charles Darwin School in Alice Springs was asked to help out. He was daunted by the task when he realised the dramatic case he was being asked to help with, but told detectives he would 'have a go'.

Using graphite and coloured pencils, Stagg spent nearly seven hours with Joanne making sketches, adjusting them, rubbing out, adding details as she made corrections based on her memory. A policewoman, Libby Andrews, sat in as Stagg worked away. Joanne was told that if there was anything she was not sure about, it could not be included in the sketches.

At one point she was asked if she wanted to take a break. For the first time in her session with Stagg she revealed her emotions, covering her face and throwing her head back, stifling a cry. She didn't want a break, she said at last. She wanted to continue. What she told him was at odds again with the account that had emerged from Helen Jones, Les Pilton and the police.

Joanne told Stagg that she was forced by her attacker from the front cabin of his vehicle into the back. Until now there had been no suggestion of her being forced from the front into the back—she had struggled into the rear by herself. In any case, she told Stagg that she landed on her side on soft material, her head towards what she believed was the back of the gunman's vehicle, although it was completely dark in there. Her hands had been manacled behind her, but she managed to slide them under her feet so that they were in front and that enabled her to feel her way towards the back. She could feel that the material she had landed on was like vinyl.

Describing the van from the outside, Joanne told Stagg that she had glimpsed it when it had first pulled alongside the kombivan, and then she had seen more of it as she stood beside it briefly before she was forced into the passenger's side of the cabin. Once more, this version of events was confusing, for she had given the impression earlier that the bag that had been thrust on her head by her assailant had come off when she was in the back of the van. But Stagg could only go on what she was telling him as he drew sketches that portrayed her ordeal like frames from a movie.

Her attacker, she said, was tall and stooped. Stagg wrote the description beside a sketch he drew of a man with long hair and dark staring eyes. She was asked to describe the dog she had seen in the passenger seat. Contradicting a description issued by police earlier, she said the dog was not a blue heeler or a red heeler. All she could say was that it was of a light colour. She was shown a book of dog pictures, but could not find a match.

As the police identikit picture was circulated nationally, the switchboard at the Alice Springs police station rang hot with possible reported sightings. Several people were astonished at the likeness between the police picture and the face of serial killer Ivan Milat, who had murdered seven young backpackers in the Belanglo State Forest near Sydney in the late 1980s and early 1990s. By coincidence, one of his victims was a young English backpacker also called Joanne; Joanne Walters, from Wales. Joanne Walters became known around Australia and the UK when her body was discovered, but it was the face of Ivan Milat that had the most chilling impact. In several photographs published around the world he was seen grinning into the camera sporting a Mexican-style moustache. He had the same dark, penetrating eyes as the sketches of Joanne Lees' attacker. But the Barrow Creek gunman could not have been Milat because he was safely behind bars, serving life for his crimes.

One report arrived at the offices of the local newspaper, the *Centralian Advocate* and came from a 24-hour Alice Springs petrol station. Their security camera had filmed a man whose description and van answered that of the wanted gunman. He was seen buying a drink and ice, and filling jerry cans with petrol some time after midnight, very early into the morning of Sunday 15 July, the morning after the attack. If he was the gunman he could have easily travelled the 295 kilometres to Alice Springs from the scene at Barrow Creek had he left an hour or so after the attack. Joanne had been unable to say when he had set off; all she knew was that she had continued lying in the bushes for several more hours because of her uncertainty about whether her attacker was still waiting for her to emerge.

Police at first denied they had been shown the security film but later admitted they had inspected it. Commander Pope, his small moustache bristling, issued a definitive, dismissive statement to the media: 'We have seen that footage but I can tell you it is not him.' What seemed like a vital lead had been thrown out with a few words, but Pope was anxious to ensure people remained vigilant.

'We don't want the public to become discouraged that the sightings are so far proving fruitless,' he said. 'We still need their help and input to help catch this man.'

Detectives also watched another film, this time a commercial movie called *Breakdown*, starring Kurt Russell. It was about a woman abducted on a lonely American desert road after the car she and her husband were travelling in had broken down. The kidnapper was a moustachioed cowboy travelling with a truck-driver accomplice. The movie had been screened on TV in Alice Springs three weeks earlier. Had the Barrow Creek gunman seen it and been inspired to pull off a copy-cat attack? Detectives were keeping an open mind.

Twenty-four hours after Joanne's return visit to Barrow Creek for the re-enactment, Paul Falconio and his father Luciano also made the emotional journey to Barrow Creek. Under grey skies, father and son stared in silent horror at the bloodstain on the road, then walked into the bush where Joanne had indicated to the police she had hidden.

'We're not going to leave Australia until we know what's happened to Peter,' Luciano told one of the officers accompanying them. 'My boy is missing. I don't go home without him.' After picking their way through the scrub for half an hour they saw no point in remaining. But, as he walked from the bushes Paul carried a small eucalyptus twig he had plucked from the trees in the area, a memento of the place where his brother had almost certainly died.

Reports continued to pour in. What seemed like a dramatic breakthrough came as Paul and Luciano were at Barrow Creek. A woman backpacker telephoned police to say she had had a frightening experience with a man who had picked her up in the Northern Territory—a man who looked like the motorist being hunted and who was driving a similar vehicle to that being sought. She had been picked up a day or two before the Barrow Creek incident. As they travelled, the man became increasingly agitated, the backpacker reported, but what terrified her was when she saw a gun. Police again declined to go into further details about how the young woman saw the gun.

She was, however, able to leave the vehicle unharmed but she told police that she had been greatly concerned about her safety while travelling with the man, who, like the driver who confronted the British couple, was travelling with a dog.

Based on information provided by the young woman, police said they had eventually been able to identify the driver of the white four-wheel drive ute. There was a feeling of excitement that a breakthrough was close as they passed the man's details to police in the neighbouring state of Queensland. But hopes were quickly dashed. The driver in this episode had a cast-iron alibi for his whereabouts on the night Joanne Lees was attacked.

Men who looked like the sketch of the gunman were being questioned all around the Territory. An employee of the Alice Springs library, married to a woman from the Warrabri Aboriginal tribe and who had been seen by police driving into the Ali Curung community a few days before the Barrow Creek incident, was questioned on his recent movements. He had a moustache, but he also had more alibis than the police cared to listen to.

Stewie Kensington, an Alice Springs gardener, also heard the police wanted to have a chat with him. Someone had dobbed him in, reporting that he looked very much like the picture of the gunman. With his long hair and handlebar moustache he bore a striking likeness and his age, 43, matched that of the attacker. But he could also prove his innocence. He was at the Memo Club for most of Saturday and at his mate Les's place after that. Even so, people stared at him all around town and he began to think that it was all getting beyond a joke.

And still there had been no public comment from Joanne. No TV appearance, no open plea for help. Journalists wanted to know where the woman at the centre of the big story was—and why the silence. Surely an appearance by her, a tearful plea for help, would keep the public watching out for Peter Falconio, alive or dead, and for the gunman.

One journalist who gained an edge over his colleagues was Mark Wilton. As the chief of staff of the *Centralian Advocate*, the small daily newspaper that fed the Alice Springs district, he kept his ear to the ground and had a large number of contacts, whose identities he faithfully guarded. While reporters from interstate and overseas were pressing the police to persuade Joanne to talk to them, Mark was off on his own, knocking on the door of a house in an Alice Springs suburb where Joanne was staying with Helen Jones.

He had received information about her whereabouts that his out-of-town colleagues would have paid dearly for. He did not know what kind of reception he would receive, but when the door was opened and he revealed his identity, he was allowed in. He was about to scoop the world with a story that would be published in the *Centralian Advocate* on Friday 20 July.

Joanne was sitting in the lounge, hands clasped tightly on her lap. Wilton introduced himself again, ensuring that she knew he was a journalist. He switched on his tape recorder. It would, she told him, be the only time she told her story for the public record and she was only doing it to clarify a number of mistakes that had been made in the reporting of her ordeal.

How was she? Mark wanted to know. What really happened out there?

Joanne took a deep breath, then began her story. 'Everyone can use their imagination about what it was like for me that night. But I was determined to escape and I feel very lucky to be alive. I honestly don't believe this man would have let me go. He really needs to be captured. I don't think he would hesitate to do it again.'

She wanted to make one thing very clear. Contrary to a number of reports, at no stage on that Saturday night did she believe that the loud bang she heard was a gunshot. The bang had simply sounded like a gunshot, but that was different to saying that it definitely was the sound of a gun. She then went on to reflect on the hours before the incident.

'We stopped and refuelled at Ti Tree and watched the sunset. And after we had been driving again for some time a vehicle drove up alongside us and Pete slowed down at first thinking it was going to overtake us.

'But he drove alongside us, his interior light was on and it was a four-wheel drive with a dog. The man pointed to the back of our vehicle and motioned for us to stop. We then stopped and he pulled up behind us. Pete got out of the car and went to the back of our van, and the two were talking amicably and I thought everything was okay.

'Pete then came back to me and asked if I would rev the engine, so I moved to the driver's seat and I revved the engine. I revved the engine again and I heard a bang, I thought it was something to do with the fault that the man was saying was wrong with the exhaust. The next thing I looked out of the window to look out the back to see what's happening and I see him with a gun.

'He then came up to me and he opened the door and he told me to switch off the engine and pushed me to the passenger side.'

But just as her story was reaching the critical point—her ordeal of being thrown into the stranger's four-wheel drive, her dash into the bush and her fear as the man came looking for her—she stopped. She didn't want to go into that. 'It's too painful,' she told Wilton.

Frustrated, he implored her to go on. 'I'm supposed to be on holidays,' she continued. 'The last thing I would have expected to hear was a gun. It never, ever crossed my mind that it was a gun shot ... things don't happen to me. You know, when you hear a bang you don't automatically think "gunshot" do you?'

The reporter gently persuaded her to keep telling her story. Her hands still clasped, she said that initially she had been wary of stopping, but after Pete and the man had talked behind the van and her boyfriend had come back to ask her to rev the engine, she relaxed.

'I thought everything was okay ... you just don't expect things like this to happen. But looking back, whether we stopped or not, I believe that he would have shot our tyres or done something anyway.'

Neither she nor Falconio had seen the four-wheel drive vehicle before it pulled up alongside them, but she and her boyfriend had seen something strange shortly before their encounter with the gunman.

'I just can't remember what the times were from memory, but the police have all our documents and they could tell you. But soon after we left Ti Tree we saw a suspicious fire on the side of the road that just seemed odd.

'It wasn't a camp fire and it wasn't a bushfire. It was just on the side of the road.' At that time, she recalled, Falconio stopped the Volkswagen intending to get out and investigate. But Joanne told him not to. It was a short time later that the man had drawn alongside them in his white four-wheel drive.

Suddenly, Joanne declared the interview was over. Wilton was shown to the door. He would have liked more details, but she was not to be drawn. Even so, he had a partial description of her ordeal from her own lips—and that was more than his colleagues had.

Chapter 4
Dead man travelling

A dead man walked into the petrol filling station and Melissa Kendall almost fainted. You had all sorts pulling in for fuel because the tiny town of Bourke was one of those 'must visit' places on the tourist map. The 'back of Bourke' was what Australians often referred to when they were talking about the middle of nowhere. Bourke was the last place on earth that could be called a bustling metropolis. Anywhere beyond and you were into the wilderness. But the tourists came, mostly because they wanted to say they had been there, although often they didn't like what they saw. When the beer flowed, there was always a threat of violence in the air.

On Sunday 22 July 2001 Melissa, 23, was running the filling station at the top end of town as usual with her partner of the same age, Rob Brown, whose parents owned the place. It was a quiet morning and Melissa had taken some time out to read the weekend papers. There was a big piece about Peter Falconio and Joanne Lees and the frightening experience the Englishwoman had been through at Barrow Creek, 1500 kilometres away as the crow flies and close to 2300 kilometres for travellers using the most accessible roads. Covering 600 kilometres a day by car, the journey could be made in four days. Illustrating the article was a photo of Falconio and

Joanne and an identikit picture of the wanted man, with his long dark hair and Mexican moustache. Melissa had a bit of a chat to Rob about it.

'A pretty shocking state of affairs when tourists can't drive around Australia without getting killed,' she said.

'Wasn't the first time, and it won't be the last,' he replied.

At 5 pm that afternoon they were ready to shut up shop. The evenings came in early at this time of the year and it was doubtful there would be any other customers now. As Melissa started sweeping up the store she could hear the occasional clatter of a plate from out in the kitchen, where Rob was clearing up.

Suddenly the console beeped. Someone had pulled into the courtyard outside and was waiting for the diesel pump to be switched on. Melissa hit the button. A few moments later the door opened and in walked a ghost. At least that's the first thought that hit her. She recognised him immediately. It was the same man she'd been looking at in the paper. Peter Falconio.

Melissa felt a chill run right through her. It was him all right, although his hair looked a bit lighter than in the picture. And it seemed he had some kind of injury to the left side of his face.

'Can I use the toilet, please?' he asked. That confirmed it. He had an English accent, although she wasn't qualified enough to place it. She handed him the toilet key, aware of her quivering hand.

As he stepped out another man entered. He was a good ten years older, about 40 she reckoned, and he had shoulder-length dark hair. He was dressed in a dirty off-white T-shirt and blue jeans. There was something about his appearance and his manner that really scared her. He asked if there was anything to eat and Melissa nervously told him the kitchen had closed.

'All right then,' he said, 'I'll just go and get some dog biscuits.'

He walked down to the shelf and collected a packet of biscuits, paying for them and the fuel with cash. Melissa was still shaking as he walked out.

While the shop was temporarily empty, she went out into the kitchen. Her heart was pounding. She told Rob that Peter Falconio, the man in the paper they'd both been reading about earlier, had just come into the shop. Rob stared at her in disbelief.

'I don't believe it,' he said. 'You've got to be shittin' me.'

He marched straight out into the shop just as the solidly built man was returning with the toilet key. Jesus, it was him all-right, except his short cropped hair was a bit more blond, as if it had been tinted. From what he recalled seeing in the paper, Peter Falconio had a bit of a mark on his lip, like a mole or a scab, and there it was on this bloke. Same place, on the left-hand side, about the size of a five-cent piece.

The customer asked for a bottle of coca-cola and a Mars bar. English accent, thought Rob, although the only accents he knew were from the TV and he wouldn't have been able to place whether they were from the south, the midlands or the north. The transaction over, the man walked out.

Rob was determined to get a better look. But Melissa had warned him that the fellow he was with looked sinister. In fact, she said, her jaw dropping at the realisation, he looked a great deal like the pictures of the wanted man, except he didn't have a moustache. The only excuse Rob could think of to walk out into the courtyard was to pretend he was looking for his dog. As he called out for Sally, his blue heeler, he could see a group of people standing by their vehicle, parked about 25 metres away. They were little more than shadows but he could make out the man he believed was Falconio and saw the shape of his male companion. There was a woman there too, but he couldn't see her clearly.

The vehicle was a four-wheel drive ute and appeared to have been very crudely painted in dark green. There were wooden sides to hold in the gear in the back and some kind of roof covering, but Rob was still able to see over the top of the sides and into the rear because the canopy had been rolled up. All he could make out was a pile of luggage. And there was a dog sitting on top of it all, but he couldn't tell what breed it was.

After a minute or two the three drove off into the semi-darkness. Rob tried to read the numberplate but it was too dimly lit. He went back into the service station and had another look at the newspaper. No doubt about it, he decided, he'd just served Peter Falconio. And the man with him could have been the fellow they said had attacked him. It was strange, all right.

Rob didn't want to make a fool of himself in case he was wrong, and so he decided not to tell the police about it—at least not right away. When his parents came home later that evening he chatted to them about it. Then he talked it over with Melissa and finally he passed the information onto the local police, but not until three days later, Wednesday 25 July. Putting aside any feelings of frustration he might have had over the delay, Detective Mick Allan showed Rob a new set of pictures of Peter Falconio. No, nothing could change his mind about what he had seen. If that wasn't Peter Falconio who came into the shop, it was his twin.

Precious time had been lost and the trio could have by now been anywhere in a dark painted vehicle, the numberplate of which was unknown. Police were already stretched looking for the original four-wheel drive used in the Barrow Creek attack; the last thing they wanted was to be distracted looking for another vehicle which might be the original and had been repainted or which was not connected with the crime at all. It was decided to keep the file open on the second vehicle in case new information came in. A lead that the police dismissed almost immediately.

X

In her laboratory on the first floor of the police headquarters in Darwin, forensic scientist Carmen Eckhoff prepared to do further work on samples she had collected from the crime scene and from the Volkswagen. She was looking forward to moving into new premises but in the meantime she remained satisfied that the laboratory had the very best testing equipment and was confident that her tests would produce results that would stand up to scrutiny in court—if it ever came to that.

As was the practice, she put on a clean lab coat, pulled on a pair of gloves and laid fresh, white paper on her work bench. Whenever she was finished with examining an item, it would be put away, fresh paper would be laid down and a new pair of gloves would be put on in preparation for the next piece of evidence.

She worked with three other scientists, Julie Garrett, Megan Hibble and a woman who had been ridiculed because of her role in the famous Azaria Chamberlain case, Joy Kuhl. Kuhl, who was due to retire soon, was an experienced forensic scientist whose lifelong career had crumbled due to a flawed analysis in the extraordinary case surrounding the mysterious disappearance of baby Azaria at Ayers Rock, 400 kilometres south-west of Alice

Springs in August 1980. Azaria's mother, Lindy Chamberlain, claimed a dingo had snatched the nine-and-a-half-week-old baby from the family's holiday tent but she was later found guilty of murder and sent to jail for life. She was freed four years later when new evidence was presented—including the discovery that a substance Miss Kuhl had said was baby's blood in the Chamberlain's car had turned out to be sound-deadening equipment. Lindy walked from jail with her head held high, and Miss Kuhl's reputation was in tatters, even though she said she had found baby's blood in other parts of the car.

But that had been years ago. Now Miss Kuhl was working in the same laboratory as Carmen Eckhoff who was being asked to look at a case that was equally as sensational in Australia as the Chamberlain affair. As far as the British press were concerned, the Falconio disappearance was even more incredible.

Forensic science had moved on since the Azaria days and equipment was far more sophisticated. DNA plays a vital role in solving crimes and is used as legal evidence in a variety of court cases ranging from identifying crime suspects to paternity suits. With the exception of identical twins, everyone is genetically unique. DNA is like a fingerprint inside the body—if deoxyribonucleic acid, as it is scientifically known, from a suspect can be matched with blood or semen or a cell found on any part of the body of a victim, the suspect will have problems proving his or her innocence.

DNA can also be used to confirm family links, for similarities can be found between parents, their offspring and siblings, but there will not be a 100 per cent match. In most cases a close match is considered good enough, given the billions of odds against another person having a similar make-up. In more recent times, a Sri Lankan baby washed away from his parents in the 2004 Boxing Day tsunami was reunited with them after DNA tests proved they were his rightful parents.

Miss Eckhoff's job was to weigh up everything she had gleaned from her examination of the crime scene, the Volkswagen and Joanne's clothing, and DNA was going to play a big part in her tests. The roadside blood had been soaked up to some extent by the earth that had been thrown over it, causing the soil to clump in places, but in her estimation Peter Falconio had lost around 100 millilitres—certainly less than half a litre. Humans could lose that amount without feeling any ill effect, unless the blood loss was caused by an injury to a vital internal organ.

On her bench Eckhoff laid out a curious item—the crude pair of handcuffs that had secured Joanne's wrists. Measuring 37 millimetres in length, 7.5 millimetres in width and a depth of 1.6 centimetres, the device looked mediaeval. The restraining implement was made up of cable ties and black tape. Two circular ties on each end were intended for each wrist and there were three loops connecting each of the outer wrist loops. Eckhoff had been told that Joanne Lees had managed to reach into her pocket and remove a tube of lip balm, which she had rubbed on the cable ties in an effort to free her hands from the loops. Miss Eckhoff could feel the lip balm's greasiness on the ties and tape. Experience told her that the substance was unlikely to affect any traces of DNA.

This barbaric apparatus, she hoped, would provide her with a vital clue. She would find Joanne's DNA on it, she expected, and also that of Vince Millar, who had cut the ties from her. If there was a third sample, there was a strong likelihood it would be that of the attacker.

To a point, her expectations were borne out. The major DNA profile on the cuffs—a significant contribution—fitted Joanne, while Millar was a minor contributor. But she found no other profile that pointed to a third person touching the handcuffs. It was not for her to conclude why, although there could be only two obvious reasons. The person who bound her had been wearing gloves; or only Miss Lees and Millar had touched the handcuffs that night. But what sense did that make?

Some people, she was aware, shed different types of cells—there were many variables—but certainly there was nothing obvious to be found on the shackles that would point to a third person handling them. Failure to find another person's profile bothered her so much that she searched the cable ties in various locations, subjecting them to various tests. She found nothing more.

There was one more vital examination to be carried out. Tests on Joanne Lees' clothing. Detectives had already told her that the top, a light green, almost turquoise, T-shirt that Joanne had been wearing looked as if it had a bloodstain on it across the front. The whole garment was in a grubby state, consistent with a woman who had been scrambling around in the bush.

Eckhoff removed the T-shirt from the plastic bag it had arrived in and held it up before her. It was a French Connection T-shirt with a round badge in the top left hand corner reading 'Try Hugs, Not Drugs'. It was a press-on slogan, so she carefully peeled it away and sent it away to another department for fingerprinting.

The T-shirt was not going to be much use to anyone by the time she finished with it. She brought out her scissors and began cutting it up, concentrating on areas that were smudged and dirty and setting aside the pieces so they could be individually examined. She also used sticky tape to lift minute samples of dirt and perhaps skin from the clothing.

An area of staining that looked like blood on the front tested positive. Eckhoff was able to extract a DNA profile from it, and found it was from Joanne. One other area on the T-shirt tested positive for blood; a small smudge near the back of the left side of the sleeve.

This time the DNA test produced a positive and exciting result. The profile was that of a complete stranger. It belonged to a male, whose genetic make-up did not belong to Falconio, to either of the truck drivers who had helped Joanne, or anyone else who had assisted her that night when she was helped into the Barrow Creek Hotel.

It was the first positive clue that someone had touched Joanne and was bleeding, if only slightly, when they had done so. Miss Eckhoff thought the smear might have come from a torn fingernail, perhaps caused by someone gripping Joanne as they struggled, because that would be the only logical explanation for the blood to be found in that location. Unless, of course, someone with a small open wound had accidentally brushed up against her in the hours or days before the Barrow Creek incident. In any case, the scientist mused, what she needed now for her examinations to move forward was a suspect whose DNA could be checked against the stain.

Eckhoff continued her tests, looking next at Joanne's boots and shorts. She found nothing more that helped. Electrical tape that had been wrapped around Joanne's neck in an attempt to gag her had a number of hairs sticking to it, but as expected they turned out to be from the English woman. Through her microscope, Eckhoff also examined tiny mounds of dirt, scrapings from under Joanne's fingernails, collected in the hope that she had scratched her attacker as she struggled to escape and there were skin cells to be found. Nothing helpful was discovered.

Eckhoff looked at swabs taken from the steering wheel. She had made presumptive tests for blood when she was in Alice Springs without any result, but now she was looking for any traces of DNA. As she had expected, she found indications that Peter Falconio had handled the steering wheel, and she concluded that although the tests did not produce a crystal clear result there was enough in her findings to show that Joanne Lees had also gripped the wheel. She had found Joanne's alleles, a multiple group of genes that make up a small section of DNA.

Although scientific debate has centred around the reliability of DNA, it has been generally accepted that every individual on earth has a combination of 26 alleles, which belong to a 'pool' of 344 known alleles. Finding a few alleles will at the very least make all the difference between a person being eliminated from or included in an investigation. Joanne, then, had handled the steering wheel, but that was of no great surprise.

What Eckhoff had to do next as her painstaking laboratory tests continued, was look beyond Joanne's and Peter Falconio's DNA on the swabs from the Volkswagen. Was there evidence of anyone else handling the steering wheel?

There was, but the profile was weak. Eckhoff tried comparing this unclear sample with the mystery person's DNA on the T-shirt. Frustratingly, because the steering wheel DNA had not produced a good profile, there was not an identical match—but she decided that there was enough of a 'DNA smear' to suggest that whoever had left the sample on the T-shirt could also have touched or held the steering wheel.

Eckhoff turned to a DNA sample she had swabbed from the knob on the gear stick. Using what is known as a low copy technique, bringing into play the minute measurement known as micrometres—an average cell nucleus is about six micrometres in diameter—she was hoping to break down the DNA profiles of those who had recently handled the gear stick. In other words, separate the profiles to provide a clearer picture.

Setting aside the strong profiles for Joanne and Falconio, Eckhoff was disappointed to find that other DNA on the gear stick was extremely weak. She was able to obtain only a partial profile and, working on the assumption the 'foreign' DNA was from one individual, she concluded it was from a male. Using sophisticated calculations on her computer, she worked out that the DNA would, on average, match one in 678 individuals in the Northern Territory—and among those would be the person who had left the DNA on the T-shirt.

Eckhoff discussed her findings with her laboratory colleagues. Science had helped her reach what she believed was a logical conclusion. There was a good chance that whoever had touched, or grabbed Joanne Lees, had also driven the couple's Volkswagen off the road and into the bush. It was not a hard scientific analysis—but it came close and it also made a lot of sense. It was not her job to come to such a conclusion. That would be down to the detectives, who would use her findings with other evidence they collected to nail down the Barrow Creek attacker.

What she did have was a strong DNA sample from Joanne Lees' T-shirt. Now all she had to do was wait for the police to bring her a sample from a suspect and if there was a match, well, then they would be well on their way towards putting the perpetrator behind bars.

Carmen Eckhoff was not alone in working behind the scenes in the hunt for the gunman. Sydney University psychologist, John Clarke, studied all that had been made public in the first few days after the incident and compiled what he believed would be an accurate profile of the attacker. Close to completing his doctorate on serial killers and criminal profiling, he concluded the gunman would have been planning the assault on the lonely road for several years. It was his belief that Falconio had been killed, removed as an obstruction, so the gunman could abduct Lees. The profile he compiled revealed a man who had a sexual fantasy of abducting a woman and keeping her for a long period as a sex slave.

To Clarke, the gunman fitted the profile of an itinerant worker who travelled from place to place, but who would have been familiar with the area, perhaps working on cattle stations. He would be of above average intelligence and fairly impulsive. The attacker would be a loner, although to those he met he would seem to be a nice person, while making acquaintances feel rather uneasy in his company.

As a child, Clarke considered, the perpetrator probably harmed animals and was perhaps fascinated by fire. He might have been bullied or his parents may have been abusive. Certainly something had turned him into a sexual psychopath and he might have a criminal history and even have raped women before.

But where could he be now? Clarke wondered. He believed the attacker would be hiding out in a place with which he was familiar, a place he was comfortable with. But he was also going to be highly stressed and very worried about what was going to happen to him because his kidnap victim had escaped.

And why had she escaped? Why had he been so careless as to allow his intended victim to break away and hide in such a way that he couldn't find her? Clarke was not the only person to wonder about such things. The circumstances surrounding the incident at Barrow Creek had raised many questions—to which there were few answers.

Chapter 5
Dark history

It was raining when I arrived in Alice Springs on the evening of Monday 16 July, 48 hours after the incident at Barrow Creek. I had arrived with the expectation that many journalists shared as news of the attack hit the world—get a story from the heroine in the middle of the outback drama. Throughout the previous day the airwaves had been filled with stories of the English couple who had been waylaid. It was obvious that the story had become too big for me to cover from Sydney.

It was a cold bleak morning the next day as I drove north to Barrow Creek. The rain had stopped but there was no tourist traffic around—reports that a dangerous gunman was on the loose were keeping everyone off the roads. Numerous police cars sped to and fro along the Stuart Highway. Officers on mountain bikes rode along the grass verges, veering off occasionally to look further inland. Heads down, eyes scanning each side, they were searching for Peter Falconio who might be lying there somewhere, dead or alive, after possibly being dumped by the attacker who, it was now strongly believed, had driven off with him.

At the small community of Ti Tree, police at a roadblock stopped me for an identity check. I asked if there was any news of Falconio or the gunman.

Not a thing, a young officer told me. Whoever was responsible was probably miles away by now, he admitted.

The road north towards Barrow Creek cuts through some of the loneliest and inhospital places on earth. The Northern Territory is a sparsely populated state of just 200 000 people which portrays to the world the image of 'the Outback'. More than 40 per cent of the Territory, which covers an area of 1.35 million square kilometres—an area as large as France, Spain and Italy combined—has been designated as Aboriginal land. It is widely recognised that these tribes are the only people who can claim to understand the wilderness, its dangers and its magic.

The car park of the Barrow Creek Hotel was filled with police cars. A caravan had also been driven there to use as a temporary operations room. Radios crackled. There was a bustle of activity as officers with high-powered guns came and went. The scene was reminiscent of a man-hunt that had been based in this very same car park 127 years earlier, although cars had now replaced horses and pump-action shotguns had taken the place of ancient load-and-shoot rifles.

In that episode violent death had come to workers at the nearby telegraph station, victims of the outback and a failure to understand its dangers. But many had also died trying to carve their way inland in the early days of exploration—and several of those who survived terrible journeys simply lost their minds. The early Europeans who did succeed in crossing the deserts have been rewarded with roads and ranges named after them but the price was often high.

In 1860, Robert O'Hara Burke and John Wills led the Great Northern Exploration Expedition traversing for the first time the land between Melbourne and the Gulf of Carpentaria. Just a few months later, Scotsman John McDougall Stuart, a draughtsman who had arrived in Australia in 1838, set out in an attempt to cross Australia from south to north from Adelaide. His horseback expedition made it to the red centre before the harshness of the interior forced the team back. He tried again in January 1861, financed by the South Australian Government, but once again he and his party were beaten by dense scrub and a shortage of rations. In October he tried yet again and this time, despite enormous hardships, he reached the northern coast in July 1862, extending further north than Burke and Wills. It was a man with broken health who managed to make the terrible return journey to Adelaide, arriving back in December 1862. He failed to recover and returned to England two years later, dying not long after at the age of 51, his sight lost, his memory gone.

Yet he had left behind a legacy—the route he had paved through that forbidding territory widened to a track and eventually a road, which became known as his road: the Stuart Highway. He had shown that the route would be practicable for an overland telegraph line. Apart from a rough track, he left one other landmark.

On his expedition through the heart of the continent he stopped in a flat area sheltered by cliffs, where a small stream flowed. He was friends with John Henry Barrow, a South Australian member of Parliament and decided to name the area after him. And so Barrow Creek was marked on the first crude maps of inland Australia. John McDougall Stuart could never have imagined the tragedies, or the mysteries, that would come to haunt that tiny place in the middle of nowhere.

Running the telegraph line from Adelaide to Darwin had been an incredible feat. Hundreds of men set up camps through the interior to construct the link, battling heavy rains in the north and extreme temperatures in the heart of the continent. They marched through land where Aboriginal tribes lived, fighting off threats with their muskets and sometimes clashing, whites armed with guns, blacks with spears.

Then in October 1872, Sir Charles Todd was able to announce with a flourish of enormous pride that 'the Australian colonies were connected with the grand electric chain which unites all the nations of the earth'.

One of the vital links was in that small clearing named by John Stuart. In contrast to the public banquets held in Sydney, Adelaide and London to celebrate what was deemed one of the most significant events in Australia's young history, there had been only a small celebration at Barrow Creek when a telegraph station was opened in August 1872. It still stands there today, an old stone structure with a high-walled courtyard and double gates at the rear, tourists learning with awe the terrible events that occurred two years after it was built.

During the warm summer evening of 23 February 1874, eight men, five of them white, two Aboriginal workers, and a Chinese cook, were sitting on the front veranda enjoying a slight breeze. Supper over, they smoked pipes and one was playing a violin. A lantern glowed nearby.

Suddenly the flickering shadows became people. From the dark bush rushed scores of tribal warriors, throwing spears and swinging clubs and before the station workers could move, linesman John Franks and one of his Aboriginal friends were struck through the heart. Running towards the gate in the hope of getting inside the courtyard, the manager, James Stapleton, was hit with spears in the chest, yet he still managed to scramble on towards the gate with his mortal wound. Telegraph operator E Flint was struck in the thigh and Mounted Constable Samuel Gason, who was based at the station, was floored by a thrown club.

Somehow the injured got inside, blood pouring from their wounds, staining the flagstone floor. Spears rained down on the roof and from the darkness the yells of the attackers became even more shrill. It was an unimaginable scene of terror for there were scores of men against a handful. Constable Gason now began firing through the slits in the wall, specially built for such an event, but he could see nothing to aim at.

Despite his wound, telegraph operator Flint lay on a sofa and managed to get through to Alice Springs by morse code. The news that came back was bad. There was no force available to send to the rescue. The only hope, it was decided, was to try to recall a party of men who had set out a day earlier to maintain the line further north. No contact could be made with them, however, unless they decided to use their portable instruments to call in. To make matters worse, the bodies of Franks and the Aboriginal worker who had died were beginning to decompose, and Stapleton, the manager, was himself now close to death.

'You need not trouble much about me,' he said with his last breath. 'Bury me in my blankets. Give my love to my wife and send my papers down.' He died shortly afterwards.

Much further to the north, Billy Abbott had been mending the line. He climbed a pole, clipped on the wires of his handset and called Alice Springs. As Ernestine Hill wrote in his book *The Territory* in 1951, 'Somebody else was calling the Alice, an insane stuttering in Morse, no hope to understand it ... then came SOS repeated again and again, and a slow spelling of one word, 'BLACKS'. Billy climbed down and looked fearfully around him, at the great silent plain peopled with shadows. He rigged his net, then caught his horse to ride a few miles off, just in case. Next morning he tried the line again, and heard the brief and tragic report from Alice Springs running through to Postmaster Little in Darwin. It came quite clearly now: BARROW CREEK TELEGRAPH STATION ATTACKED BY BLACKS 8PM SUNDAY JOHN FRANKS KILLED STAPLETON SERIOUSLY WOUNDED SENDING HELP'.

Men had indeed been rounded up at Alice Springs, while from the north came the workers who had left earlier but had since called in by chance. Spears continued to fall on the station until the rescue parties arrived, although even they came under attack as they passed through dense scrub. The Aborigines then fled.

The following morning a party of 13 men set out to hunt them down, but the tribe had vanished. There was no hope of finding them in the thick undergrowth. In time, as Ernestine Hill noted, Franks and Stapleton and the murdered Aboriginal worker were avenged, the innocent suffering for the guilty. A punitive expedition of police and bushmen, headed by a police trooper called Wormbrandt, rode for 480 kilometres herding all blacks before them, from Ellery's Creek Gorge on the Finke River to the Haartz mountains, 160 kilometres east of Barrow Creek. And out there is a range of hills which, for grim and sufficient reason, is known as Blackfellows' Bones.

If Barrow Creek and the surrounding bush was not already stained with enough blood, another terrible event was to follow in 1928. An old dingo hunter, Fred Brooks, had a falling out with a tribe over the right to cross certain lands. When Mounted Constable William George Murray, who was then in charge of the tiny Barrow Creek Police Station, heard that Brooks had been slaughtered he gathered up a posse of European men to hunt down the killers. This was despite his official title of Chief Protector of Aborigines.

There was no mercy. Whenever the hunters came across a group of Aborigines, they were gunned down. At least 70 were killed in the bloody reprisals, which marked the last major Aboriginal massacre in the Northern Territory. When Murray travelled to Darwin to report his actions, he was greeted as a conquering hero. As a formality, he was charged with murder and when asked why he had taken no prisoners, he expressed the racist attitudes which existed in the Northern Territory at the time by telling the Darwin court, 'What use is a wounded blackfella a hundred miles from civilisation?' He was found not guilty of the charges and totally exonerated.

No-one knows exactly how many Aboriginal people died in the punitive hunt for the killers of the telegraph station men and the dingo hunter, or whether their bodies were buried by friend or foe. Many of their bones, it is said, lie in the bush undiscovered. But, their descendants who live in small communities scattered around Barrow Creek know that the shadows of their ancestors still walk.

Now, ten miles past the car park of the Barrow Creek Hotel, police cars at the roadside marked the spot where the stain of Peter Falconio's blood covered the road. The stain was easy enough to see in the sun that was now bursting through the last of the clouds, although it looked now as though much of the earth that had been thrown over the blood had been washed away by the previous day's rain. Police were still walking through the tall, wet grass as if hoping to miraculously find Falconio where they had searched numerous times before.

The hum of police motorcycles somewhere beyond the roadside bushes broke the silence. TV cameramen scurried around looking for some action to film and settled on training their lenses on the riders. There wasn't much else.

The following day, renowned Aboriginal tracker, Ted Egan, was brought to the crime scene in the hope that perhaps he could find something that the Aborigines from Ali Curung had missed. Egan was an old man, well into his sixties, with a shock of white hair under his wide-brimmed hat. His reputation went back to the age of six when he revealed incredible tracking skills, following the trails of lizards and snakes as he travelled through the bush with members of the Warlpiri tribe. Since his late teens he had worked for the Northern Territory Police, one of his most celebrated cases being the hunt for an Aborigine named Billy Ben who had murdered another man and taken off into the bush with his dog.

Billy Ben had covered his movements, wiping out his tracks as he went and assuming that his dog's pawprints would be lost among the vast number of dingo prints. But Egan was not to be discouraged. For 18 days he followed the dog's tracks and was finally able to lead police to the wanted man. Now, Egan was being asked to look for another man and a dog—except that this perpetrator also had a vehicle. It could be a blessing or a curse, for if he had parked on soft ground Egan would find the tracks, but if he had stayed on the hard bitumen he would have a problem, unless there was an oil leak or something fell off the tyres.

Egan was led into the bush where the Aborigines had searched earlier. Human footprints told many stories to him, the weight of a person, the direction travelled and even if anything had been carried. Egan could read the most subtle of signs. But he came up with the same conclusions as the earlier trackers—there was no sign of a man or a dog walking around here, but that could be because the police had walked over everything.

Later that afternoon, standing beside a police car a few kilometres south of Barrow Creek, Egan's voice was almost a whisper as he complained about the length of time that had passed before he was called in to help. 'The police shouldn't have waited three days,' he said. 'It was a waste of time calling me in after they'd buggered it all up.'

But he believed he'd found traces of the tracks of a vehicle that had stopped near the place where the bloodstain was now located. 'Looked like he had a flat tyre, or a soft tyre. Don't know if it was his vehicle but if it was there was something wrong with the tyre.' And that was about the extent of Egan's discovery. Even so, the way things were looking any information would be useful.

X

Joanne Lees was continuing to refuse all requests to appear on TV or give any interviews. Finally, on Friday 20 July she agreed to appear at a press conference; however, it was made clear to me and to other journalists interested in hearing her story, that she would not be saying anything. It would be Paul Falconio, Peter's older brother, who would be reading out a statement she had prepared.

This would be the first time the media had seen her, apart from a glimpse as she was driven back from the Barrow Creek re-enactment in a police car. She entered the room in a building across the road from the police headquarters wearing a light-coloured top bearing the slogan 'Cheeky Monkey'. The fun clothing struck many in the room as being ironic for such a serious occasion.

She sat beside Paul Falconio, staring at the desk in front of her as he read her words that said she wanted to thank her family, friends, the public, and the people who knew her and Falconio in Sydney, for their support.

'I'd like to ask people to concentrate their efforts more on finding Pete than trying to speak to me,' she urged, 'and on finding the man. The police are 100 per cent focussed and devoted and trying to do their best.'

Her statement added, 'I don't want to lessen the severity of what happened, but I believe there has been speculation I was sexually assaulted, but this did not occur. I consider myself very lucky to have escaped and to be okay.' Until she had raised the subject of sexual assault, there had been little speculation about it, aside from few idle comments in pubs around Alice Springs pubs and Sydney University psychologist John Clarke's suggestion that a sexual deviant was the perpetrator.

Joanne thanked all the people who were phoning in with information, 'and if they can just continue to do that because he's still out there and could do this again.' If it was not already clear that she was not willing to discuss the incident, she added, 'I also want to say I am not prepared to sell my story to the media.' The statement over, Peter Falconio's brother and girlfriend rose and left the room, her hand in his.

It was a full 11 days before Joanne Lees appeared before the cameras again, but not to answer any questions. It was merely to read another statement and appeal for continued public assistance—a move that many believed she should have made much earlier. She sucked in deep breaths as she made her way down the corridor. Then, with the cameras trained on her, she began reading her statement.

'I am feeling positive and strong and believe it's only a matter of time now before the man responsible for what has happened to Peter and myself is caught. I am confident everything that can be done is being done and I am hoping one of the leads police are following up will lead to Peter being found. I am confident Pete will be found.

'The re-enactment was unpleasant, but I feel it was necessary. I have asked police to tell me only positive news and remain hopeful of finding Pete. If I could say one thing to the man who did this, I would ask him to let police know where Pete is.'

She had not yet decided how long she would be staying in Alice Springs, she said, or in Australia. 'At the moment I don't think further ahead than what I will do tomorrow.' She urged people to continue phoning police with any information about the man and the vehicle. She thanked the police and Paul Falconio for all the support she had been receiving 'and I hope now that people will respect my privacy and allow me to get on with my life.'

There was a finality in that statement. I wondered how she could talk about getting on with her life when surely she realised the focus had to be on her boyfriend. Had she given up on him already? Had she already made other plans for the rest of her life?

Her hopes for peace and quiet were not to be, of course. A man was missing, presumed murdered, and a gunman was on the loose. And Joanne Lees was the only other person who had been there. No-one was going to let her get on with her life until there had been a result from the police investigation.

Joanne's determination to keep a distance from journalists left the media wondering what she was so afraid of. Leading criminologist Paul Wilson, who had helped police compile profiles of hunted killers, particularly the cold-blooded murderer Ivan Milat, urged her to reveal more information. 'She should be more open, and she should stop manipulating the media as she has been doing,' he said after watching her brief appearances on TV. 'She is controlling the media and the media and the public don't like that.'

But why was she controlling the media, if indeed that was the case? Why was she being so evasive? Certainly a number of police officers found her difficult to deal with. She was continually pressed by her police minders to sit down and answer a number of burning questions to satisfy the public hunger, and finally she agreed to do so. There were conditions, however. She would not speak to anyone from the British media after learning that one journalist had asked Commander Bob Pope if she suffered from mental problems.

'I find that question offensive,' she had retorted and the damage was done as far as relations with the UK reporters were concerned. So it was a small group of Australian journalists that Joanne Lees finally met to answer just three questions out of more than a dozen that had been submitted for her to consider. They related to her treatment by the press—nothing more, nothing less.

The incident at Barrow Creek was slowly evolving into a one of Australia's greatest mysteries which might, in time, be written into folklore along with the outback drama centering around Lindy Chamberlain and her baby Azaria. To this day, the nation remains divided over Mrs Chamberlain's (now Lindy Creighton–Chamberlain) involvement in the baby's disappearance at what was then known as Ayers Rock. even though she has been exonerated. After her conviction for murder, the courts finally accepted Mrs Chamberlain's story that a dingo had taken her nine-and-a-half-week-old baby, although the child's body was never found—just a jumble of her clothing outside a dingo's lair.

A new phrase was emerging now in Alice Springs. People were beginning to talk of the 'Lindyfication' of Joanne Lees, whose behaviour and limited public accounts of the Barrow Creek incident had given rise to rumour and speculation. A gradual change from public sympathy to a deepening mood of suspicion was beginning to enshroud the woman at the centre of the affair.

Two weeks had gone by and police were admitting they were no closer to solving the mystery of the stranger's whereabouts and what had happened to Peter Falconio. There was a sense of frustration about their repeated admissions that they were getting nowhere. Along with huge searches, which by air, foot, car and motorbike had covered half of the Northern Territory, they had received hundreds of phone calls from the public suggesting possible sightings of the gunman and his ute. But there had been no sign of Falconio's body; nor had there been any arrest. As for the Falconio look-alike who had purchased a Mars bar and a soft drink in Bourke a week after the incident, detectives had all but dismissed the report as an Elvis sighting.

In fact, reports that Falconio had been seen in other parts of Australia added to the police burden. Those that could be checked out were followed up, but most turned out to be cases of 'now you see him, now you don't'. One report suggested that Falconio had been seen limping around Tennant Creek, 224 kilometres to the north of Barrow Creek, his leg heavily bandaged.

Chapter 6

Too many questions

As I wrote my stories for the *Daily Mail*, I found myself shaking my head at what appeared to be curious aspects, if not discrepancies, in Joanne's story. I was to learn later that several officers were also asking questions about the case. If the gunman had searched for Lees—just how long was not entirely clear for she had said she did not know for sure when he had left—why did he and his dog leave no footprints, at least none that the Aboriginal trackers could find? Commander Pope had dismissed this mystery by stating that the ground was very hard in places. But Joanne, in her dash into and out of the bushes had left at least one clear footprint. Why had the stranger, walking up and down, left no prints at all—anywhere? The police had stamped over vital evidence, but even so, a print from Lees had been found. So where were the stranger's tracks?

There were numerous other questions that begged answers. Why had the stranger tied Lees up in such a way that she could escape? Why had he left her in his ute with an opportunity of getting away while he went off to do something nearby—presumably move Falconio's body? And if he was moving the body, where had he moved it to? He could not have put it in his own vehicle during that time because Joanne was soon to escape from it, scrambling over the front seats where he had dumped her and then crawling her way through the rear of the vehicle and dropping down onto the road.

By a great stroke of luck she had managed to find undergrowth in the pitch darkness that was thick enough to hide her from the stranger who had then come looking for her with a torch, his dog at his side. And he must have been desperate to find her. She had seen his face. She had seen his dog. She had a reasonable idea of what his vehicle looked like. She knew enough to be able to identify him. He had to find her—and he had all the time in the world. No-one knew what had happened. Any passing motorist would assume the two vehicles parked at the roadside were travelling together and had stopped for any number of reasons. It was highly unlikely anyone else on the road that night would stop to check out the vehicles. No, the stranger had all night to look for the woman who had escaped his clutches. She was the only witness to his crime; all he had to do was wait for dawn to arrive and he would surely find her. Then it would be a simple matter of eliminating the only witness.

Despite this advantage, the gunman had given up the search, even though he knew the woman must have been in the undergrowth. And why hadn't his dog found her? No matter whether the dog was a frisky, curious animal or a docile pet, dog owners around Australia were suggesting that the gunman's dog must have been blind and deaf with no sense of smell to have not found a woman hiding in the bushes close by

There was also the question of what the stranger had done with Falconio's body. Joanne had been able to give police a reasonably good description of the attacker's vehicle, suggesting that the sack he had thrown over her head had come off in a struggle before she was thrust into his cabin. In that case, as she was dragged past the rear of the Volkswagen towards the other vehicle she would have passed the spot where Falconio would have fallen if he had been shot. Perhaps Falconio had stumbled, or fallen, off the road—but in that case, why had no other blood been found aside from the small pool on the bitumen?

The disappearance of Peter Falconio's body was one of the greatest puzzles. As it wasn't to be found anywhere near the bloodstain, only one conclusion could be drawn—the gunman, having curiously abandoned the search for

Joanne, had made another strange decision. He had picked up the body, dumped it in his own vehicle and driven away into the night with it. That was the assumption. But it raised another question: why were there no drops of blood on the road to indicate a bleeding body had been moved? Did the gunman wrap the wound, or the body, so no blood trail would be left? Why would he have bothered to do that anyway, for the pool of blood already told the story that someone had been hurt there. If Falconio was dragged, why were there no scuff marks from his shoes? Was the attacker so strong that he was able to physically lift Falconio and carry him to the four-wheel drive? To have been able to haul the bulky body of Falconio up off the ground and into the van required great strength, yet it seemed the man who had struggled with Joanne had not even been able to overcome her entirely and had failed to tie her feet securely.

There were other peculiarities. It would also have been an enormous risk for a killer to drive away with a bloodied body in the back of his utility. A mishap on the highway, perhaps striking a kangaroo and disabling the vehicle, would be a major problem. In any case, why take the body away at all? Falconio meant nothing to him. Why not just roll the body over to the side of the road and, having lost the woman, make his escape? It would become obvious sooner or later, whether there was a body or not, that Falconio was dead.

There could be only one or two reasons, it seemed, why the body had been removed. The gunman may have feared he had left his DNA on Falconio in a brief struggle before he was shot. Yet Joanne Lees had said nothing about a struggle before hearing what could have been a gun shot. On the contrary, she had told police that from the snatches of conversation she could hear the two men were talking amicably at the back of the van. The other possible reason for removing the body could have been the stranger's belief that the bullet from his gun was still lodged in Falconio and ballistic checks could pinpoint him as the weapon's owner. However, police considered this reason for moving the body to be unlikely—anyone owning a revolver and using it for a crime would not be on any official weapons register.

There was one other curious fact. Joanne and Falconio had kept meticulous records of their journey, noting the kilometres at each fuel stop and recording how much they had spent. Police checked the distance from the fuel stop at Ti Tree to Barrow Creek against the kilometres recorded by the Volkswagen, and found the vehicle had travelled an extra four kilometres. Had the gunman started driving it away, perhaps looking further down the highway for his ecaped victim, then returned it to the bushes near the scene? Had Joanne and Falconio driven some distance off the road at some point? She certainly had not told the police that. The extra kilometres were a mystery.

As police continued to question Joanne, hoping to drag from her the tiniest detail that she might have overlooked, Falconio's mother, Joan, appeared on TV from the UK asking for the Australian public's help. Her face revealed her grief as she made her desperate plea. She suggested that the wanted man 'must live somewhere ... he must have contact with someone, somewhere.' Referring to the police identikit picture she urged the public to, 'Think of his face. Is he your next door neighbour? Does he live down the street? Someone must know him somewhere. Think, think ... do you know this man? Connect him with the dog, with the vehicle, put them together. He has to be found.'

But still the Northern Territory police had to concede that they were no closer to finding Falconio or his presumed killer. Hundreds of phone calls were coming in from the public offering advice and clues, but Commander Max Pope had to admit that there had been no breakthroughs.

Then a new mystery arose. Truck drivers Rod Adams and Vince Millar had already told how they had found Lees with her hands tied together at the front of her body by the crude black handcuffs. But Lees had told detectives that her hands had been tied behind her back. She later explained the discrepancy by pointing out that she had been able to wriggle her buttocks and then her legs through her arms, so that her hands were then at the front of her body. Even so, when it came to the moment that she was able to manoeuvre her hands there had been another change in her story. Initially she had told detectives that she had accomplished this while lying in the bushes, yet when asked by artist David Stagg when she had slipped her body through her hands, she said it had been while she was lying on her side in the back of the gunman's ute.

She had also described to the police earlier how the gunman had thrust a bag over her head, but that when she was being pushed into the front of his vehicle the bag had somehow come free. Her story indicated that she saw nothing between the time she was dragged from the Volkswagen to the gunman's four-wheel drive—yet she was able to give a good description of his vehicle to Stagg, including the polished, unpainted bull bar and the appearance of the rear canopy.

Joanne's more detailed description to the artist suggested that she had been led to the gunman's vehicle without a covering over her head, but in that case, why had she not seen the body of her boyfriend lying at the rear of the Volkswagen where his blood had been spilled? If she was led from the driver's seat of the Volkswagen to the gunman's four-wheel drive, parked behind, she would have passed the rear of the Volkswagen and it must be wondered why she did not see her boyfriend lying there. If there was enough light to see her assailant's vehicle, there must have been enough light to see his body. She had heard a bang, which could have been a shot. Why had she not swung her head from side to side looking for her boyfriend whose welfare would have been of prime importance at that moment? Why had she failed to see him, yet had noted a number of features on the gunman's vehicle?

Aside from the many doubts that had arisen, the British public and the police had learned from bitter experience that even the most convincing victim can dupe the experts. This was not to say that Joanne had not been truthful with her account, but no-one could forget the earlier British case of Tracie Andrews, who claimed her lover had been killed by a mystery road rage attacker, but who was later found guilty of his murder. It was inevitable that comparisons would be drawn between the Andrews case and the Barrow Creek mystery.

X

Tracie Andrews, 30, from Alvechurch, Cheshire, claimed she and her lover, Lee Harvey, had been chased by another motorist as they drove home from a pub late one winter's night in 1996. Andrews claimed that Harvey was stabbed by a passenger in the other car, a man with 'starey eyes' who looked as if he had taken something. With the carotid artery in his throat severed, Harvey died in her arms at the roadside. Miss Andrews graphically described the other vehicle as a dark-coloured Ford Sierra and said the assailant was a 'porky' man in a donkey jacket and was called 'Jez'.

A massive police search was launched for the killer, with appeals for public information going out around Britain. In time, doubts began to surround Miss Andrews' story. Bloodstains in the neck of Miss Andrews' snakeskin-effect leather boot matched the shape of a knife, indicating it might have been hidden there, and the distribution of blood at the scene did not match her account. Police re-interviewed her and charged her with murder. She was found guilty and sent to prison for life. The case was said to be remarkable both for the inventiveness of the defendant's alibi and the steadfastness with which she refused to deviate from it, even when faced with what was said to be 'very strong evidence' to the contrary.

Later, in a letter she wrote from prison and published in Britain's *News of the World*, she provided details that were not heard at her trial. She told how she had plunged the knife again and again into her lover's body, how she felt sickened as she gazed at his butchered body by torchlight and how she had concocted the road rage story minutes after watching Harvey die in her arms.

In her description of that bitterly cold night she said she and Harvey had a row about her ex-lover Andy Tilston, the father of her daughter, as they drove home from a night at the pub. 'I told Lee to stop the car,' she wrote. 'I would rather walk home. He did this, I got out. Lee drove off. He then reversed back and shouted at me to get in the car.

'I was being stubborn and wouldn't get in. He swore at me and drove off again. As I reached the house where the incident happened, Keepers Cottage I think is the name, Lee was waiting in the car, again shouting at me to get in. I told him it was over and I wanted my keys to the flat. Lots of nasty, nasty things were said. He wouldn't give me the keys to my flat. I told him I would call the police.'

She went on in her letter to say that the argument reached boiling point, with Lee accusing her of sleeping with other men. She taunted him about her ex-lover. It was at this point, she said, that Lee got out of the car and pulled a knife. 'I was crying. He came straight up to me and grabbed my hair. He said "See if Andy wants you with a fucked up face." He had a knife and I was scared.

'With that, I kneed him, he fell down and pulled me down too. Then he grabbed me and pulled me, we fell over to the grass verge opposite the car. He hit me, I fell back. I got up and tried to hit him back. We was shouting at each other all the time. He punched me again. I fell. I saw the knife on the floor, picked it up and when he went for me again I just reacted with the knife. I must have stabbed him, then he stood still and shouted "You fucking bitch", then hit me so hard I fell again. I got up halfway and all I can remember is seeing red. I just went mad.'

When police examined the body later, he was found to have died from a frenzied attack of 35 stab wounds to his head, neck and body.

Andrews' letter of confession continued: 'I knew the police would take me away. I was so scared and there was my boyfriend, who I loved, lying in the road because of the stupid fight that had got out of hand. My whole life had ended. I think deep down I knew he wasn't alive. I went back over to Lee. He wasn't breathing. I knew I had to make it look as though we had been attacked.'

She described how a man came from a house and the alarm was raised. She was in a state of shock as the ambulance came. She had been running on adrenaline and now it was wearing off. All she wanted to do was go to sleep and not wake up, to turn back time.

'They took me into a house. I made up a story about us being attacked. I went to the hospital. I flushed the knife down the toilet.'

'I was told that Lee had died. I went to the police station; I made the statement. I made it up as I went along, trying to remember what I had told the police beforehand. I wasn't in the right frame of mind. Why I didn't just tell the truth I don't know—scared of what would happen to me. I couldn't let my family, Lee's family, know what I had done. I hated myself so much. I still do.'

Andrews went ahead with a televised press conference, appealing for the public's help in finding the killers. 'I did the press conference,' she wrote. 'I wanted to die before doing that, but I didn't have the chance. I waited until early morning and went to my flat. I got every tablet I could find. At my mother's house I got all her tablets. I wrote some notes as best I could to my family and my daughter. I told my mum a little later I was going for a lie down. I took all the tablets, along with the ones the doctor had given to me. It was a serious attempt to end my life.'

She was rushed to hospital where she was interviewed by police and was watched 24 hours a day. 'I just couldn't bring myself to tell the truth. I was petrified and felt so alone. All through questioning I kept to the story I had told at my first interview.'

In a tragic self-examination, she confessed: 'I have been a stranger to myself for so long. I only hope I can find myself again. Maybe if I face my fears I will begin to find myself. I know I have a very long road ahead of me ...'

Andrews later appealed against her conviction, her lawyers claiming she did not receive a fair trial because of the adverse publicity surrounding the case. She caused outrage by arriving at the hearing dressed in a figure-hugging white poloneck top and a split skirt. Lord Justice Roch, sitting with two other judges, dismissed the appeal saying, 'The conclusion we have reached is there is nothing unsafe in her conviction.'

The *News of the World*, in an editorial, stated: 'Tracie Andrews told lie upon lie when her fiancée was stabbed to death. She lied to the police, she lied on TV and she lied to the courts. Time and money were wasted looking for the mystery man she blamed ... And the irony is that she has nobody to blame but herself, and her lies.'

The Tracie Andrews affair is, of course, related in no way to Joanne Lees or Peter Falconio. But the Andrews' sensational event, and its bizarre parallels, explains why so many people in the UK began to question aspects of Joanne Lees' account of the incident at Barrow Creek. Comparison of the two cases led to wild speculation among those who knew of the unexplained four kilometres on the Volkswagen. One suggestion was that Joanne and Falconio had had a blazing row, one of them had got out and the other had driven off into the night, before having a change of heart and returning. There had been a fight and Falconio had died. A plausible theory but for one problem—what had Joanne done with the body? Armchair detectives dared to suggest that she had been found by the stranger she said had attacked her and he had helped her dispose of the body. There is, of course, nothing to support this, but such were the rumours and theories that surrounded Joanne Lees as the case was debated on both sides of the world.

Superintendent Jeanette Kerr who was among several police officers who questioned Joanne after the incident, was worried about elements of the British woman's story. She asked Joanne if she would agree to be hypnotised in an attempt to draw out more details from her. Rather than helping the inquiry, the hypnosis revealed inconsistencies—particularly in Joanne's description of the inside of the attacker's ute. Up until then, in all the checks of four-wheel drives that matched the description she had given, police had failed to find a single vehicle that allowed access from the front cabin into the rear. Detectives had also made extensive inquiries with panel beaters and mechanics but they had all stated that they had never come across such a vehicle. In their opinion, taking the panelling out between the cabin and the rear would result in the vehicle collapsing in on itself, unless special reinforcements were built in and that would be such a major job it would not make the change worthwhile.

The failure to find a vehicle with access to the rear was a considerable worry, but detectives were also concerned about the lack of footprints in the bushland, other than those of Lees. There was certainly no sign of anyone walking up and down looking for her with a dog

X

On 28 July 2001, I wrote a story for the British *Daily Mail* carrying the headline: 'Is the Outback Heroine Telling the Truth?' The article raised my concern over the issues—the missing footprints, the absence of spots of blood, the failure of the gunman and his dog to find her. The article was circulated in police departments where discrepancies in Joanne's account were already being examined. She had told of hearing Falconio and the stranger chatting amicably, but tests conducted by investigating officers had found it was extremely difficult to hear a conversation at the rear of a Volkswagen from the front seats. And if a kombivan's notoriously noisy engine was running, it was just about impossible.

There were further elements to Joanne's story that had not been made public. Superintendent Kerr and her team had discovered that a scrolling pattern on the revolver Joanne had said the gunman pointed at her bore a striking similarity to a pattern on the handle of the Volkswagen door.

A doctor who examined Joanne shortly after the attack was confused about the apparent lack of consistent injuries on her body. There were grazes on her knees and elbows, but the doctor had expected that someone who had struggled with an attacker, fallen to the road from his ute, stumbled into the bush and then thrown herself down to hide, would have revealed many more scratches and bruises. She had also revealed no early signs of frostbite, which the doctor might have expected to find on someone who had spent several hours lying absolutely still in temperatures that dropped to close to zero in the desert in the middle of winter. Forensic scientist Carmen Eckhoff had found the cold almost unbearable when she arrived at Barrow Creek two nights later, and others who were in central Australia within 48 hours of the incident had also noticed how bitterly cold the nights were.

There was more—Kerr had examined a length of electrical tape that had bound Joanne's wrists and ankles. The tape, measuring 70 centimetres, was insufficient to tie her legs together the police officer concluded. Lees did not have an answer for this, apart from insisting that her legs had been tied. There was nothing much she could say, either, to the suggestion that the Aboriginal trackers who had examined the scene at Barrow Creek had given the opinion that no-one had remained hidden in the bushes for any length of time.

Further concerns were raised in the mind of Superintendent Kerr when she asked Joanne to describe the bag that had been thrust over her head by the gunman. Her detailed description matched a canvas mailbag that she may have seen at the Barrow Creek Hotel after she was picked up by the truckies.

While the lack of physical evidence remained a major worry for detectives, it was possible that Joanne's recall was confused because she was suffering from stress. Research by Associate Professor of Psychiatry, Charles Morgan III, based at the Yale School of Medicine in the US, found that it was quite normal for eyewitnesses who have been in stressful situations to be incapable of accurately remembering what happened, even if questioned as soon as 24 hours after the event.

'Contrary to the popular conception that most people would never forget the face of a clearly seen individual who had physically confronted them and threatened them for more than 30 minutes, a large number of subjects in this study were unable to correctly identify their perpetrator,' Professor Morgan stated in a report. His conclusions might explain why there were discrepancies in Joanne's story, but whether they were aware of problems of recall in some witnesses did not dispel the doubts that some officers had about aspects of the British woman's account.

But while doubts lingered among some detectives and uniformed police, the job had to go on. It had to be assumed that Joanne Lees had told the truth because there was certainly no question that Peter Falconio had vanished and that it was his blood that had spilled on the road. Vehicles that matched the description Joanne had given of the gunman's four-wheel drive continued to be checked and men who looked like the attacker were given second looks. If there was anything about them that suggested the police should look into their backgrounds and lifestyles they were secretly watched. One man who looked similar to the moustachioed assailant and who was seen drinking later at the Barrow Creek Hotel was discreetly photographed and checked out before he was eliminated from inquiries.

Chris Malouf, who had been grabbed by police when he pulled into the Barrow Creek Hotel the morning after the attack, had had his share of troubles as he'd continued on his way north. He was stopped so many times by police that he finally had to beg for a special card from a senior officer with a note that explained he had been stopped and cleared at previous road blocks and should not be searched again. Even so, people in small towns stared more than once at him as they recalled the face in the wanted pictures.

As he sat by the banks of the Katherine River at the top of the Northern Territory one afternoon, two fishermen, former security guard Greg Pollard and his mate Bruce Dejersey, watched him as he whittled Aboriginal music sticks, one of his favourite pastimes. 'That bloke is a dead ringer for that murderer,' Pollard whispered to his friend.

Dejersey stared hard at the man. 'Don't reckon we should be hanging around here,' he said after a moment or two. 'It's him all right.'

Even so, they had a chat with Malouf, talking about the pleasantness of their riverside surroundings but neither of the two friends wanted to be a hero. When they packed up their gear, they thought about telling the police but decided against it. Their concerns were shared by others who in the course of time saw look-alikes but decided against going to the police—no-one wanted to show any bravado in case there were comebacks.

For his part, Malouf just wanted to get away from the harassment. But he could well understand why the police had been so interested in him. He had a dog lead in the back of his vehicle, a memento of a previous pet, and his appearance and that of his four-wheel drive were similar to the gunman's he'd been hearing all about. He'd had enough; he was going to drive to Broome, 1500 kilometres away, where he could stay at a men's shelter and hang loose for a while until he got his life together. There would be many other people like him he could fit in with, men from broken homes, some on the run from the law, drop-outs, renegades of one kind or another. He rolled up his swag, tossed it into the back of his canvas-covered ute and headed out along the Victoria Highway.

Some time earlier, another white van had also hit the road towards Broome. Unlike Malouf, the driver had not taken the road north to Katherine. Instead, Brad Murdoch, a burly man with a Mexican-style moustache similar to Chris Malouf's, had turned onto the Tanami Track, just north of Alice Springs, and his ute was bouncing along the corrugated dirt surface. If he managed to keep up a good speed, despite the rough track, which tested even the most experienced driver, he could be in Broome by dawn the following day, Monday 16 July.

Chapter 7
Picking up the pieces

When Joanne Lees eventually flew back to Sydney from Alice Springs after days that ran into weeks of police questioning, she returned to the embrace of the friends she had made previously at Dymocks bookshop.

She had been considered such a good worker that she was taken on again, telling her employers that she would like to remain in Sydney for a while in case there was any news of her boyfriend. Dressed in a pale blue, short-sleeved shirt—the Dymocks' uniform—she politely attended to customers in the shop, which was below street level. Passers-by would occasionally stop to stare through the knee-high window at the dark-haired woman whose face had appeared so often in the newspapers and on TV. Although she had shied away from the media in Alice Springs, the relative brief glimpses that photographers and cameramen had of her were repeated often in the newspapers and on television. But any customers who dared to ask her about her experience was given short shrift—she would excuse herself and head off to the back of the shop.

Her friends at Dymocks had no doubts about her story, one angrily dismissing rumours that she might have been involved in Falconio's disappearance. Workmate Tim Ford, 27, who spoke to Joanne almost every day since the incident, described her and Falconio as 'the perfect couple' who were set to become engaged. Falconio, said Mr Ford, was planning to propose to Joanne when he disappeared.

'They were just wonderful together,' he said. 'I know she was hoping Pete would propose to her in Hawaii, which was going to be their last stop before they flew home to England. There was never any tension between them. The last five months I spent in Sydney working closely with Jo were the happiest times possible. They were both such easy personalities. They would never argue. You would never see anything to indicate that anything like this would occur. They were one of the most perfect couples you could come across.'

Mr Ford, himself from England, said he felt he knew Joanne better than anyone else who had met her in Sydney. 'I can say she is not that kind of person. She's not violent and she's not irrational. I never saw anything amiss between them. There was never any reason why they would have anything to argue about.'

When asked about the ugly rumours that she might have been involved in Falconio's disappearance, Mr Ford said: 'Joanne did not kill Pete. It's insane. Anybody who has spent any time with Jo would find it completely ridiculous to suggest that she had anything to do with it.'

Then there was Gary Sullivan, Joanne's boss at the bookshop. He remembered the way she was before the incident. 'She and Peter were like a married couple,' he recalled. 'She was the outgoing, vivacious one while he was the quieter, thoughtful, more analytical one.'

Perhaps her friends had decided they needed to help take her mind off the ordeal, but in any case shortly after her return to Sydney Joanne was to be seen in bars around the city, drinking, dancing and laughing. The memory of Falconio would have still been strong, for it had been less than a year since he had left his workplace near Darling Harbour after collecting his weekly wages and made the 20 minute walk to the city to meet her.

Her friends from the bookshop gave her the greatest protection whenever she left the premises. At least one girlfriend would walk at her side as they made their way along George Street to catch the ferry around the harbour to the beachside suburb of Manly, where they shared a hilltop house. One of

Joanne's favourite drinking spots in Manly was a pub at the end of the pedestrian mall named—ironically, given that she and Falconio had lived in Brighton—the New Brighton Hotel. She could be found in the upstairs bar, surrounded by a large group of friends, and would often stay there until closing time. She appeared to be suffering from mood swings. Sometimes she would be laughing and joking with them; at other moments she would sit alone to one side, her face glum.

Her resumed job at Dymocks put her on a duty list that meant she had some weekdays free. She would grab the opportunity to walk down the hill from the house she shared to an internet café and there, sitting anonymously among other backpackers, she would tap away at the keyboard for an hour or more. Joanne Lees cut a lonely figure as she wandered around Manly while her friends were at work. It was only when she was back in their company, back in the pubs, dancing to live bands, that she appeared to come back to life.

She returned to England just before Christmas 2001, staying briefly with her parents near Huddersfield before returning to Hove, where she had previously lived with Falconio. She sought solace with old friends, first moving in with air hostess Sarah King, before renting a two-bedroom Georgian flat of her own. She took up her former job as a travel agent, telling friends that one day she hoped to buy a house.

'She's keen to keep her anonymity,' said one of her friends. 'She's fed up with people staring at her, people thinking they know her but unable to recall exactly who she is. She's obviously hoping it's all going to go away, all this staring. She just wants to put the past behind her and start a new life. She talks to no-one about what happened and seems quite introspective at times, although she is generally quite happy and relaxed.'

The friend said that Joanne and her former flatmate Sarah had become very close, Sarah being one of the only people Joanne had confided in since Falconio disappeared.

Sometimes Joanne could be seen walking on the Brighton sea front. An onlooker said, 'She seemed happy, confident and very much back in control of her life, although there were moments when she appeared to be a bit detached from the rest of the group.' Just as she had seemed detached at times when out with friends in Sydney on her return from Alice Springs. It was anyone's guess what she would have been thinking.

Chapter 8

The drug runner

He knew the inland roads as well as anyone. He was familiar with the shortcuts—if thousands of kilometres could ever be a shortcut—and he had a good knowledge of what routes to avoid when it was raining, for even the experienced could become bogged on unmade tracks in the wet season.

The outback was Brad Murdoch's backyard, his four-wheel drive his home, although he preferred to call it his bus. He travelled with his beloved dog, Jack, an inquisitive, face-licking dalmation and sometimes a black and grey cat called Tom—actually a female, Murdoch discovered, after calling it by the male name for years. The dog and cat were his usual companions, although Murdoch would sometimes leave the cat behind in Broome and there were occasions when a mate would go along in the cab with him.

Murdoch's father, Colin, endearingly referred to his big son as a 'gypsy of the inland', for he could cope with any problem that came his way. Meticulous, neat and well organised, as the rear interior of his Toyota four-wheel drive testified, no-one was more capable of keeping on the move and fixing the problem if anything went wrong with the motor. Although not a trained mechanic, Murdoch had picked up a vast experience over the years, working as a truck driver and travelling hundreds of thousands of kilometres to visit his family in Perth. He had found jobs at a number of engineering works, honing his skills and earning a reputation as a good worker. Murdoch was a Toyota man, at least in later years, swapping over from an F100 Ford to a late 90s model Toyota Land Cruiser, an HZJ-75, although some time earlier he drove an older style model, an HJ-47. He kept the latest four-wheel drive, a former Telstra vehicle, in immaculate condition, but wanted it looking even better. In June 2001, a month before the Barrow Creek incident, he asked Wayne Holmes, who specialises in powdercoating vehicle parts, spraying them with a special paint that does not chip, to work on the wheels. He talked to Holmes about his plans to put security mesh doors on the rear canopy, under the canvas, at some time in the future.

In his early 40s, Brad Murdoch was big and strong and it was said that if he was your mate you could rely on him to back you in the worst of circumstances. He even suffered fools as long as they were loyal. For above all, Murdoch believed that loyalty was the greatest of all assets. But he made no secret of his dislike for Aboriginal people. On his tattooed arms was a picture of an Aboriginal hanging from a noose above a fire and the letters KKK. And once he walked into a pub wearing a T-shirt bearing the slogan, 'I Hate Niggers'.

A road that daunted many travellers but which Murdoch knew like the tattoos on his arms was the Tanami Track, mostly an unmade dusty stretch cutting across desert from a few miles north of Alice Springs to Halls Creek in Western Australia. The brutal route eventually meets the Great Northern Highway for the final stretch along bitumen through Fitzroy Crossing and on to Broome on the north-west coast—a total distance from Alice Springs of 1800 kilometres. The track is one of the most treacherous roads in Australia, deep ruts and severe corrugation reducing travelling speed at times to 30 kilometres per hour. Fuel supplies are few and far between, the isolated roadhouses where it is available open at reduced hours so astute motorists carry cans of spare fuel.

Murdoch used the Tanami, as it is popularly known to locals, for two reasons. Despite its hazards, it was the quickest route to Broome from South Australia where he often stayed. More importantly, however, was that there was less chance of running into a police patrol set up to breath test drivers or hit them for speeding—for Murdoch's principal occupation was drug runner, carrying large supplies of marijuana from his suppliers in South Australia to Broome. From here it was distributed among the bikie gangs who in turn moved it around the north and sometimes back down to the coastal towns further south by road or sea.

The gangs knew where to set up their own distribution centres without attracting too much attention from the authorities. As well as buying and distributing cannabis that found its way to the north from South Australia, courtesy of Brad Murdoch and other less notable runners, the bikie gangs grew their own marijuana and sent it by boat along the coast. In the mid-1990s, bikies living on Aboriginal land near the remote coastal community of Kalumburu, on the Western Australian border with the Northern Territory, had been running a big cannabis plantation until the area was raided by police. But the bikies, members of the Coffin Cheaters gang, came back, mooring two boats and, it was claimed, flying light aircraft to and from Indonesia. The Aboriginals said they had learned that there was a pilot in the gang and they had heard unidentified planes landing near one of the bikie camp sites at Lull Bay, some 70 kilometres from Kalumburu.

In any case, what Brad Murdoch brought into Broome helped to keep the supply ticking over. For he and his partner it was a profitable business and well worth the 3600 kilometre journey, which could take up to four or five days driving. He never stopped in hotels or motels; his converted utility with the canvas canopy on the back and all manner of camping gear neatly stacked inside served his needs perfectly. Jack, the dalmation which he had bought as a puppy several years earlier, needed company during the night, for Jack was Murdoch's constant companion whether he was on the road or helping out in a workshop somewhere. Everyone Murdoch was acquainted with also knew and loved Jack, a friendly, full-of-life dog.

Murdoch had done a stint in jail years earlier for the incident of firing a gun in a public place when a group of Aborigines had blocked his road and he had shot over their heads. He wasn't keen on going back to prison. So when he was on a drug run he took the greatest precautions. There could be absolutely no mistakes that could cause trouble from the police or criminal elements. He carried many thousands of dollars in the ute to make his purchases, and extra amounts of cash should the opportunity arise to buy a bigger stash. Sometimes he would be carrying marijuana worth $100 000. There was no way he was going to drive around outback Australia with all that dope, or money, or both, without some form of protection. So he got himself 'tooled up', fitting himself out with a couple of hand guns. He wore one in a shoulder holster and hid a second weapon in the side panelling of the ute door. It was just a matter of taking precautions. Made sense, he would tell people close to him, considering the kind of business he was running.

Murdoch was also aware that he could be arrested at any moment if he were to make the slightest mistake—pulled over for speeding, dangerous driving, or having something wrong with the ute that would cause a police patrol to wave him down, resulting in his vehicle being searched. Not that the regular police patrols concerned him so much as state narcotic squads. If for any reason they had been tipped off about his activities he wouldn't put it past them to use every means at their disposal to trap him. He was an ex-con after all. Murdoch believed that with modern equipment he could be traced through his mobile phone, so he would frequently change the SIM card. As an extra precaution he purchased a bug-detecting device which he carried in a small bag. If he had stopped at the same petrol stations during his trips, he would switch on the device knowing that it would scream if any voice-monitoring equipment were operating. As far-fetched as these precautions may have seemed to others, Murdoch was a careful and meticulous man.

He did not even want to stop outside the house he was sharing in Broome in order to open up the gates and drive in off the road. It was his practice to call his flatmate of three years, burly Maori taxi driver James Hepi, as he drove into the small town.

'Hey mate, it's me. Be there in five ...'

Hepi would then open up the gates and Murdoch would swoop right in, much of the driveway being hidden by bushes and trees. It was a perfect base for Murdoch to operate a business in which arrest, robbery or death was a 24-hour risk.

A few times on his run, Murdoch had taken a mate known as Sheriff with him. They travelled from Broome to Adelaide for what he would describe as 'business', although one of the main aims of their second trip, in Murdoch's original Ford, was to pick up the newer HJZ-47. But whatever the vehicle, Sheriff, Brian Johnston, would share the driving and the sleeping. Whoever was sleeping would be able to lay his swag out across the gear that Murdoch had in the back. This included plastic tubs, an esky, a fridge, primus stove, two chairs, a 20-litre water container, a 60-litre water container, and plastic crates full of tools and clothes. When either man wanted to sleep, he would have to get out of the cabin and walk around to the back of the vehicle to climb into the rear canopy. Jack the dog also slept in the back, usually stretched out on blankets lying across the top of the long-range fuel tank.

Another ex-biker, Darryl 'Dags' Cragan, who has known Murdoch since they grew up together in Northampton, also did a bit of travelling with the big man. After losing touch with each other they met up again in Geraldton. The two men eventually ended up sharing a place in Broome. There, Cragan was introduced to all of Murdoch's friends and associates, including James Hepi. On one occasion, some two years before the Barrow Creek incident, Cragan travelled with Murdoch to South Australia. On that journey he found out the most popular route Murdoch would use— along the Tanami Track, stopping off for fuel and some food in the small community of Fitzroy Crossing. Their first and only trip together from Broome to South Australia took two and a half days with hardly any stops along the way, and Murdoch did all the driving. Cragan remembers that most stops were to let Jack out for a walk, but the journey was desperately slow along one stretch of the Tanami south of Halls Creek where there are washaways, rocky outcrops and corrugations. In order to lessen the severe shaking and to obtain better traction, they had to let pressure out of the tyres. If there was something that Cragan learned about Brad Murdoch on that trip, it was that he felt utterly confident that no matter what happened to the vehicle, he would be more than capable of getting them out of a jam.

Peter Jamieson, another friend, had got to know Murdoch when they were working as truck drivers together in the late 1980s, and later took over as manager of the BP roadhouse at Fitzroy Crossing. Fitzroy

Crossing was a small mixed community of Aboriginal and white Australians, famous as the base for the search for a notorious Aboriginal outlaw known as Pigeon, and his gang at the end of the 19th century. Murdoch would sometimes stop off at the roadhouse to refuel, have a snack and a bit of a chat with Jamieson before continuing on the last leg of his journey to Broome.

On his drug run in July 2001, at the time of the Barrow Creek incident, Murdoch stopped over for a sandwich and a cup of coffee with Jamieson. With Jack the Dalmation at his side in the Toyota's cabin, Murdoch then set off for Broome with the precious cargo in the back of the vehicle.

'The bus has taken a battering,' Murdoch said to Hepi, referring to his ute, as he shook the dust of his clothing and entered the shared house. 'It needs looking at.' No-one would be surprised to learn that Murdoch's vehicles needed regular maintenance. He had the use of Hepi's property in South Australia but he also had friends in Adelaide and his elderly parents and brother lived in Western Australia. He and Jack the dog were likely to pop up anywhere at any time in his four-wheel drive.

Later that same morning of Monday 16 July, Murdoch and Hepi drove around to see another mate, Brett Duthie, who owned a vehicle repair shop called West Kimberley Diesel. Murdoch often worked with Duthie, filling in when times were busy, and Duthie couldn't speak highly enough of him. He even allowed him to keep a caravan at the back of his workshop.

Murdoch and Hepi picked up four heavy-duty batteries, two for Murdoch's Toyota HZJ-75 and two for Hepi's vehicle, an early HJ-75 model. Then Murdoch set about having work carried out on his ute in different places in town—jobs that were to come under intense scrutiny in time.

Also closely analysed later was a conversation Hepi claimed to have had with Murdoch shortly after his arrival back in town from that trip to South Australia in July 2001. Hepi was to tell the authorities that the two of them got into a conversation about the attack on Falconio and Lees because the story was 'all over the place'. Murdoch, according to Hepi, volunteered the information that it wasn't him, that he wasn't the person who had attacked the couple.

Even more intriguing was the conversation Hepi said he had with Murdoch about the disposal of bodies. It just happened to come up one day, Hepi reckoned, when Murdoch asked about the most efficient way of getting rid of a body. He had even suggested the quickest and safest method was to bury a corpse in the soft earth of a run-off drain at the roadside, a cutting that allowed excess water to flow off the surface of the road.

Hepi thought the police might be interested in hearing this kind of information. But the truth was that James Hepi was in a bit of trouble with the law over drug possession. He needed to come up with something, something that would help get him out of trouble. He would be doing himself a favour if he were to go to the police with everything he knew about Murdoch. Perhaps he could even strike a deal ...

X

Julie Harrison (name changed at request of court) had had enough of serving drinks and entertaining the guys at the exclusive drinking club in Broome, used by members of the outlaw motorcycle gang, the Coffin Cheaters. It was there that she had earned the reputation of being able to drink the hardiest of them—big tough men with tattoos on their arms, guns under their arms, and dope in their pockets—under the table. And she was only 18. She did a few other jobs around town, working in an electrical shop for a while, but she wanted a change, so she headed first to Darwin, then down to Adelaide and then across to Perth, where her family was living. She was an attractive woman, with long dark hair, but she hit the bottle regularly and her friends realised that Julie had a serious alcohol problem. She simply told them that she liked beer—she found it refreshing.

Unable to settle in Perth, she decided to head east again and at 5 am on the morning of 19 June 2001, roughly a month before the Barrow Creek incident, she set off for Adelaide, 2750 kilometres away, in her Suzuki Vitara. Her route would take her across the Nullabor Plain, a seemingly endless stretch of road the name of which is a corruption from Latin for 'not any trees'. In time her journey was to become of great interest to the police and a team of defence lawyers. Both would try to find some benefit from what she was to describe of her journey.

For motorists reaching even the smallest outpost on that long road from Perth to Adelaide there is some relief from the endless horizon. Julie reached the last 'big' town, Norseman, with a population of 3000, where she bought fuel, coffee, beer and cigarettes. It was the beer she really wanted, purchasing two sixpacks of stubbies from the service station, and she drank as she continued her journey.

Shortly before dusk, with the two sixpacks consumed, Julie reached the small community of Caiguna, which, because of its location roughly halfway between Perth and Adelaide, keeps its own time zone. As she was driving into the outpost she noticed a four-wheel drive with a canopy on the back parked just a little way off the road. A big man was walking around the vehicle with a dog and Julie had the impression he was camping there.

She pulled into a small hotel and drank a few beers. She also bought more beer for the road. She accelerated to 100 kilometres per hour, but because she had continued drinking and it was now dark she did not want to risk driving faster—there would be kangaroos out at night and she did not have spotlights. She noticed two pinpricks of light in her rear-vision mirror. They were growing larger. Then the vehicle was right up behind her. Moments later the lone woman driver was being overtaken. She raised her hand to the side window to acknowledge the other driver. She caught a glimpse of a dog sitting in the passenger seat and realised the white ute was the vehicle she had seen parked at the roadside as she'd approached Caiguna.

As the other vehicle pulled away ahead of her Julie saw how well its lights were illuminating the road. She thought it safest to try to keep up with the other driver, using his vehicle as her guide along the hazardous highway. She followed the other driver into the petrol station at a tiny place called Madura. As they tended to their vehicles she thanked him for the use of his lights.

'That's okay,' he said. 'If you're still heading east you can follow me again.'

He was a big man, well over six foot, with short, greying hair and a grey moustache that came down over the sides of his mouth. He was wearing jeans and a jumper with a zipper in the neck. She gave him her name, said she was going through to Adelaide, and he introduced himself as Brad. He grinned as he said he recognised the Western Australian shire where her numberplate had been registered. She noticed that he also had Western Australian plates, yellow and black. Their conversation was friendly and he suggested they drive along the road a bit and then stop for a beer and a chat. She followed him along the highway until they reached a truck pull-in. For police, this meeting with Brad was important as it gave them a fix on his movements in June 2001.

Julie handed him one of her beers and they started chatting about places they had been to. It wasn't long before she learned he was living in Broome. She told him she had worked there for a while and they bounced around the names of people they knew.

'You know, I've got a pretty good idea I recognise you,' he told her, his thumbs casually stuck into his belt as he chatted. She couldn't be sure about that, even though he said he knew the Coffin Cheaters club, where she had worked, very well. As they were drinking their beer Brad offered her a line of speed. Julie didn't hesitate to take up his offer. They drank more beer, had a few cigarettes and then they smoked a joint. His dog, a dalmation which he called Jack, pottered around. From being a lonely woman on a lonely road with only her stubbies for company, Julie now felt very comfortable with her new friend.

He said he'd driven down from Broome and she asked why he hadn't used the Tanami and then headed down the Stuart Highway to South Australia. He told her he had people to see in Perth.

'Well, if you go back to Broome on the Stuart and you decide to go further north than the Tanami to cross to Broome, you should make a point of stopping off at Barrow Creek,' she told him. 'There's a hotel there, run by a guy I know called Les Pilton. They call it the Pilton Hilton. Quaint little place.'

Finally, with alcohol, speed and marijuana coursing through their veins, they set off on the road again. Brad had told her she could put her headlights on as she travelled behind him because he had curtains in the back window of his cab and he could pull them across so he wouldn't be blinded from the reflection in the rear-vision mirror.

As the night wore on they stopped from time to time beside the deserted highway for a drink, a smoke and another line of speed. They passed across the border to South Australia shortly before 1 am, then pulled into a small post, called Border Village. Julie was grateful to be over the border; it signified that a large part of her journey was behind her, although there was a good 1000 kilometres still to go. Although she was tired, she wanted to keep going and hit the highway behind Brad, grateful that his powerful lights were opening up the road. Finally, an hour or so before they were due to reach the town of Nullabor, Julie confessed she needed to sleep. Brad suggested they could stop a little further along, close to the Head of the Bight, where treacherous cliffs plunge into the sea.

They pulled into a clearing where Julie found a flat piece of rock where she could lay out her swag. She fixed up a roll of tarpaulin from her bullbar to form a crude shelter. Brad parked his ute a short distance away in front of her Vitara, positioning it at an angle so it gave her some protection from the wind. They had a smoke and chatted a little more.

'You feel safe travelling on these roads like this?' he asked. 'A girl on her own, you ought to be careful.'

She chuckled and said that one day she'd find herself a gun, a small magnum revolver, something like that. A lady's type of gun, one that looked nice, perhaps with a mother of pearl handle, but with a lot of kick. It wouldn't be for protection as such but more for sport, she told him, because a friend of hers had joined a shooting club and she wanted to do the same. 'Something small but powerful would be good,' she said.

'That would probably do the trick,' he said with a smile, before clambering into the back of his ute for a sleep. She noticed all his camping equipment and a mattress when he rolled up the side of the canvas awning. Julie crawled into her swag. She didn't even notice where Jack the dog was sleeping. She'd had a lot to drink, smoked countless joints and taken speed. She was out to the world as soon as she lay her head down.

She woke to the sound of his voice just on dawn. He was a huge man, she noted and seemed even larger than the night before as he towered over her offering her some coffee he'd brewed up. Jack was wandering around nearby. She gratefully accepted the mug, then they set off in convoy to the small community of Nullabor. They found a caravan park where they took showers before they hit the road once more, the rising sun in their eyes. They stopped a few more times to take speed and smoke cannabis.

Left: Peter Falconio and Joanne Lees in England after he graduated with a building and construction degree. *Courtesy of AAP images.*

Below: Joanne and Peter lived life to the full, in England and Australia. *Courtesy of AAP images.*

Above: Peter Falconio found work with a design company in Australia and was never without his cigarettes. *Courtesy of AAP images.*

Below: At the start of their outback adventure, Peter and Joanne pose for a friend in their renovated campervan in April 2001. *Courtesy of AAP images.*

Left: The original
artist's impression
of the gunman,
based on Joanne
Lees's description.
*Courtesy of AAP
images.*

Below: A four-wheel drive fitting the description of the gunman's
vehicle described by Joanne Lees stops at a petrol station in Alice Springs
at 12.45 am. *Courtesy of AAP images.*

Above: The poor-quality security camera frame of the mystery driver who arrived at the Alice Springs truckstop several hours after the Barrow Creek incident.

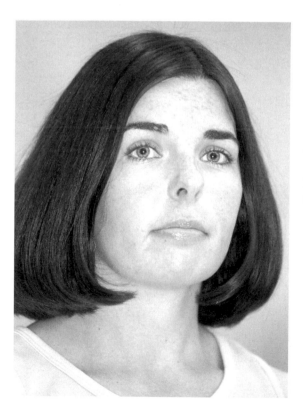

Left: Joanne Lees in Alice Springs a few days after the incident at Barrow Creek. *Courtesy of AAP images.*

Above: The orange and white volkswagen at the centre of the incident at Barrow Creek. The dark smudges on the side of the vehicle are fingerprint dust and the squares at the right rear reveal where forensic scientists made a painstaking search for spots of blood or gunshot residue. They found none. *Courtesy of Richard Shears.*

Below: This photo taken in November 2001 shows the whiteboard behind Superintendent Kate Vanderlaan, in charge of the Alice Springs investigation. Officers were looking for a man with shoulder-length dark hair and of medium build, with a red heeler cattle dog. *Courtesy of Richard Shears.*

Above: One year to the day after the Barrow Creek incident, the dark stain of Peter Falconio's blood could still be seen on the road. The picture was taken on 14 July 2002. *Courtesy of Richard Shears.*

Left: When Joanne Lees returned to Sydney after Peter Falconio disappeared she went back to her former job at Dymocks bookshop in Sydney. She rarely left work without being in the company of at least one co-worker.

Above: Bradley Murdoch's converted ute after his dramatic arrest in South Australia.

Below: A rare photograph of Brad Murdoch and his dog, Jack, the dalmation. The picture was taken in South Australia after the incident at Barrow Creek and reveals a close relationship between the burly outback traveller and his dog. *Courtesy of the Murdoch family.*

Left: Brad Murdoch as a 14-year-old schoolboy attending his 24-year-old brother Gary's wedding in Western Australia. *Courtesy of the Murdoch family.*

Below: A wedding photo without the bride ... Brad Murdoch, aged 26 in 1984, poses with his father Colin and his mother Nance. The cut where the bride was removed with scissors can be seen between mother and son. *Courtesy of the Murdoch family.*

At Ceduna, a tiny town of white stone buildings with the blue-green sea in the background, Julie said she wanted to stop off to check her bank account and draw out some money. Brad kept on going but she didn't think for a moment that she wouldn't see him again. And just as she had expected, he was parked at the roadside, waiting for her. Together they drove off the road for what she expected would be to smoke more dope. She followed his four-wheel drive into a sheltered area, a gully surrounded by nearby hills.

'You remember you were saying you were interested in getting hold of a gun?' he said. 'Well, it so happens I've got one for sale.' He reached into the ute and brought out a small, silver-barrelled revolver. She noticed the spin-around chamber. He told her to fire off a shot, just to see how it felt.

Julie didn't feel comfortable about that and turned down the offer. So he fired a round off into the bush, not aiming at anything, just firing it so she could see how it worked. For the first time since she'd been travelling with Brad she felt a little uneasy to be with this man and a gun in a place where no-one could see them from the road. But he simply put the weapon away and told her he was happy to continue being her escort on the journey east.

This alleged incident was of interest to the police because it was evidence that Brad Murdoch carried a small revolver. But for a team of lawyers who were to be brought into the Barrow Creek case later, the journey Julie made with him was evidence that while there might have been every opportunity to take advantage of a drunken, doped-up woman on a lonely road, he had not done so.

At Port Augusta, the centre of a semi-arid grazing and wheat-growing region 330 kilometres north-east of Adelaide, it was time for them to go their separate ways. He was going to travel on to a small community east of the wine-growing region of the Barossa Valley beyond the Mount Lofty Ranges, and she had to travel down to Adelaide.

She was sad to say goodbye to him. Despite that moment of unease she'd felt when he'd fired the gun, she considered he'd been the perfect gentleman. She wished she could see him again some time, and Jack the dalmation.

'If you're ever in Adelaide,' she said, passing him her phone number, 'please give me a call.' She watched as the ute headed out of town, the big man at the wheel, his lovely dog at his side.

In the coming weeks she wondered if it was Brad whenever her phone rang. But June turned into July, he never called, and she gave up on him.

Chapter 9
Journey into darkness

It was early July when the orange Volkswagen chugged through the northern suburbs of Adelaide. Peter Falconio, 28, and Joanne Lees, 27, had been making the most of their trip to Australia and there was so much more ahead to see—the incredible outback, a Mecca for any visiting couple. But although they had been going out together for seven years and there had been talk about settling down and getting married after their trip, time would reveal that in the more immediate future, Joanne had other plans. Plans that perhaps Peter Falconio would have been shocked to learn about.

The Yorkshireman doted on Joanne, even though there was no doubt among those who knew the couple in England and had befriended them in Australia that it was Joanne who 'wore the trousers', as one acquaintance put it. They had met at a nightclub in Huddersfield in 1994, although Falconio had by then already left the industrial region of West Yorkshire to work in Brighton, returning for family visits.

Joanne, who has a younger brother, Samuel, had grown up in Almondbury, a small West Yorkshire town a couple of miles south east of Huddersfield. Almondbury has more importance as a historical region than a modern-day centre, for it was an important Tudor settlement. It remains a popular area of exploration for archaeologists, while other visitors just enjoy the climb up Castle Hill, the site of an old fort, to enjoy the surrounding landscape. Joanne attended Almondbury High School (Motto: Together We Achieve) where she was described as being an intelligent and attentive student. While there, her mother, Jennifer Lees, went into a second marriage with Vincent James and it was a family decision to remain in the area.

Peter Falconio, meanwhile, attended Holmfirth High School, which lies in the Holme Valley, the setting for a popular British TV series, *Last of the Summer Wine*, a few miles from the centre of the grim textile town of Huddersfield. Huddersfield stands proud of its architecture, sport, (including the Huddersfield Town Football Club), festivals and culture. A master at Holmfirth remembers Falconio as being 'a smashing kid' who was 'popular with adults and students alike'. Falconio continued his studies at Huddersfield Technical College, which promises its students that no matter what their age, if they want a dream job, a place at university, promotion or just want to do something for pleasure, the staff can help. Falconio studied to be a chef but later decided he wanted to go into building construction and made up his mind to move south. Fellow students described him as an easy-going fellow, very relaxed and a good friend.

Impressions change. When Falconio moved to Brighton to take a degree in building and construction management, there were mixed opinions of him. Dr Kassim Gidado, his personal tutor and course leader, recalls him as being one of the high fliers on the course and very popular. But he had also struck Dr Gidado as being a very determined young man and his intensity caused some of his fellow students to keep their distance from him.

After meeting and dating Joanne, they moved to Brighton, where they lived together and built up a circle of friends and acquaintances. With his qualifications as a chef, Falconio earned praise for his cooking skills whenever the couple entertained at home. But some of those friends saw them as being mean and money-hungry. It was certainly true that the couple were saving hard for their dream trip to the Far East and Australia, but some of their friends believed their determination to build up their funds sent out the wrong message. In particular, Falconio was described by one acquaintance as mean and 'a bit dodgy'.

Whether they were aware of the opinions that had built up about them in some circles, they began planning their trip, for Joanne had started work in a travel agency and had all the details of every country they planned to visit. 'On Sunday mornings,' she was to recall, 'we would have breakfast in bed and get out the atlas and plan where we wanted to go and it would change every Sunday. Being a travel agent I calculated the cost and chose the final route.'

Colin Chivers (name changed by request) met Falconio in Hotshots bar, Brighton, soon after the Yorkshireman arrived in the seaside town. It was the bar's opening night and Chivers and Falconio had been taken on as staff. The two men had been paired up, as had other staff members, and although they had got on reasonably well together Chivers was to admit later that he had not taken an instant liking to his work colleague. The words 'dodgy northerner' came to mind although there was nothing in particular that Falconio did that led him to think that.

Falconio told him he had a girlfriend who was living with him, but that didn't prevent the two men becoming friendly enough for them to go out on the town on occasions, hitting the nightclubs. About a year after the two men met, Falconio found himself a job on a construction site, while still working at the bar part-time. He needed all the money he could get, he told Chivers. Falconio's work was at the site of the new Royal Sussex County Hospital and when he changed jobs there and his previous position became available, he arranged for Chivers to take over. It was a full-time job and better pay than the pub.

Falconio stayed with the same construction company, but now, instead of working as a drawings administrator he was a planner. He and Chivers worked out of an office, with Falconio's desk directly behind Chivers'. Between this work and the part-time bar work, Falconio was also continuing his studies at Sussex University. There wasn't a lot of time to devote to Joanne, who was working hard at the travel agency in any case, but even so their plans to make the big trip abroad proceeded. Chivers hung about with Falconio more than the other young men on the building site, many of whom found him to be rather dull—'hardly the life and soul of the party', was how Chivers was to remember him later. Not the kind of person you would want to spend every weekend with. At the same time, Chivers was grateful that Falconio had got him the better job.

As the months rolled by, Chivers decided that if he had to sum up his occasional friend in a few words, it would be 'dodgy, sly, brash, deceitful'. Despite this, Chivers hung out with Falconio because of their close work relationship and there were some fun times when they drank together. And if truth be told, Chivers felt a little sorry for the north countryman.

Although not outgoing, Falconio was very outspoken which was why, Chivers believed, Falconio found it hard to find true friends: he just didn't get on with people because he said what he thought and did not consider the consequences.

The group of young men from the site who tended to hang around with Chivers saw Falconio as something of an outsider; they tended to wind him up with jokes that he often didn't get—but the implications were mainly along the lines of him being a tight, mean northerner. They gave him a nick-name, 'Dodgy Pete', because he was always looking for ways of scamming and making a quid here and there. The standing joke among the group was that Falconio would sell his own grandmother for a tenner.

Chivers found out that Falconio was allegedly involved in piracy of DVDs, CDs and videos. Sometimes he would go across to France on the ferry or hovercraft and bring back beer and cigarettes to sell. He would return with his old VW Polo piled high with duty-free goods and he made it known among his work colleagues that there were bargains to be purchased.

Chivers came to realise that his assessment of Falconio as being a money-grabber was correct when a group of them, at closing time in the pub, suggested going on to another establishment. Falconio told them, 'You don't want to waste your money in a club. Come back to mine and Jo's and we'll have a good old session there.'

At the couple's flat, Falconio asked everyone what they wanted—wine, beer or spirits—and then he said to each of them, 'That's 40p, that's 50p' and so on. His friends started laughing, thinking it was one of Falconio's rare jokes. But then they realised he was deadly serious.

'I'm charging for the drinks. You don't think I'm going to give them away, do you?' he said.

His mates were astonished to think that Falconio, with alcohol piled up in the flat, should charge them for entertaining them in his home. But then, they agreed, he had always been mean with the drinks; none of them could recall him ever buying a round. Money was an obsession with him and it didn't seem to matter how he made it.

Joanne was the same, Chivers considered. When he and Joanne became involved in a discussion about the various ways Falconio was building up his funds on the side, she told him, 'You've got to make the money somehow'.

Falconio admitted to his mates that he was much happier in Brighton than Huddersfield. He didn't like his life in the northern city and he had no plans to return. But Joanne, Chivers learned over the months that he knew her, was different. She missed the north and would often complain of feeling homesick and missing her parents. Sometimes she would pack a bag and head off home for the weekend, but Falconio didn't go with her. He just wasn't interested in going back. Chivers thought it was almost a kind of punishment when she left him a note with things for him to do before she set off each time for the north.

Their friends saw their relationship as fiery, like a couple who had lived together too long and the cracks had appeared, yet who remained with each other because they had become so accustomed to being with one another. Joanne would call him at work five or six times a day sometimes, and Chivers gained the impression from Falconio's answers on the phone that she would be nagging him. He could tell that at times their conversation was quite heated. There was no doubt in his mind that Joanne was the dominant one in the relationship and in their verbal battles she always seemed to come off best.

Often, it seemed to the group of friends who hung around with Falconio, the tension eased when his older brother Paul came down from the north to visit him and Joanne. They'd all go out for a few drinks together over the weekend and then Paul would head off back to Huddersfield, although the building site men heard that sometimes he went across to France for a few days.

To Chivers it seemed that Falconio would be happy to be free of Joanne. Now and again, particularly when he was drinking heavily, he left his friend in no doubt that he wanted out. In any case, it became apparent to Chivers that they had discussed splitting up during their travels if one wanted to go to a particular place and the other wished to visit a different area. 'They agreed they would separate for a while if it came to that and then they'd meet up again later,' Chivers was to say later as he recalled his late night talks over drinks with Falconio. 'None of my mates would have been surprised if they finished up not seeing one another. I certainly don't think Pete would have been surprised.'

In time, Falconio was moved on from Brighton to work closer to London, but he fell out with his new boss and moved on again, before yet another falling out. Friends said Falconio didn't get on with his bosses, being called in to be disciplined on a number of occasions for being late and looking scruffy. But that was the way he was, his friends agreed, he just didn't get on with people.

When Falconio returned to Sussex, where Joanne had continued to live, and resumed his work with the construction company, he fell back in with his mates. He was soon back into his 'off-licence' beer selling trade. He turned up at Chivers' house one night asking if he wanted to buy a few cases of beer. On another occasion he arrived at Chivers' home wearing a pizza company's T-shirt. Chivers learned Falconio was using the construction company car to deliver pizzas in the evening and Chivers and his friends realised that the Arthur Daley in Falconio had never left him—he was always after a quick quid, sometimes with an air of desperation about him.

As a joke his friends decided to put a bit of a scare into him. They wrote up a letter on headed company notepaper reading: 'Mr Falconio, We have noticed that your mileage is higher than average. Can you explain this?'

The group of friends arranged with someone from head office to put it through the company postal system so the envelope would be properly franked. But the last paragraph of the letter read: 'We think you are a complete spanner!'

That was meant to be the clue to Falconio that the letter was a spoof. Unfortunately, he took it as a serious communication from head office and telephoned the accounts department with a lame excuse for using the company car to deliver pizzas, which only landed him in further trouble.

Falconio wasn't the only one working at two jobs. Chivers was doing the same thing himself. While working by day on the construction site he was busy three nights a week as a temp at an insurance office, inputting data into a computer. On one occasion his supervisor told him that she was setting up a fraud team because of a scam that was being operated at the time. She told him that people were taking out life insurance policies, paying the fees for a couple of months and then going away to foreign countries and allegedly getting themselves killed. Then someone close to them would cash in the policy. The best places for obtaining a false, cheap, death certificate, Chivers heard, was Africa, but there were other parts of the world where it could be done, too. You didn't even have to show a death certificate, he learned. If you were missing for a certain period of time, seven years he believed, the company would pay out anyway.

Chivers was told by his boss that she had been asked to set up a fraud team to investigate bogus claims by people faking their deaths or disappearing in circumstances that suggested they had died.

In their favourite bar one night, Falconio got around to his favourite subject of working scams and making easy money. 'That's nothing,' Chivers suddenly piped up. 'You should hear what I found out today.'

He proceeded to tell Falconio about the insurance cheaters. Chivers wasn't surprised to see Falconio's eyes light up. Falconio questioned Chivers about how it was done but it didn't end there. Back at work on the site Falconio brought the subject up again, asking what else Chivers could tell him—how it was done, how people were caught and whether people were still doing it. Chivers was asked three times about the scams until Falconio seemed convinced that there was nothing more he could learn from his friend.

Eventually, Falconio was made redundant but the payout put him in a good mood and he realised that he and Jo would have a nice tidy sum to take away with them on their dream holiday. He told everyone that he would arrange a leaving party, but in the end very few turned up and it became just a few friends having a drink together in the flat. Chivers thought the low number might be because people thought they would be charged for attending.

Shortly before they were due to fly off on their year long trip, the couple travelled north to say goodbye to their families. Joanne's mother, with Joanne's brother, young Samuel, aged 14 at her side, gave them both a big hug, and Joanne gave the family dog, a tan and white mixed breed, a farewell pat.

'They were so excited,' Mrs James recalled later. 'I could see how much in love they were with each other—very much in love I would say.'

On 15 November 2000, Joanne and her boyfriend took off from England on their adventure. They had saved thousands of pounds, mostly due to putting aside their wages and partly thanks to Falconio's drinks business. Joanne had planned everything meticulously, arranging the cheapest air fares and finding the most exciting and interesting places to visit.

Their first real taste of the Far East was in the capital of Cambodia, Phnom Penh, and from there they travelled north to wander around the ruined temples of Angkor Wat. They sent emails and postcards to their families and friends telling them of their excursions. Then came a distressing message to Vincent and Jennifer James.

Joanne's parents had not been happy about them going to Cambodia, where apart from its recent history of mass murder under Pol Pot, there had been horror stories of backpackers being murdered there between 1994 and 1996, including Australians Kellie Wilkinson and David Wilson, as well as five Britons, Mark Slater, Dominic Chappell, Tina Dominy, Christopher Howes and Robert Burndred. But the message Joanne and Falconio sent home was not about personal harm—they had lost all their belongings to a thief. Nevertheless, they were able to rearrange their lives with help from the British Embassy and continue their journey to Australia.

In Sydney, Falconio found work with an office furniture design company close to Darling Harbour while Joanne got a job working in Dymock's bookstore in George Street, the city's main shopping thoroughfare. They rented a flat at Bondi, a short walk from the famous beach and the coffee shops of Campbell Parade, and quickly built up a circle of friends, spending the late-night hours drinking and dancing either separately with their friends or together. Joanne was held in high regard at Dymock's and while Falconio also proved to be a good worker with the furnishing company, there were mixed opinions of him among his workmates. One co-worker found Falconio brash and difficult to get along with and, during one heated clash of personalities, Falconio raised his fists and suggested he and the other man step outside 'for a blue'.

On the other hand, another workmate, driver Paul Dale, found Falconio to be a good friend, so much so that Dale and his partner went out on the town several times with Falconio and Joanne. They dined in the North Bondi Returned Servicemen's League club and drank in pubs around Darling Harbour. They also enjoyed evenings at a favourite hang-out among the young Sydney set, the Woolloomooloo Bay Hotel. On occasions they sat on the wharf eating pies from a kiosk called Harry's Café de Wheels, a world-famous yet humble eatery that has attracted names as big as Elton John.

'With Peter, you couldn't wish for a better mate,' Dale recalls. 'He was a straight shooter. He would talk from time to time about the trip he and Joanne were planning and said they were looking around for a good van, something that would get them around Australia. Finally they arranged to have a look at a kombi that was up for sale and the owners brought it along to where we were working in Botany Road. He had a look over it and thought it would do fine, even though it needed quite a bit of work done on it.'

Falconio and Joanne paid $3600 (£1328) for the Volkswagen and then he and Paul Dale started restoring it. 'Mechanically it needed a few bits and pieces doing to it,' Dale recalls. 'But it was the interior that was in the worst mess. We spent a lot of hours working on it, relining all the door panels and putting in new curtains and lights, generally tidying it up inside. I was sad to see them go in the end.'

Joanne's friends told her the same and as the time approached for them to set off she appeared to be almost reluctant to say goodbye, despite all the planning and preparation that had gone into the trip. She even admitted later, 'I was really settled and didn't want to leave. I could have quite happily stayed there.'

She had made two special girlfriends in the store—Lisa, from England and Amanda, originally from New Zealand—but she had impressed staff in other Dymocks stores, too. Paul Jones, who worked in a nearby shop, spoke to her most days for work reasons and found her to be chatty and 'a real breath of fresh air—she was so different to all the other travellers who work at the store. Lots of tourists know they are not going to be there for longer than six months so they don't care much about staff relations and customer relations, but Joanne wasn't like that. She cared. She formed close friendships with so many people at the shop. They made a point of going out every Friday after work and her boyfriend joined them, too. She was obviously a nice, sweet girl.'

When the time came for her to leave, the Dymock's staff organised a going-away party for her, when many tears were shed. Her friends also gave her a gold chain as a memento. She thanked them all, thanked them for their close friendships.

But Joanne had become closer to one particular man than Peter Falconio had ever suspected. It was a secret she was to keep as she and her long-term boyfriend drove out of Sydney for their outback adventure.

X

The old Volkswagen headed south-west along the Hume Highway, that early stretch of road notorious for a series of hideous crimes that had occurred in the late 1980s and early 1990s. The highway had been the hunting ground for backpacker killer Ivan Milat, who picked up hitch-hikers, including two young British dark-haired women, and raped and murdered them in a forest. The Volkswagen carrying Joanne and Peter roared past the forest road, the Milat crimes far from their minds.

They travelled to Canberra, a trip that took two days and a city Joanne found 'quite boring', before travelling on to Victoria and South Australia. They often stayed in caravan parks where they chatted with other travellers, before turning the Volkswagen north, where their real outback adventure would begin. They stopped off in the desert town of Coober Pedy and Joanne wrote a postcard to her family in Huddersfield.

Hi Mum, Vin, Sam and Jess,
We are currently in Coober Pedy an opal mining town. It is also where they filmed *Mad Max III*. Then we are on up to Ayers Rock, Alice Springs and Broome. The weather has been cold and crisp, so it will be nice to get to warmer climates. Have only seen one living kangaroo. Unfortunately all the rest have been dead along the roadside. Just about getting used to living out of a rucksack again. We have been skiing in the Snowy Mountains. We went to a place called Brighton

in Melbourne. They had lots of colourful original Brighton Beach boxes. Lots of love, Jo and Pete.

Despite Joanne's stated intention to travel to Broome, the couple's plans were not clear-cut. Falconio had had his mind set on visiting Papua New Guinea, lying to the north of Australia, but Joanne was not so keen. They discussed the possibility of his making a side trip to the country and meeting up with her later. But that was something for the future. In the meantime they mixed with other travellers on popular outback routes, visiting the spectacularly beautiful Kings Canyon and climbing to the top of Uluru, where they asked another visitor to take a photo of them sitting close together—she in a green windcheater and he in a grey top and both wearing sturdy walking boots—looking the picture of happiness against the big blue sky.

The Volkswagen had been passed from traveller to traveller before they purchased it and as they headed towards Alice Springs the engine began to splutter. This was bad news. It meant dipping into the holiday money to get it fixed, but it had to be done.

Around 10 July, mechanic Rod Smith was working in Desert City Motors, a popular workshop in the centre of Alice Springs, when the Volkswagen pulled up outside. He and his mate Jason Scott watched as the two occupants came in—or marched in, as Jason would have put it. The woman, who he learned was Joanne Lees, was in a foul mood and Scott guessed they had been arguing. From her demeanour, Scott considered she was the dominant one of the partnership, demanding that their Volkswagen be fixed up quickly and expressing dismay when they told her it would have to be kept in the workshop for at least 24 hours.

Smith found that the Volkswagen was running on only three cylinders, which meant that every time the accelerator pedal was lifted the vehicle would backfire. Aware of the woman's mood, he set about working on it as quickly as possible but when the couple returned the next day, Joanne began arguing over the bill.

In the workshop's yard was a dog called Jess, belonging to one of the mechanics. The dog snapped at Joanne as she was arguing over the bill, which caused her to ask what breed it was. She was told it was a red heeler.

In a curious twist, parked outside the workshop was a white Toyota four-wheel drive, similar to the one she would say pulled up later beside the kombi. The red heeler dog and the Toyota were to come together in Scott's mind later that month and he would pass the information to the police.

On Saturday 14 July a curious incident occurred. Joanne and Falconio decided to change their travel plans of driving around the country together. Instead, she and her boyfriend went to a travel agent where she bought a single ticket for herself to fly from Brisbane to Sydney. She was to describe it later as a 'holiday within a holiday'.

Later that day, they went to the famous Camel Cup, jokingly referred to as a horse-race for camels. While this remains an oddity for overseas visitors, the locals regard it as a perfectly normal attraction—as normal as the Henley-on-Todd Regatta, an annual yacht race held on the dried-up bed of the Todd River and in which contestants run with small boats attached to their waists. As for the camels, they have been around in Alice Springs since the early explorers, who brought Afghans and their 'ships of the desert' to Australia to help penetrate the uncharted wilderness.

A tourist's video sweeping across the crowds caught a fleeting glimpse of Joanne at the cup, standing among spectators at the rails. Later that afternoon, around 4 pm, she and Falconio left the cup event and started heading north out of Alice Springs with Joanne at the wheel and Falconio resting in the back. Locals warn travellers not to set out for the lonely outback at this time, particularly in the winter months of July and August, because the sun soon sets and darkness brings many dangers from wandering animals. There are also few places to camp safely and the advice has always been to set off out of Alice Springs in the morning. Even so, Joanne and Falconio decided for their own reasons to head out of town, their distinctive kombi being nonchalantly noticed by a motorist who was parked at Colliers Creek, just north of Alice Springs. That same motorist, with idle indifference, also noticed a white Toyota four-wheel drive heading up the highway some 20 minutes later.

At 5.30 pm, a motorist travelling south as the sun was low in the sky, noticed the Volkswagen heading north, a few miles south of the small community of Aileron. Half an hour later, the same motorist saw a white Toyota also heading north.

It was at 6.22 pm, just on sunset, that the Volkswagen pulled into the petrol station at Ti Tree, a popular stop where hot meals and take-away snacks can also be purchased. Everyone who fills up at the self-service pumps is noticed twice, for the employee on duty watches through a window in case anyone tries to drive off without paying and then eyes them again when they enter the shop to pay.

The British couple bought toasted sandwiches, pulled back onto the highway, then stopped to watch the last rays of the sun spread out across the endless landscape. They smoked marijuana before winding the window up as the chill of the winter night descended.

Chapter 10

The net tightens

When Brad Murdoch split from Julie after their drugs-and-beer journey across the Nullabor, he headed for a rural property in the Riverland district, owned by James Hepi. It was not unusual for Murdoch to turn up at the property at all hours of the night or day, depending on which direction he had come in from.

In the second week of July Murdoch headed north again with marijuana hidden in an empty long-range fuel tank in the rear canopy in his Toyota. On this occasion, though, it was to be an historic journey—for what was to happen hundreds of kilometres to the north on the Stuart Highway was to became one of Australia's most debated crimes. By the time Murdoch reached Broome on Monday 16 July and Hepi swung open the gates of the house they shared, police were searching for a killer in a white four-wheel drive.

Within a short time of arriving in Broome, Murdoch was being questioned by the police about his movements on and around the night of 14 July. Murdoch was able to satisfy local officers working on behalf of Northern Territory police who had included him in a wide sweep of four-wheel drive owners that he had a very good alibi for not being involved in any attack on Peter Falconio—although the police refused to reveal what it was.

In the days that followed Murdoch's arrival in Broome, he drove to a workshop and asked for the canvas canopy on his Toyota to be replaced with an aluminium covering, with security wire mesh on the interior, around the sides and back. Hardly had that work been completed when police released photographs of the suspected gunman, taken from the security video at the Alice Springs truck stop. The pictures showed a man with a moustache walking into the store at the filling station to pay for fuel for his four-wheel drive Toyota. A lot of people studied those pictures, including Broome vehicle upholsterer Loi Odore. He had done work for Murdoch in late 2000, fitting green PVC curtains on the sides of the canopy of his Toyota. He was convinced that the canvas on the vehicle in the truck stop photo was one he had fitted for Brad Murdoch earlier that year.

To his surprise, not long after that photo was released by police on 6 August, Murdoch turned up at Odore's workshop. Odore was interested to note that his canvas had been removed and replaced with aluminium. There were mesh sides with hinges at the top of each mesh so they could swing open and upwards and there was an aluminium roof. Murdoch told Odore he wanted PVC curtains put over the mesh to stop rain getting in, but Odore was more interested in his customer than in the work he wanted done.

'Mate,' Odore said cautiously, 'the vehicle in that truckstop photo looks a lot like yours because I recognise my work.'

Murdoch shrugged. 'Yeah, it could have been me,' he said, 'I stopped to get petrol around that time but I had nothing to do with that stuff at Barrow Creek. The cops have been hassling me about it but they're pretty satisfied it wasn't me.'

The men who worked with Odore were impressed with the Toyota. It had a larger than usual exhaust and a powerful, modified engine, which was noticed when one of them had to reverse the vehicle from the workshop.

As the hunt continued for the gunman, information began to pour in to police stations around the country. At the Alice Springs police station, Megan Hood Rowe, an intelligence manager, began working with a number of officers collating the tip-offs and general information. People answering the gunman's description were checked out and several were detained for questioning before being released. If a person was said to have been in the

Barrow Creek area at the time, data from roadblocks set up in the area was crosschecked, as were credit card transactions and withdrawals from ATMs. Vehicles reported as stolen were also searched for in case they showed up on any roadblock data. What Rowe was looking for was not only people of interest but vehicles of interest, a job she knew would demand all of her patience and expertise.

But that was only part of her work. She and her team in the intelligence cell built up a database of 17 000 people who were staying in lodges or caravan parks that Joanne Lees had told police she had visited with her boyfriend. Police collated details of everyone who had stayed in those places a week before and a week after the Barrow Creek incident. Checks were also made of people who had used an ATM within minutes of Joanne Lees using the same machine, in the hope that they might have seen her or Falconio, perhaps in the company of another person—or were being watched by another person.

As a result of this comparison of data, some 75 'people of interest' were listed in addition to the 2500 that had been mentioned as possible suspects by people ringing their police stations. But it was not enough to have a single person of interest or a single vehicle—the two had to come together. This matching generated around 30 people, who were then placed on a priority list. Police officers were sent out to their homes; their friends and relatives were questioned. Some 15 even provided DNA samples, eliminating them from the inquiries.

One by one, the potential suspects from the hot list were removed because they had alibis or their DNA, compared against the small speck of blood found on the sleeve of Joanne's T-shirt, did not match. Only one person who was questioned but who did not supply DNA could not be eliminated. His vehicle matched the description provided by Joanne and while there were discrepancies with his appearance, he had admitted to being in the region at the time.

That person was Bradley John Murdoch.

Although there was no transaction evidence to put him in the area, detectives concluded it would have been easy for him to slip under the net. The time had come to put him under surveillance.

In the meantime, police had to deal with a number of confusing leads, among them suspicions that Peter Falconio was still alive and had been seen in different parts of the country. Officer Rowe, aware that Falconio had a joint account with Joanne, monitored the account but there was no indication that he had accessed it in the months following his disappearance. So intense were the follow-ups to information that he might still be alive that police even checked pawn shops in case Falconio—alive but perhaps broke—had tried to sell his diver's watch or St Christopher medal.

X

As the investigations continued over the following months, Joanne was settling back to an anonymous life in Britain, having returned at Christmas 2001. The world was still reeling from the attacks on New York on 11 September, so the focus had totally shifted away from her. It was under this protective shield that she went against all her promises never to sell her story and struck a deal for AUD$120 000 with a British TV show, *Tonight with Trevor McDonald*. She was to be interviewed by Martin Bashir, the journalist who had famously interviewed the Princess of Wales when she revealed the problems of her marriage to Prince Charles.

Joanne flew secretly to Australia with the TV team early in 2002 but, according to a police source, refused to travel with them to Barrow Creek. In fact, the police themselves did not even know she was in Australia at the time. Even so, Joanne was ready to tell her story all over again, causing uproar among many who asked, 'How on earth could she go back—for money?'

'I feel guilty that the man didn't want Pete—he wanted me,' she said in the interview, much of which was recorded in Sydney. No-one was put off by the fact that the Falconio story was being aired again, for each time it was told, particularly with any input from Joanne, there were subtle variations that continued to raise questions about her account.

'He just wanted a female and he had to get Pete out of the way,' she told Martin Bashir. She had a funny feeling, a sense of foreboding, she said when the stranger waved her and Falconio down. She didn't want to stop. 'I can't explain it. It was just so dark and remote. But Pete said it will be fine—he loved his campervan so much and we'd had faults on it before. The man looked aged forty-plus, like a local man ... he was driving a four-wheel drive utility truck. He seemed totally friendly. He kept pointing to the back of our van. He was bigger than Pete, six foot, I'm not sure.

'He had lots of layers of clothing on. He had longish, shoulder-length, grey, streaky hair—someone who didn't take much care in his appearance. He looked to me that he maybe had an outside job. He had a grey, long moustache, drooped down the sides. There was a red or blue heeler dog, typically Australian dog. Medium-sized, short-haired, pointed ears. Similar to a Staffordshire bull terrier.'

'Pete told me to wait [in the VW]. It was cold and I was just in shorts and a T-shirt. Pete took his cigarettes and went and had a chat with the man. He came back and asked me to rev the engine. He said that everything was okay. The door was open. I heard him talking to the man. It all seemed amicable, joking. I could hear Pete saying "Cheers mate, thanks for stopping." I was thinking, "Oh, this nice man".'

Joanne said she caught glimpses of the man and at one point her eyes met the stranger's. There was a wildness to his stare, she said. 'It made me feel nervous again. It just made me feel a little uncomfortable.'

She described hearing a bang, thinking it was the exhaust—'I never thought in my wildest dreams it was a gunshot,' she said. Then she turned to look around and saw the man who 'stood outside the driver's door. I saw the gun in his hand pointing at me and he started to open the door. He looked big and crouched over. Calm. Not aggressive. Very controlled and commanding.

'He says, "Switch the engine off". I think he turned it off because I was shaking so much. He pushed me over to the passenger seat and said "Put your head down and your hands behind your back". Then he put a gun to my head and that's when I thought, I'm going to have to do as he tells me.

'He had a revolver. I haven't seen a gun before. It was a handgun, not very big, and I remember it had scrolling in a rectangular box along the barrel. I couldn't smell anything from the gun. Later people said, "that's because you are in survival mode".' She had also felt no sense of heat from the barrel when it was held to her head, but what she remembered was her overwhelming fear. 'I was asking him, "Where's Peter? What have you done with Peter?" I was screaming for Pete. I just thought that at any moment Peter was going to come and save me.

'The man pushed me out of the car onto the ground, face down. I am so angry—he's trying to tie my legs together—and I won't let him. I just kick and kick and he can't do it. He got so mad that he hit me on the side of the face. I just keep thinking, "this is over" and "this is the end of my life".

'He drags me or lifts me up and tries to put tape across my mouth—some kind of masking tape—but I move around and it just goes in my neck and in my hair. He walked me towards his vehicle, lifted up a side of the canopy and got a sack out of his truck and put that over my head. Then he pushed me through a passenger door of his car.

'There was his dog. I was screaming and screaming but he grabbed me and pushed me through the seats into the back. He tied my hands together behind my back, using four cable ties. I think they were black. There was some kind of tape in the middle as well. At one point I was trying to bite it off. He didn't manage to tie my feet together. I told him I couldn't breathe and somehow the sack came off. I tried to get out the passenger side. His dog was there which didn't make a sound and he just pulled me and grabbed me and pushed me into the back of his vehicle which had some kind of bed in there or mattress.

'Once I was laid in the back I really thought that was the end of my life. He went 'round to the side of his vehicle. I kept shouting to him "What have you done to Pete? Is he hurt?" He came to me and told me to shut up or he'd kill me. I just said "What is it you want from me? Is it money? Do you want to rape me?" He just told me to shut up. I asked him then if he'd killed Pete and it took him a long time to answer. He said no. Then he went back to whatever he was doing. And that's when I just thought this is it. This is my chance. I'm going. I slid down the truck, down the base of the truck and jumped out and ran into the bush.'

She couldn't see anything. She tripped. She tripped several times. She knew he was behind her and she realised she couldn't outrun him.

'I just crawled into a bush and hid about 30 or 40 metres away. When I jumped down on the gravel it seemed to make so much noise I was sure he was behind me. My hands were still tied behind my back. It was so quiet that every noise I made on the branches and trees made such a noise. My heart made such a loud noise.'

She could not estimate how much time passed as she hid. She was not wearing a watch and she dared not move. She told the interviewer she could hear the gunman, but not the dog. She 'presumed that he had followed me into the bush with the dog, but I never heard the dog. I heard his footsteps crunching the branches and saw the torch. He came past me three or four times. I just put my head in my knees and covered my legs with my hair and held my breath. He got three or four metres away, maybe closer.'

Some time later she heard both vehicles—the man's truck and the VW—move. 'That's when I thought he's in his car and I brought my hands from behind my back to the front of me.' It had not been difficult to do that, she said. 'I just brought them from underneath me.

'I thought, he's leaving, he's going. I was going to come out and then I heard him come back on foot. I just kept thinking, is this ever going to end? I thought that he is going to be so mad when he finds me.'

However, on his return the man had sounded further away. 'I could hear him slamming doors of his utility truck. Then he seems to be doing something ... I just hear his footsteps, branches crushing and creaking and felt he was dragging something and I really thought it was Peter. I thought he was dragging him into the bush near where I was.'

She had no sense of how bitterly cold the night was or of her injuries, she said. 'I didn't feel cold at all. I didn't feel. I knew there were cuts and bleeding all over me but I didn't feel any pain at that point. Grazes on my knees, elbows, cuts from twigs and things in the bush.

'After a while I heard the vehicle drive away. I really wanted to come out but didn't know what to do. Best to just stay there, hidden really well and I felt safe in my hiding place. I came out a few times but got back in. I never thought it was safe. I just thought Pete was close by, injured, and I wanted to get to him and get help. That was my motivation, otherwise I would have stayed there till daylight. I walked towards the road but I couldn't see it. Then I saw the white line. I walked across the road and fell in some grass on the other side of the road. I couldn't see anything. A few cars passed but I didn't feel brave enough and didn't know who would be driving those cars. Could have been him.'

At last she decided to flag down a truck and waved down a road train. 'I ran alongside. My hands were tied together so I kept holding them up so he [the driver] could see I needed help.'

She went on to tell the interviewer that when a man sprang from the cab she told him that her boyfriend had been shot by someone and that she needed help to find him. The driver woke up his mate who was sleeping in the cab, cut her free and then all three of them started searching.

'They disconnected their loads and with just the cab they came back to the crime scene with me. We looked for Pete, got torches out, but couldn't find him.' They did notice two piles of dirt and she later found out that that was where the stranger had covered over the blood.

They drove to the Barrow Creek Hotel where she was given tea. One of the drivers cleaned her knees and put ointment on them while the other phoned the police. When he got through, she claimed, the officer put the phone down because he thought it was a hoax call. It was four hours before police arrived.

Helen Jones had stayed with Joanne in the days after the ordeal, loaning her a T-shirt and trousers, but Joanne had no kinds words for her in the interview. Expressing her distaste at Helen Jones speaking to the media later, Joanne said: 'I'm quite disgusted that she can get off on someone's tragedy.'

She recalled how police photographed her cuts and bruises and continued to interview her until 10 pm the day after the attack.

As the TV interview proceeded, she told how she and Falconio had spent a few days in Alice Springs because there had been a minor problem with the VW, which kept backfiring. 'We just wanted to pass through, but there were a few jobs we needed to get done so we booked it into a garage. I also booked my flight back to Sydney and Pete spoke to Dan [a friend] arranging the trip to Papua New Guinea.'

On that fateful day of 14 July they had been preparing to leave the camp-site they were staying at on the outskirts of Alice Springs to start heading for Darwin, but had then decided to go to the Camel Cup.

'It was a lovely hot summer's day and I really liked it,' she said, appearing to have overlooked the fact that it was the middle of the Australian winter, although Alice Springs was sunny. 'It reminded me of the local galas and family fetes that we used to have in our village.'

Asked about rumours that she and Falconio had argued, she said there was no truth to them and said the police had 'mixed us up with another couple'. They had been on the road—by that she meant since leaving England—for eight months and insisted their 'relationship was stronger than ever'.

Between 4 pm and 5 pm they set off for Tennant Creek, a good five hours drive away. Joanne drove between Alice Springs and Ti Tree and then Falconio took over the driving. 'There were hardly any other vehicles on the road,' she said. The next thing she knew there were headlights close behind them. 'Pete slowed down and said to me, "I wish this car would just overtake".

'After a few minutes it drove alongside us and we looked into the vehicle. We could see a man and his dog. The man was pointing to the back of our vehicle and motioning us to stop.'

It was then that her ordeal, the apparent gunshot, the attack started. Yet commentators who watched the TV interview in the UK were not impressed. One said that her decision to give it did not dramatically improve her image. The overriding impression was one of self-pity.

'Nobody knows what I've gone through,' she told viewers. 'Nobody can begin to imagine it. I am a private person and I do bottle up my emotions. I guess that with no friends or family near me to talk through these things I did become withdrawn and felt that I was in this on my own.'

The comment about having no family or friends was inaccurate. Her friends from Dymocks flew to Alice Springs. Her stepfather Vincent James flew from Britain, as did Falconio's brother, Paul, and his father. Helen Jones stayed with her all the time. And the media begged her to talk to them, for in doing so it might help to find the attacker. But she had refused all requests for a detailed interview at the time—yet now, finally, she had given her version of events in a TV interview—for money.

Meanwhile in Darwin and Alice Springs, the police teams agreed to proceed on the basis that Peter Falconio was dead. One person above all others appeared to be a prime suspect—Bradley Murdoch, the man who had been in the area and had changed the appearance of his vehicle after arriving in Broome.

But having a suspect was not enough. Police needed more evidence and, if possible, a sample of his DNA. There was pressure from within the Northern Territory government and from the public for an arrest to be made, and, unlike in the bungled Lindy Chamberlain case, there could be absolutely no mistakes. If Bradley Murdoch were to be pulled in, police would need to have a very good case to throw at him.

But where was he? As the inquiries hotted up and other people of interest were eliminated, Murdoch vanished from Broome. James Hepi suggested police look for him at the property in the Riverland in South Australia, but he couldn't be found there. Murdoch, suspecting treachery from his former friend, realised the police would soon find him there. He would not have been aware if police had gathered any evidence against him—even if it may have come from his former partner—but given the nature of his drug-running operation he was not prepared to hand himself over for any kind of grilling.

So he stayed at various addresses in South Australia, including a shed in a community called Angle Vale. In May 2002, ten months after the incident at Barrow Creek, Murdoch spent five days at the Bolivar Caravan Park in South Australia before an acquaintance in Port Broughton suggested he rent his dilapidated stone farmhouse on the York Peninsula. It was a perfect hideaway. He moved in with another man, Darryl 'Dags' Craigan.

'Don't know how they reckon it's you,' Craigan told him. 'You don't look anything like that bloke in the picture.'

Similarly, Murdoch's mate Sheriff, who knew all about Murdoch's drugs and guns, couldn't work out why the cops were now looking for him, as he had a crew cut, was six foot four inches tall and 'weighed a thousand tons'. The English woman had described someone of medium build with long hair. 'Someone has really fucked up,' Sheriff told one of his other mates.

In fact, there appeared to be nobody who could remember Brad Murdoch with the long hair that Joanne Lees had described her attacker as having. Even James Hepi's former girlfriend, mother of four Rachel Maxwell, who saw Murdoch six months before the incident, could not help noticing his short hair, beard, very broad shoulders and his missing front teeth whenever he spoke. His forearms were heavily tattooed. Why hadn't the Englishwoman mentioned any of these features? she wondered. Maxwell was interviewed by police who wanted to ask her about some articles she may have seen in Murdoch's possession. Yes, she said, she had seen him using black tape and cable ties to wrap around bags of hemp. She had also seen a gun—an old-style silver gun with a wooden handle, 'like John Wayne would have used, like a Wild West gun with a ten inch barrel'. On another occasion that she met him, around about May or June 2001, his hair was still cut short, what she would describe as a crew cut.

Only one of Murdoch's former girlfriends, Beverley Allan, was to tell police that his hair was longer than a crew cut, although nothing like the length described by Joanne. And of course there was Julie Harrison who had travelled across the Nullabor with him some three weeks before the incident at Barrow Creek. He had short hair during that drink-and-drugs journey and a number of police officers readily agreed that there was no way he could have grown his hair to shoulder length in that brief time.

Occasionally, while he was hiding out in South Australia, Murdoch would be seen walking into Port Broughton to buy newspapers and groceries. He got on well with the local people who, unaware of his time in jail and his drug-running activities, generally agreed he appeared to be a decent sort of fellow.

In time, Murdoch decided to move on—and called in on James Hepi's neighbours in the Riverland, a former brothel owner, his de-facto wife and her 13-year-old daughter, people he had befriended on his numerous trips to Hepi's South Australian property. And there, in a guesthouse, he put his feet up and kept his head down, for he told the daughter: 'I've been framed and I'm on the run.'

Continuing to fear treachery, particularly from Hepi who had argued with him several times over money and who had once borrowed his vehicle and badly damaged it, Murdoch dared not tell even his best friends where he was. He kept in touch only with his older brother Gary, with whom he remained close. There is speculation about whether it was James Hepi who tipped off the police on the likely places that Murdoch could be hiding.

X

While Murdoch was keeping a low profile in the Riverland, I flew to Darwin to speak to John Daulby, the Northern Territory's Assistant Crime Commissioner. With me I carried a statement that had been signed in

Britain by Falconio's former workmate, Colin Chivers. In it Chivers, who emphasised he would co-operate in passing all his information to the police, had suggested he would not be surprised if the man he referred to as 'Dodgy Pete' had pulled off an insurance scam. It would be interesting to learn what Mr Daulby thought of that.

A tall, softly spoken man with a tendency to carefully compose his words, Daulby scanned the document studiously. Then he asked an assistant to bring in some other papers, which he showed to me. Papers that had been stored in police files for many months. They were letters from other people in England, making similar suggestions—that the circumstances surrounding Peter Falconio's death were so bizarre that the events supported their beliefs that he had faked his disappearance. They had written independently of one another, but, interestingly, all had the same suspicions.

Such an incredible suggestion, of course, would have required the complicity of Joanne—unless the mysterious gunman was in on the 'disappearance' scheme and she was an innocent dupe. There were so many possibilities, and John Daulby did little to shoot them down with his admission that the amount of blood found on the road was 'not necessarily fatal'.

He did reveal, however, that police had not dismissed a 'faked death' scenario: early in the investigation they had made inquiries about any insurance policies that may have been taken out on Falconio's life. It was a bombshell admission, for it suggested that police had indeed had their doubts about Miss Lees' story—at least in the first stages of the investigation. And now? The 51-year-old investigator with 28 years experience, smiled and merely said, 'We still believe Joanne's story.'

Shuffling the 'insurance scam' documents neatly together he added, 'We've questioned her thoroughly, over and over, and she has given us a very full and believable description.' If the faked death scenario was eventually proven beyond doubt to be untrue we both agreed it would have been another cruel burden heaped on the shoulders of Joanne, whose 54-year-old mother Jennifer had died that same week, not to mention the Falconio family.

Looking at the CCTV photos of the man in the service station once more, Daulby said he did not believe that this was the gunman or his vehicle; there were significant differences between that vehicle and the description provided by Joanne of the attacker's ute.

The man in the truckstop video appeared to be about six feet tall—certainly not medium build—with average-length dark hair, appeared to be wearing glasses and thongs and was aged between 40 and 50. Joanne, said Daulby, said her attacker had long, dark, shoulder-length hair, appeared to be younger and was not wearing glasses. He believed she would have noticed if he were wearing thongs, which were not the best kind of footwear to carry out an attack and then hunt for a runaway woman in any case.

But the most significant differences were between the truckstop vehicle and the gunman's. The vehicle at the service station was a Toyota Land Cruiser trayback dropside four-wheel drive ute with a square green canopy. It was believed to be a 75 series vehicle manufactured between May 1991 and November 1999. It had non-standard tyres and rims, the rims being white and the tyres being wider than normal. There seemed to be flares on the front wheel guards and a cow-catcher type of bullbar on the front. On the bonnet was what seemed to be a 'bug deflector' while the exhaust had a turned-down tail pipe. The bullbar and bug deflector were the types commonly seen on trucks. Police had been able to see that there was no gap between the front seats.

In contrast, Daulby said Joanne described the attacker's vehicle as having a chrome, not black, bullbar. She could not recall seeing flared guards and a bug deflector. The vehicle had a gap between the driver's and passenger's seat, leading police to believe this was work that had been specially carried out.

The question of the delay in police releasing those CCTV pictures came up, but Daulby attempted to explain it away by simply stating the original video had to be enhanced. He merely shrugged off a suggestion that the video was a poor back-up version because the original, which would have clearly shown the four-wheel drive's numberplate, had been automatically wiped after a period of time. No, he insisted, the police had not been slow to react from a call from the service station to come and examine the original tape. They had to work with what they had received.

What had been gained from the tape had been important information in any case, resulting in police finding conflicts in Joanne's description and the pictures of the man and vehicle in the service station. Daulby recalled the man's purchases—two bottles of water, two bags of ice, a 600 ml carton of iced coffee and 117 litres of diesel fuel. He paid for it all with cash.

Significantly he was on the premises for 12 minutes, what we agreed was a long time for a man to hang around a public area after having recently committed a murder. Yet Daulby admitted he was baffled why the man had not come forward to eliminate himself from the investigation, for he would have certainly been aware of the nationwide publicity.

'We are confident we are approaching this affair properly and efficiently,' he said. He suggested I wait in Darwin for a few days when the results of a review into the way police had handled the case to date would be revealed.

A number of Darwin-based journalists were at police headquarters when Joanne Lees' pastel-green T-shirt was spread out a few days later. It was protected by a plastic bag, and had stains on the front, side and back. Some of the stains were blood and some were dirt, it was explained. Parts of the garment had been cut away by the forensic scientists.

As for the official review into the handling of the case, it was little more than a pat on the back for the Northern Territory police. The investigation had been carried out over a six-week period by Superintendent George Owen of the Northern Territory and retired South Australian Assistant Police Commissioner Jim Litster. They had concluded that there was strong evidence to support Joanne's story that a gunman had attempted to abduct her and was responsible for the disappearance of Peter Falconio.

The review, Mr Daulby was anxious to point out, should not be seen as an attempt to apportion blame on any one or any group of people, but should be recognised as a process which would support and strengthen the existing investigation. It also aimed to ensure that all aspects of the case had been thoroughly investigated, make sure appropriate procedures had been followed and to determine the continued resource requirements.

The review team, said Mr Daulby, had read more than 100 statements and had examined nearly 23 000 pieces of information. They had also interviewed police, witnesses from the public and forensic specialists. Then followed the praise. The review team found that Alice Springs police had responded quickly to the incident, considerable efforts were made to locate evidence at the crime scene and searches were carried out in a logical and orderly fashion and the general handling of the crime scene was in line with accepted practices.

There were some departures. The team found that the police information system had trouble initially coping with the tremendous influx of information, although this was soon rectified. While a re-enactment by the team, using crime scene measurements and photographs, corroborated Joanne's story, it was reasonable to expect some inaccuracies in her statement, given she had undergone extreme trauma.

Another criticism was pushed away, the team stating that 'while creating some contamination' police made the right decision to enter the crime scene in the first instance for the purpose of saving Peter Falconio had he been alive and in the vicinity. One point the team was agreed upon —if Falconio's body was anywhere around the crime scene, it would have been found.

While the roadblocks were set up in a timely fashion, it was possible the gunman could have escaped the police net due to the five-hour time difference between the incident and the report to the police. But overall, the praise was there for the police and others working with them. The performance of the forensic personnel, the team found, was professional. There was no need to carry out further forensic tests on the VW after the luminol testing, as it had already been subjected to tests for blood using the chemical orthotolidene, which is a more effective method of locating bloodstains.

There was more to come at this meeting in the police headquarters. Police strengthened their belief in Joanne's story by producing a timeline showing how the Volkswagen had been seen travelling up the highway late in the afternoon and in the early evening of 14 July 2001, with a white Toyota about half an hour behind. The diagram revealed how at 7.45 pm, some 15 minutes after the Volkswagen was waved down, a witness travelling north saw the Kombi parked at the roadside with a Nissan or Land Cruiser ute behind it. This, of course, was a significant piece of evidence, although Daulby was not prepared to reveal who that witness was.

At 8 pm, 15 minutes later, another witness, travelling south, saw the Kombi parked at the roadside and a second, unidentified vehicle, leaving. An hour later, a second witness travelling south, told police of seeing the kombi off the highway in the bush and possibly a torch light. At 10 pm another witness, also travelling south, drove past the scene but saw nothing. And finally, there was the sighting by 'witness H' who saw a white Toyota in the Shell truckstop in Alice Springs at 12.47 am on 15 July, a little over five hours after the Barrow Creek incident. But there was, of course, more than one witness, for the four-wheel drive was captured at that time on the truck-stop's CCTV.

Two of the on-road witnesses, Mrs Pamela Nabangardi Brown and Mr Jasper Jimbajimba Haines from the Npuriya Aboriginal community, described how they were travelling south along the Stuart Highway near Barrow Creek at about 10 pm. Mrs Brown saw a white vehicle come out from the right hand side of the road and onto the bitumen, its lights sweeping onto their own vehicle. 'Where did that car come from?' she asked Mr Haines, as the vehicle continued heading north at what she estimated to be 50 or 60 kilometres per hour.

Shortly afterwards in their own lights they noticed an orange kombi with a white roof, also on the right hand side as they continued south. It was parked near the bitumen and facing north. It had no lights on and there was nobody in sight. Mrs Brown and Jasper stopped to pick up some people at Barrow Creek and it took them a further hour and a half to reach Ti Tree, where they had to turn off to drive to their community. It was now at least 11.30 pm and no other vehicle had passed them as they headed south.

Their sighting seemed to dampen the chance of the man in the truck-stop being the Barrow Creek attacker, aside from the differences described earlier by Daulby. For if the gunman had been driving the white vehicle seen by Mrs Brown, it might be wondered how he could have then taken the kombi off the highway and hidden it and still reached the Shell truckstop by 12.45 am, a distance of 180 kilometres. He hadn't overtaken the witnesses' car and to cover that distance in a little over an hour, even if he had come speeding down the highway behind them, would, in fact, have been impossible.

The affair was becoming increasingly confused. On the one hand there appeared to be firm evidence of a white van travelling up the highway some distance behind the kombi and later being seen parked behind it and possibly being filmed at the truckstop in Alice Springs. On the other hand, Daulby had told me at our private meeting that there was no question of the vehicle in the truckstop being the same one that had been involved at Barrow Creek. The timings given by Mrs Brown and Mr Haines also suggested that the man in the Shell truckstop could not have been the gunman.

There were still many unanswered questions about what had actually happened there at the roadside, 10.7 kilometres north of the tiny Barrow Creek community.

Chapter 11
Unanswered questions

They say that Tennant Creek was created when a beer wagon, carrying those vital supplies to the north in the 1870s, broke down at that site. In any case, 500 kilometres from Alice Springs and 650 kilometres from Katherine, it was chosen as a telegraph station on the Overland Telegraph Line—then suddenly boomed when gold and copper were discovered nearby.

Today it's a bustling town of 3500 and a welcome stop-over for anyone travelling up and down the centre of Australia. It is also a place of significance for the Warumungu Aboriginal people, who make up a large part of the population. It was here that Joanne Lees said she and Falconio planned to stop for the night after setting out from Alice Springs.

There's a small local newspaper, the *Tennant and District Times*, run by Jasmine Afianos, who keeps 1500 urban and rural readers informed of local events once a week. She was examining pictures on a computer when I called in to see her and learned she had a thousand stories to tell about the Falconio case, although she admitted with a grin that 99.9 per cent of them were rumour and innuendo.

Her phone had been running hot with 'tips', that varied from Falconio being seen in Tennant Creek a few days after the Barrow Creek affair with a big bandage around his leg. Preacher men, clairvoyants, spiritualists, people who belonged to another time and another place, all made their way to her tiny newspaper office in the main street to tell of their visions and offer their advice on whodunit and where Falconio could be found; some said dead, some said alive.

There was a local man, she said, who fitted the description of the wanted gunman. He had been interviewed by police and she thought he was still considered a suspect. And then there was Paddy, the ice-cream seller at an outback attraction called Devil's Marbles, some 130 kilometres north of Barrow Creek, who swore she served Falconio and Joanne Lees a couple of days before the incident. If that was true, they would have had to return to Alice Springs for the Camel Cup, and then drive north again, and the question arises: why they would have done that? The area was alive with rumours—and for some sleuths they were too tempting to ignore.

Such was the desire of Jasmine and a reporter from Darwin to scoop the world and find Falconio's body that the two of them followed up a tip that a freshly-dug grave had been found in the scrub about 100 kilometres from Barrow Creek, a short distance north of the small community of Wycliff Well. Jasmine and the reporter, armed with shovels, walked 300 metres along a track, where they found a hump of earth amid the spinifex.

She watched as the reporter started shovelling earth. 'This is weird,' she told him, but encouraged him to keep digging. They found nothing. As time went by, she learned she was not the only person to head out into the bush with a shovel on the word of a tipster or a clairvoyant. At least one 'seer' approached a woman's magazine with her plan of where to dig, but once again the vision failed to turn to any kind of reality. Another woman spent weeks travelling through the outback with an Aboriginal tracker who reckoned he would find the body, while yet another female sleuth dug up mounds of dirt all around the Northern Territory without finding so much as a hint of a dead roo, let alone an Englishman. Peter Falconio had vanished, that much was certain.

Jasmine said she accepted that she was on a fool's errand on most of her follow-ups, but in Tennant Creek where the local agricultural show gets big coverage, a tip on a murder is given every consideration. She cited another occasion when she drove to a lonely place where a motorcyclist said he had seen a man answering the gunman's description camping. She found evidence that someone had camped there, but nothing that indicated he could have been the gunman.

Such then were the rumours that Jasmine followed up, week after week, month after month. There was one other report she received from what she said was a 'very credible source', an old school friend who was close to the investigation. The friend had told her that in the couple's Volkswagen police had found an airline ticket for the couple's travels through Asia and on to Australia, along with a separate ticket for Peter Falconio to fly from Sydney to Bangkok in the months before the Barrow Creek incident. That ticket, according to Jasmine's friend, had been used. This was an astonishing claim for it meant that Falconio had travelled to Thailand on a mysterious trip during the time he and Joanne were staying in Sydney. It conjured up a number of scenarios, such as Falconio travelling to Asia to pick up a false passport, which he could then use after faking his disappearance to start a new life. It was a suggestion that would not have been instantly dismissed by his former workmates, those who had heard him asking how people faked their death, in Britain. However, after some investigation it seemed that the false passport idea was just another unfounded rumour, which might, or might not, have any basis.

At 11 pm on 14 July 2002, the same time that Joanne Lees said she was hiding in the bushes a year earlier, I stood amid the same spinifex. What did I expect to find there, alone in the dark in the middle of nowhere? Nothing really, except that my curiosity had led me there. There was a pale moon, the stars sparkled like they never do from a city aspect—and the air was bitterly cold. So cold that even though I was wearing a winter jacket I was shivering uncontrollably. The night seemed to be on top of me, like a heavy blanket, but it brought no warm comfort.

I tried to imagine a 27-year-old British woman curled up here, wearing just a cotton top as a killer came looking for her. How could she have lain so silent and still for hours with cold and fear gripping her body? The spot where she hid was said to be about 20 or 30 metres from the road and I wondered how someone with a torch walking up and down, accompanied by a dog, could have failed to have found her.

Added curiosity led me back to my rental car. I opened my bag and brought out a small torch I carry everywhere. I shone it into the bushes. The lighter-coloured grasses stood out against the darker shrubs. Then some interesting thoughts struck me. Joanne had been wearing a pale-green, or light turquoise top. Surely a sweeping torchlight would have illuminated that clothing? She had also told how she had covered her legs with her hair so the skin wouldn't stand out in the torchlight. How, with her hands still behind her back, according to one of her accounts, had she managed to undo her hair and throw it forward over her legs? And, I asked myself again, how had covering up her legs have helped when she was dressed in such a light-coloured top? The longer I looked at this whole affair, the more puzzled I became.

I swept the torch over the edge of the road. It was still there ... the dark stain of Falconio's blood. Rain and sun over the months had failed to eliminate it. There was something spooky about standing there in the silence of that long and lonely highway looking at the bloodstain of a man who police were convinced had fallen there exactly a year earlier.

Yet as I continued on to Alice Springs the questions I had asked so many times before bounced around in my mind, refreshed by that short excursion into Joanne's hiding place. Why had the gunman left no footprints? The ground would have been hard, but then Joanne had left two prints and she had not walked up and down like the gunman. Why was no evidence found of the man's dog, the red heeler cattle dog as described by Joanne? Why had the dog failed to find her?

Even Connie Redhead, vice president of the Cattle Dogs Association of South Australia, had commented: 'That dog must have been deaf, dumb and blind not to have found her—red heelers have a natural curiosity and a very keen sense of smell and hearing.' What could be surmised from this was that the gunman had been travelling around with a very dependant pet, which could not see, hear or smell.

More questions came at me. The one that persisted was: why did the gunman, knowing Joanne had seen his face, drive away without waiting for daylight, when he would have certainly found her? He had the advantage of knowing that nobody was aware where she was. All he had to do was wait until the sun came up and then rid himself of his only witness. But instead he had driven away.

Assuming he had shot Falconio, why did he take the body with him when an accident or a breakdown could have resulted in him being caught red-handed by police? There is no doubt he did drive the body away, for it would have been found at the roadside as soon as the alarm was raised, or even sooner when Joanne and the truck drivers who picked her up had made their cursory search.

Yet, if the gunman had driven away with the body—because where else was it—why were there no signs of it being dragged into the gunman's vehicle? Falconio, by all the evidence, had bled after apparently being shot, yet there were no spots of blood beyond the patch at the roadside. No drag marks, no scuff marks from his shoes as he was hoisted up into the gun-man's four-wheel drive. And if he had fallen at the back of the VW, as Joanne believed, it meant the gunman would have had to have carried or dragged Falconio to the back of his own vehicle. He certainly didn't turn his four-wheel drive around to make it easier to pick Falconio up, because Joanne would have said so. Where then, was the evidence that a body had been moved from the road and lifted up into a vehicle?

Did Falconio suddenly and inexplicably stop bleeding, or did the gunman care enough about his victim to bind his wounds? Did the killer wrap his victim in tarpaulin or plastic before moving him? Again, if he had done this, there would have been traces of tarpaulin and pieces of plastic on the road as the body was dragged to the back of the four-wheel drive. Why had he thrown a bag or sack over Joanne's head after she had already seen his face? Why had she failed to see Falconio's body before the sack was thrust over her head?

Which part of Falconio's body was hit by the bullet—assuming he was indeed shot and that the bang Joanne had heard was the sound of the weapon being fired? There have been countless discussions about the effects of gunshot wounds and there appears to be no pattern. Some victims die from excessive bleeding, shock and severed vital organs, while others have survived. Victims will bleed heavily or shed very little blood. Sometimes bullets, even those of heavy calibre, will remain in the body while others will pass through. A US law enforcement officer, asked to explain exactly what happens when someone is shot, points out that much depends on the calibre of the gun, the length of the barrel, the type of bullet, the distance from the weapon to the victim, and even the physical build of the shot person. A bullet to the head will usually cause instant death or certainly immediate unconsciousness, and death will be instant if a bullet penetrates the heart, causing a massive drop in blood pressure.

'You could fire a gun at 20 different people and get 20 different results,' the officer explained.

In one extraordinary case in Las Vegas in 1997, Juan Lopez, 36, was shot in the front of the head when two men randomly fired semi-automatic handguns into a crowd. Incredibly, the bullet ricocheted off his skull but the blood flow was sickening. Towel after towel was drenched as people tried to stop the bleeding. Yet one day later he was released from hospital. Falconio shed much less blood than that.

Imagine the scene based on the description of events provided by Joanne ... Falconio jumps down from the Volkswagen and wanders around to the rear of the vehicle where the stranger is waiting to point out a problem with the exhaust. He is smoking a cigarette. They have a brief chat, the other motorist telling Falconio, perhaps, that he has seen sparks coming from the twin exhaust pipes. The engine is still running, but Falconio cannot see any sparks, which is why he returns to the front of the VW to ask Joanne to rev it up. Then he wanders back—and is shot.

If the bloodstain is any guide and if the VW was parked on the hard shoulder, it would appear that Falconio was shot when he was close to the rear driver's side of the kombi. It might also be assumed that the gunman was standing back a metre or so, allowing Falconio to have another look at the exhaust as Joanne revved the engine. At this point, perhaps, the stranger produces his revolver and shoots the Englishman. If the gunman was facing the rear of the vehicle there was a chance the bullet would go straight through Falconio and hit the back of the Volkswagen. There was no sign of any bullet damage on the vehicle when police later inspected it, so the suggestion is that the gunman was either standing to one side when he fired the gun, so that the bullet went through Falconio and continued on into the bush. Or it stopped in the Englishman's body. This is assuming that Falconio was indeed shot.

Was he was standing up when hit? Had he and the gunman become embroiled in an argument that resulted in a struggle and the weapon had been fired? Or was he bending over, examining the exhaust when the gunman stood over him and coolly shot him in the head?

Whatever transpired, the scene was apparently played out in the spooky headlights of the gunman's vehicle for it would be inconceivable for Falconio to examine the rear of his vehicle in the dull glow of the VW's rear red lights. If he was shot in the head or heart, he would be in no position to cry out, and it must be assumed that he would have certainly been unconscious by the time Joanne said she was dragged from the cabin. Otherwise, she would have heard him calling for help or moaning. In her interview for the British TV programme Joanne had mentioned that Falconio had taken his cigarettes and gone for a chat with the stranger. It seems likely he would have lit up as he discussed the problem of the exhaust. But police had insisted they found no discarded cigarette butts at the scene.

There were so many questions, so many scenarios. Were the police thinking along the same lines? In the main incident room in Alice Springs, just across the road from the central police station, there was no hint of any doubts about the case. Detectives took phone calls, perused computer screens, compared details from one caller with another. Some calls resulted in police in a faraway town travelling around to an address to check someone out.

It was a long shot, but several days after arriving back in Alice Springs I asked if I could look at the Volkswagen, parked in a police yard a short distance from the town centre. I was surprised to receive permission and was taken up the highway and led across to the dusty, orange and white VW, with its pop-up top. It had South Australian numberplates, registration WOI 597, and was parked among a number of other vehicles that had been stolen, impounded or brought in for specialised examination. There was a long white stripe on each side and a spare tyre attached to the front. The bumper bars were painted white.

The rear of the vehicle on the driver's side, above a rusty towbar, was inked with graph lines, indicating a painstaking search of that area by forensic scientists, letters of the alphabet across the top of each square, the numbers down the side. There were stickers from Western Australia, placed on the window by a previous owner. The van had certainly been around. Inside there were numerous cardboard boxes, provided by police, containing the couples' personal items and two fold-away chairs. There was nothing about it that gave a casual onlooker a clue to the drama it had been involved in and the police had also admitted finding nothing that could help them.

'She can have it back whenever she wants,' said a police officer as I sat in the driver's seat, clutching the steering wheel, imagining that journey up the highway in this old vehicle. 'Although I'm not so sure that she does want it.'

In the meantime, pressure remained on the Northern Territory police to make an arrest—and it would be only a few weeks before it came.

Chapter 12

The arrest

Hiding out in the Riverland, Brad Murdoch was edgy. He knew the police were looking for him because his movements and behaviour—being in central Australia when the Barrow Creek incident occurred and changing the profile of his Toyota—had made him a suspect. He was also convinced that Hepi, his former friend, had pointed the finger at him. Then he learned that the police had called on his brother, Gary, and had asked for a DNA sample. If he had had any doubts that they were looking for him, they were now dispelled. He was a fugitive.

Murdoch told the house owner's 13-year-old daughter, who is known as Melissa because her real name cannot be revealed for legal reasons, that he was on the run but that he was an innocent man. The girl and her mother had a dramatic story to tell to a court later, but their account was thrown out and to this day the truth of it comes down to their claims against Murdoch's denials. But there is no doubt about the drama of his subsequent arrest.

Murdoch, so streetwise, was to claim to trusted friends later that he was certain he had been under surveillance for at least several days before he was arrested, but the evidence that police put together for his court appearance told a different story.

At 11.30 am on 28 August 2002, Detective Geoff Carson, based in the Riverland, received an anxious call on his mobile phone from the 68-year-old former brothel owner, who claimed that his de-facto (common law) wife and her daughter had been kidnapped by Brad Murdoch six days earlier. The two had since been freed, but Murdoch was still in the area, said the caller.

Accompanied by Constable Rebecca Milne, Carson drove to the man's home where they heard that Murdoch had allegedly raped the 13-year-old girl before blindfolding her and tying her up in the back of his white 1999 four-wheel drive. The man added that Murdoch had then forced the girl's mother into the back of the vehicle and driven for 20 hours before dropping the couple off at a Shell service station in Port Augusta. He had given the woman $1000 in cash to get a taxi to Adelaide.

Carson contacted his superior officer in the town of Berri, Detective Sergeant Mark Boileau, asking him to set in motion an urgent police alert around the state. Carson said he had been told that Murdoch was armed and would retaliate against police if challenged or cornered. Sergeant Boileau called in the help of other detectives. As part of the operation, a check was made of videotapes from service stations to see if Murdoch could be recognised.

At 4.50 pm that same day, Senior Constable Robert Michael and Constable Peter Stirling were waiting in an unmarked Holden Commodore at a BP service station on the main highway near Port Augusta. They saw a Toyota four-wheel drive matching the description of Murdoch's vehicle and towing a camping trailer, drive past. They started following, asking for a registration check at headquarters. Within minutes it was confirmed that the vehicle was owned by the wanted man.

The officers followed the vehicle into a car park near the Woolworths shopping centre. Senior Constable Michael decided they were facing a 'high risk incident' and radioed for immediate armed backup from all available officers. He warned them all to come wearing bullet-proof vests. Nearby streets were cordoned off.

From a used-car business, the two police officers watched as Murdoch climbed from his vehicle, unlocked its steel-mesh canopy and spent some minutes doing something at the front of his pants before adjusting his jumper and walking into the supermarket. The officers feared he might have been concealing a weapon.

Shortly afterwards, the two police officers were joined by a trained marksman, Senior Constable Mark Cowling, who positioned himself in the car yard with a powerful rifle. Then Senior Constable Sean Everett arrived with a 12-guage pump-action shotgun. Brad Murdoch would have little chance if he dared confront police with any kind of weapon he might have been carrying.

More police arrived. They were warned that Murdoch was considered to be highly dangerous and believed to be carrying a number of firearms, including a pistol and a high-powered rifle. With a pistol probably hidden in the front of his pants, he was likely to shoot it out with police rather than be taken into custody because, the assembled team were told by Senior Constable Michael, he was a suspect in the disappearance of Peter Falconio.

It was at 6 pm when one of the watching police, Probationary Constable Ben Timmins, radioed to the others that he could see Murdoch paying for his groceries at the Woolworths checkout. He was on his way out. The moment had come for a confrontation. Senior Constables Cowling, Dredge and Everett positioned themselves behind a stand of gum trees while two other officers, Sergeant Troy Kaesler and Constable Justin Nichele, quietly ordered shoppers to move into nearby shops in case the bullets started flying.

At 6.07 pm Murdoch walked from the store towards his Land Cruiser carrying a white plastic bag of groceries in each hand. This was encouraging for the police, as he would not be able to grab any hidden firearms quickly.

'Go, go, go!' Senior Constable Michael yelled into the radio.

Senior Constable Everett raced across the car park, aiming his pump-action shotgun at Murdoch. 'Down, down, down!' he shouted at Murdoch, as other officers surrounded the wanted man.

Murdoch hesitated, his hands remaining at the front of his pants, although they were still holding the shopping bags.

'Get on the fucking ground now!' demanded Everett.

The police officer was to say later that Murdoch appeared very calm and did not appear frightened by the raid or the firearms that were pointed at him. 'I would describe his reaction to our presence as calculating,' he would say. 'I formed the belief that the suspect was about to produce a weapon from a concealed position under the front of his shirt.'

But seconds later Murdoch lowered the shopping bags and raised both hands into the air. Then he dropped to his knees but did not obey the order to lie face down. So Everett shoved him hard in the rear lower back with his foot, keeping Murdoch pressed flat to the ground.

The big man was handcuffed and his ankles were bound with plastic restraints. Senior Constable Dredge then searched him and found a shoulder holster with a gun, which had ten bullets in the clip. Murdoch was hauled to his feet. He and Senior Constable Michael glared at one another. Then the officer told him, 'I'm now arresting you on suspicion of the offences of abduction and rape. You are not obliged to say anything further. Anything that you do say will be recorded and may be given in evidence. Do you understand that?'

'Yep,' said Murdoch.

The running and the hiding were over. And a new, dramatic series of events was about to begin.

X

For the next two days, police crawled all over Murdoch's 'bus'. It was more than a home on wheels—it was an adventurer's wagon, filled with every-thing that a man living in the outback for months or years on end could need. The rear of the long-wheelbase 1999 Toyota diesel was equipped with bedding, water bottles, cooking equipment, a variety of tools, wires, ropes, cable ties, a CB radio, an electric cattle prod, a jockey whip, five pairs of disposable gloves and long-handled shovels. There was a .308 Mauser bolt-action rifle with a powerful telescopic sight, a number of boxes of ammunition, two pistols, several knives, a crossbow with 13 bolts, and Russian-made military-style night-vision goggles. Hooked to the rear was a trailer filled with camping equipment, ice-boxes filled with food, full fuel cans and a Kawasaki trailbike.

The search of the ute had to be carried out with the outmost care, for police believed that if Murdoch had indeed murdered Peter Falconio and carted his body off in the Toyota there might just be a chance that some clue remained. Although they all suspected that after 13 months it was highly unlikely they would find anything that would link the vehicle to Falconio's disappearance.

The investigation of the van was overseen by a forensic expert, Senior Constable Peter McKenzie, who began by searching the front cabin. Between the seats he found a backpack containing a holster that was fitted with a fully loaded .38 Beretta semi-automatic pistol, which had had its serial number punched out. Also in the bag was a list of names and telephone numbers, a pouch with 29 .38 bullets, disposable gloves, a black shoulder bag with $3000 in cash and $2000 wrapped in yellow cloth.

In the rear canopy, McKenzie and his team found several lengths of chain, a pair of bolt cutters, a tin containing cannabis, six rolls of tape and a .308 R.Famage bolt-action rifle loaded with three rounds of ammunition. There were also four bags containing between them 308 bullets for a .38 pistol and 9 millimetre pistol, a crossbow and six knives. A blue plastic tray held seven rolls of tape and a plastic bag with ten cable ties.

Next, McKenzie turned his attention to the camping trailer, covered with a green vinyl top. It held a camp-bed base, a spare tyre and a canvas tent. McKenzie also found two long-handled shovels, a box with thirteen cross-bow bolts, two tins of cannabis and a pair of size 11 shoes.

The forensic officer decided to make an even closer examination of the main canopy. Studying a fuel tank attached to the floor and the front wall that was between the canopy and the cabin he realised the tank could be moved away from the wall. The tank, he found, had a hidden compartment extending from one side to the other. While the front half of the tank was sealed and contained diesel fuel, the back half had been made to allow a metal compartment, about 24.7 centimetres square and 1.5 metres long, to be fitted inside the space behind the fuel. Inside the false compartment was a black plastic box that contained a Glock pistol. The Glock 9 millimetre is made of durable lightweight steel and largely regarded as one of the most reliable weapons in the world and the first choice of many law enforcement agencies. The newly formed Iraqi police forced received 10 000 of them in October 2004.

Meanwhile, at Port Augusta police station, other officers were examining the contents of several bags taken from the vehicle. They found three West Australian registration plates, a cross bolt quiver, 33 pearls wrapped in tissue paper and a Nokia mobile phone with the SIM card removed.

Murdoch's arrest made headlines around Australia and Britain. Everything about him fitted the picture of the man wanted for holding up the British couple at Barrow Creek. Or did it? His burly appearance was vastly different to the description of the medium-height man who pointed a gun at Joanne Lees. And while his vehicle was fitted with all the weapons, tools, tapes and shovels that could have been used to perpetrate and then conceal a murder, there was one major problem with it—there was no way anyone could squirm from the front cabin into the back. And judging from an investigation of the metal structure of the vehicle, there never had been.

Even so, police in South Australia and the Northern Territory were ecstatic. They had made an arrest in an unsolved murder—or at least disappearance—that was never going to go away until someone was hauled in to answer a lot of very serious questions.

Bradley John Murdoch was charged with the alleged offences for which South Australia police had been alerted—kidnapping the mother and daughter on the remote Riverland property. He was formally accused of two counts of rape, two of indecent assault, two of false imprisonment and one charge of common assault. But that impending case was merely a sideshow.

What the world wanted to know was whether Murdoch was the Barrow Creek killer. Every man and woman in the Northern Territory police force certainly wanted to know that. They wanted Murdoch back in their territory but they needed more than a vanload of guns and tools as evidence; a rape charge in South Australia was not going to be enough to pin a murder onto the suspect. They wanted hard evidence linking him to the attack—and the best hard evidence would be a DNA match.

Forensic scientist Carmen Eckhoff, working in her Darwin laboratory, had already extracted a small DNA trace from Joanne's T-shirt. The wait for a suspect to match it with appeared to be over. Except for one problem. Murdoch told police he would not cooperate in providing a DNA sample, although he was to say later that he suspected police would get a sample anyway. That would be easy enough, by taking swabs from his van or even 'borrowing' his toothbrush he was using in jail, where he was being held on remand pending the outcome of the rape trial. And had they not already taken DNA from his elder brother? In fact, police had secretly collected a cigarette butt from an ashtray Murdoch had used at the Riverland house.

Whatever decision was handed down in the South Australian case, it seemed that Murdoch would be dragged back to the Northern Territory under an extradition order. If he were found guilty of rape in South Australia, he would have to serve a jail sentence in that state and could only be extradited once he had completed his time. If he was freed, it was likely he would still be extradited—but a DNA match would turn a 'likelihood' into a certainty.

Murdoch, through his newly appointed lawyer, South Australian solicitor Mark Twiggs, appealed against the Northern Territory application for him to provide a sample on the basis that samples could not be sent from one state for use in another. But on the advice of his legal team he eventually dropped his appeal and provided a swab from his mouth. The sample was immediately sent to Darwin. Within two days there was a jubilant announcement from Darwin. Murdoch's DNA matched the sample on Joanne's T-shirt.

At least, that was the interpretation the world had put on the finding, although Crime Chief John Daulby was cautious in his announcement, saying the results of the scientific analysis meant that Murdoch could not be excluded from the investigation. Daulby would not confirm there had been a 100 per cent match, saying he did not wish to prejudice future court cases.

After the doubts about elements of Joanne's story, enhanced by the feelings of the Aboriginal trackers, the news was received by many, with mixed emotions. While I was satisfied there might now be a solution to the baffling case, there were still lingering doubts about the loose ends—the failure to find any sign of a dog at the crime scene, the missing footprints of Joanne's assailant and the enormous differences in the height of her attacker and Brad Murdoch. Even so, it was time for me to publicly put my hands up and write in London's *Daily Mail* that I was happy for Joanne that someone had been arrested. I reported that 'I am the first to admit that there were elements of her story that caused me to doubt her.' I added, 'Today, she will be able to face her critics and hold her head high.'

The following day I was asked to appear on the ABC's *7.30 Report*. I was asked how I felt about earlier doubting Joanne. I could only repeat my previous thoughts that there were many elements of her story that had not added up, and which I felt still did not add up, and that there would probably be many more surprises to come in this extraordinary saga.

The following day I received a call from an ABC reporter in Perth, who had been contacted by an old friend of Murdoch's. The man wanted to speak to me urgently. When I called, he explained he had seen me on TV and urged me not to stop my inquiries because 'you have been on the right track all along'.

Of course, any friend of Murdoch would be more than anxious to get a reporter on side and perhaps help to support his defence. On the other hand, I could hardly ignore the invitation to meet the man. I agreed to fly to Perth once the Adelaide hearing was complete.

Bradley Murdoch appeared before Judge Michael David in mid-October, his hair shorn. The identities of the witnesses—the mother, her 13-year-old daughter and the brothel owner who called the police—were supressed.

The hearing produced colourful evidence in which the woman claimed her daughter had told her that Murdoch had raped her in the house. Then, it was claimed, he had abducted both the mother and daughter for 25 hours, driving his vehicle into a ditch and chaining her and her daughter to fold-out chairs.

'He went and snorted some speed, smoked cannabis and checked things in his vehicle,' said the woman. 'He walked around the outside to make sure no-one was there and he was checking his guns.' She added that Murdoch told her he wanted to have sex with one of them and she volunteered.

'I did not want to have sex with him but I didn't want him to harm my daughter again so I said I would do it,' she told the court.

As the case continued, the 13-year-old he was said to have raped and chained up for six hours was called to give evidence via closed circuit TV. She explained how her relationship with Murdoch had grown.

'On my birthday, he gave me $500 and he hugged me. He had never hugged me before. Sometimes he said I looked nice.' She had visited

Murdoch on a number of occasions when he lived in Adelaide and he had stayed with her and her parents at other times. They had often talked about school, animals and other things. He told her how he travelled around Australia and asked her to help sort out some maps. She knew he had a pair of handcuffs and it was these that he allegedly used to bind her hands behind her back before raping her.

'He was kind of leaning on me, trying to get them at the back of my hands,' she told the court, adding that her mouth was taped and material was put in her ears before she was raped.

When the mother's husband stepped into the witness box, barrister Grant Algie, working with Mr Twiggs for the defence, asked if he sought to profit from the kidnapping incident, given that it had taken five days for him to report it.

'You must be joking,' said the man. 'My daughter is worth more than that. If I had a gun in my hands I would shoot him in the head right now. If the media approached me, of course, I wouldn't talk to them. Unless they paid me.'

Several weeks later, the mother agreed to tell her story of life with Murdoch to Adelaide's *Sunday Mail* newspaper. Because her identity could not be revealed due to her daughter being under-age, she called herself Tania. She left the readers in no doubt that Brad Murdoch was a 'dangerous animal' who was obsessed with drugs, guns and other weapons such as an electric prodder.

In the days before Falconio's disappearance, she claimed, she saw him practising tying cable ties and chains in her neighbour's shed. Her daughter had watched as he had drilled holes in the steel-mesh canopy of his Land Cruiser before he left on what he said was a drug run to the Northern Territory.

He returned to the Riverland property about six weeks later, she said, some seven weeks after the Barrow Creek incident. 'Brad is a dangerous animal and he's capable of anything,' said the woman. 'He told me he harmed people. I walked into the shed at the neighbour's and he was sitting down at the table trying out the cable ties, pulling them tight.'

Referring to her daughter under a false name, she added, 'Melissa later told me she saw him drilling holes in the canopy of his Land Cruiser but she didn't think anything of it, you know, because he's a mechanic.'

Tania and her de facto husband, the former brothel owner, met Murdoch in 1999 through an acquaintance Murdoch said was his partner in the drug trade. Shortly afterwards, Murdoch started using a guesthouse on their property and they would see him wearing his night-vision goggles and watching people by the Murray River.

The woman and her husband worked as 'gofers' for the big man, doing his shopping, buying food and phone cards in Tania's name and generally running his errands. He was treated as part of the family, but he was no ordinary guest.

Tania claimed he repeatedly used drugs, especially speed, in front of them and was often so high he would stay awake for up to five days. On his return to the Riverland in the weeks following Falconio's disappearance, she noticed that his vehicle had been modified and his behaviour was paranoid. He became irate while watching the TV news whenever it featured the Faclonio case, and complained an acquaintance—who he had fallen out with—and police were trying to set him up. The acquaintance was James Hepi.

Bob recalled that the person in the identikit picture wanted for the Barrow Creek incident looked a bit like Murdoch, but the description of the vehicle was entirely different. He left the property on the same weekend as the Falconio disappearance with the ute's trailer on the back and when he returned a few weeks later there was a new canopy on the vehicle. It had been spruced up, with a turbo charger added.

'We knew the guy but we didn't think he did it. He came back and we saw the photo but we thought it was bullshit. They were trying to set him up,' he said.

Tania said that she knew Murdoch was dangerous, but up until then he had been generous and protective towards her and her daughter. He gave the girl money, atlases and an encyclopaedia. He also brought Tania cigarettes and alcohol and for her birthday gave her $500. Tania added that Murdoch would give her marijuana and a hundred dollars here and there when they needed it.

'We thought he was a good guy,' she told the newspaper. 'Looking back now, he was the best actor I've ever seen.'

On 10 November 2003, the jury hearing the case against Murdoch decided the evidence of the mother, her de facto and the 13-year-old was flawed.

Murdoch's lawyer, Mr Grant Algie, had told the court the rape charges had been 'made up' as part of an elaborate three-state (Western Australia, South Australia and the Northern Territory) conspiracy to 'frame' his client for Falconio's murder.

The charges against Murdoch, Mr Algie said, were part of a plan drawn up solely so that his DNA could be obtained. The conspirators, he claimed, had gone to great lengths, including breaking into Murdoch's home and stealing some of his possessions, to frame him. This was a reference, in part, to someone collecting cigarette butts from the Broome house he shared with James Hepi.

In any case, Murdoch was found not guilty. He was a free man—for less than a minute. He was immediately arrested inside the court under an extradition order from the Northern Territory. He would be sent to Darwin under close escort to answer a charge of murdering Peter Falconio.

But his lawyer was anxious to emphasise that Murdoch had been framed—and he said as the court closed its doors at the end of the dramatic trial that the jury's verdict 'clearly confirmed' his client's claims he had been set up in a conspiracy.

'Mr Murdoch wants the media and the public to know that the verdict of the jury is a confirmation of his innocence,' Mr Algie told a large group of reporters. 'His defence has always been that he was falsely accused and set up, and he believes the verdict is a clear confirmation of that.'

Murdoch was driven off to jail to await his extradition. A new chapter surrounding the incident at Barrow Creek was about to begin.

Chapter 13
Friends and family

I met the man I will call Macca in a pub on the outskirts of Perth. He settled for a beer with a meal of sausage and mash. He and his wife had known Murdoch for the best part of sixteen years and he wanted to say right away that his old mate was no angel. But neither, Macca insisted, was he a killer. He carried guns, which he would use if anyone seriously threatened his life because in his line of business, running drugs around the country, anything could happen.

Macca was anxious to explain why he believed Joanne Lees' descriptions were inaccurate and which left him without any doubt that his friend was not responsible for the attack. What he had to tell me reinforced several of the discrepancies that had already arisen in Joanne's account, but he was eager to emphasise them—and add a number of points that no-one else knew about. He had been looking at the picture of the bespectacled man in the Shell truckstop. Murdoch, he said, did not wear glasses when he drove. Whenever he travelled through the outback he towed a trailer with a motorbike in it—there was no such trailer in the truckstop picture.

Murdoch, said Macca, had never had long hair in all the years he had known him and he was nothing like the identikit picture originally put out by police. He was baffled by the startling difference in the original picture and a second identikit, released a few weeks later, showing a man with very short hair and protruding ears—a face that looked very much like the Brad Murdoch Macca knew. This worried him. He wondered if, early on in the investigation, the police had already decided that Murdoch, whose travels through the outback which he felt would have almost certainly been known to the authorities, was going to be their man. But he conceded these were only the thoughts of a friend of the arrested man and what would they be worth to the authorities?

There was one important fact that Macca wanted to emphasise and it was more important than any of the features on the van or whether the attacker had long or short hair: Brad Murdoch travelled everywhere with Jack the dalmation. There was never a trip that Jack wasn't with his master. 'That dog, with its white hair and dark spots was as different from the red heeler that Joanne Lees described as chalk is from cheese,' said Macca. 'I've heard that she later described the gunman's dog as being like a bull terrior, with short pointed ears. Either Brad picked up a hitch-hiking cattle dog and dumped Jack at the roadside, or Joanne Lees's account needs a second look. You can speak to scores of people who know Brad and they'd all tell you the same thing, that he never travelled anywhere without Jack. They were inseparable.'

Later I met Macca's wife, who had also known Murdoch for years, for the three of them had often knocked around together in and around Perth. Joanne, she said, had missed out one very important feature when describing her attacker in such fine detail. If the gunman had been Murdoch, why hadn't Joanne noticed that he was missing his two front teeth? No-one failed to notice this; the missing teeth were obvious every time Murdoch uttered a word and it was well known that he had spoken to the Englishwoman, for he had ordered her to lie down across the Volkswagen's front seats and had issued other commands. Why, too, had she failed to make a point of Murdoch's enormous size?

'Why didn't she tell everyone what would have been obvious to her the minute he supposedly appeared at the side window of the kombi, that the gunman was a giant of a man, so big that she had no hope of competing with him?' said Macca's wife. 'Brad's size and missing front teeth are the first two things you notice about him, but all she gave initially was a description of a medium-built person with long, dark shoulder-length hair and wearing a baseball cap. I think it changes a bit later but you have to go on first impressions, don't you?'

Macca and his wife agreed that Murdoch was 'not everyone's cup of tea', as his background known to them testified. When he was in his early 30s he rode a Harley with the feared bikie gang Gypsy Jokers. Husband and wife grinned as they recalled he had joined the gang after they had broken his leg in a fight in the car park of a Perth brothel. He had a string of girlfriends, for while he could instil fear with his size he was also a charmer with the ladies. There had been a wife, Diane, and they had a son, but Diane's very religious mother was not enamoured with Murdoch, there was pressure on his wife to leave him, and by the time the boy was 18 months old the marriage was in its death throes. Diane found a new husband; a New Zealander who was also deeply religious.

Looking at the CCTV picture again, Macca said that if anything, the man featured in it looked more like Murdoch's brother Gary than Bradley himself. Could it have been Gary, who also worked and travelled through the outback?

'Don't think so,' said Macca's wife. 'Even though the person in the photo is wearing glasses, I think it could be Brad. I think I can recognise the sweater he's wearing, but of course, I could be wrong. And I don't think he ever wore a baseball cap. As I recall he would wear a type of woollen cap with a bobble on it. What I do wonder is this: assuming Brad had filled up with fuel in Alice Springs to head towards Broome and had then got involved in this Barrow Creek thing, why on earth would he drive all the way back to Alice Springs to fill up again? That would be like someone setting off from Perth to drive to Adelaide and then driving back to Perth to get more fuel as the tank emptied. That doesn't make any sense to me at all and this is one of the reasons why there is so much confusion over this whole business.'

X

Colin and Nance Murdoch lived in a neat cottage at the end of a short driveway in a Western Australian beachside suburb. Their faces portrayed their concerns about their son's future when they invited me in for what was to be their only interview. Both in their 80s, they had been married for 60 years and had seen the raw side of life as they scratched out a living in the early days. There was a walking frame in the room, which Nance used to get around with following a heart operation. As a companion, they now had a small, friendly dog, Molly, who sat in her basket wearing a pet's blanket. In a cabinet in the Murdoch's small front room were their memories—colour photos of their three sons, Robert, the oldest, who was now dead; Gary, the second brother, and Brad, who was twelve years younger, staring out in black and white from a silver frame. They would tell me about Robert shortly, they said, and that might help to explain why Brad had gone off the rails and become something of a renegade—although, they insisted, they could not and would not accept that their son was a murderer.

Also behind the cabinet's glass door, along with pictures of Brad at his brother's wedding and at a niece's wedding, were photos of his own marriage. But the bride had been cut out of the picture with scissors. 'We don't want to be reminded of Diane,' said Colin. 'It was another bad time for Brad, the problems he had with her and her family. He just happened to marry the wrong kind of woman.'

On top of the cabinet was a certificate presented to Colin Murdoch by the Returned Servicemen's League of Australia for 50 years continuous service as a member of the league after joining up at the age of 21 and seeing service in the Middle East with the 2/11 Battalion.

'I didn't meet Nan until I came back from the Middle East,' said the tall, softly spoken father of the man accused of the outback murder. 'I was in Ceylon for three months on the way back and then I went to New Guinea in 1942, so I did my bit for king and country. I had to get out of the army in the end and come back to Australia because my father was dying of cancer.

'My parents had a farm in Donnybrook, about 140 kilometres south of here, and Nan was living in Lord Street in Perth and we just happened to meet up through a cousin. She was a good looking sheila was Nan, and we started going out with each other. We were by now the only ones left in our families and we got married in St Albans Church in Perth.' He chuckled as he added, 'I can still remember that day, with the vicar, an old bloke, shaking in his shoes with age.'

The newlyweds travelled down to the Murdoch farm because there was no-one else in either family to manage it. In time they moved to the small town of Northampton, 150 kilometres north of Perth, where they watched their three boys grow. Brad had been born in nearby Geraldton, 'an easy birth' Nance recalled.

They had been hoping for a daughter at some time but accepted after the birth of their youngest, Brad, that they would now be the parents of three brothers. Their years in Northampton were during what Colin described as 'the days of the rabbit'.

'The place was lousy with rabbits. People would go out shooting them, laying traps for them, but it made no difference. They were everywhere, eating everything in sight.'

Colin made a living travelling around Western Australia, working as a mechanic and helping to fight the rabbit plague. Robert and Gary went to high school in Geraldton, while Brad waited to be old enough to attend the local school in Northampton. While still only five, he made friends with boys who lived a short distance away and he would often visit them at their home, stomping across the paddock in his father's big rubber boots, an image which still caused Colin to laugh.

But there were racial tensions in the town, which penetrated even the youngest groups. Colin spoke of two neighbouring Aboriginal families who were always drinking and if they ran into any problems they would blame the whites. 'They were always blaming us Murdochs for one thing or another when really we had nothing to do with them.

'Things turned from bad to worse on the day Robert had his 21st birthday party. Our black neighbours couldn't get their car to start and so they pushed it downhill but it stopped in front of our gate. In no time we had people from our party coming out to stare at the Aborigines, who were all quite drunk. Sensing trouble, I rang an old policeman friend, old Jack, who has since passed on, and asked if he was coming to the party because he would find quite a reception of all races waiting for him.

'One of the Aborigines was lying drunk in the gutter and old Jack said he was going to arrest him, but one of the women ran at him and said Jack couldn't arrest him because he didn't have any pyjamas to wear in prison. Jack was stunned by the whole scene because across the road was another bloke drunk and entangled in a wire fence. In the end Jack kicked the bloke outside our gate and told him to get on home, but that started a bit of a war between us, and Brad, being the youngest, was on the receiving end of their punishment.

'He would often come home from school telling us the blacks were always ganging up on him and one day he got pretty badly beaten up. I think that was probably something that stayed with him for a very long time. Could be that explains why he turned out to be a bit of a wild fella himself because he learned from a very young age that it all came down to a survival of the fittest.'

But there may have been more in Brad Murdoch's early life, which led to him distrusting Aborigines and eventually having that KKK tattoo indelibly inked into his arm. For Colin would tell Brad of the problems his own father, John, had with the blacks in the West Australian gold rush days in the 1890s.

'I would tell Brad that my dad believed the blacks were a pretty wild bunch. Dad walked once with a mate from Port Pirie to Coolgardie during the Gold Rush and on that occasion he said he learned to always look behind, never in front, because the blacks would always be following you. They were about to drop off to sleep one night when they heard a rustling in the bushes, so Dad's mate fired a shot over the top of the bushes and a whole mob of them fled, screaming as they went. I told Brad all about this and I think he decided that if he had any trouble, especially with the Aborigines, you fire a gun over their heads and the problem goes away.'

This story might explain an incident later in Brad Murdoch's life, which saw him being arrested for firing a rifle over the head of a group of Aborigines.

When Brad was eight years old his handsome, dark-haired eldest brother Robert was sent home from the grain bulk handling company where he was working because he was feeling ill. His mother, who was running a hair-dressing business, noticed a lump on his neck and he was sent to a specialist. On receiving the results of the analysis the family reeled with shock. Robert had Hodgkin's disease. The lump was malignant and the prognosis for the 22-year-old's future was grim.

After having lived in Northampton for 16 years, the family moved to Perth so that Robert could receive regular chemotherapy and radiation treatment. 'He only lasted 12 months,' said Nance, brushing away a tear. 'He went from being a boy who was even bigger than what Brad grew up to be, to nothing. We all watched him waste away. Our hearts were breaking up.'

Brad was ten when his brother died, a great loss Nance recalled, for the younger boy had looked up to him. Even so, Brad was denied the chance of saying goodbye to Robert at his funeral. Colin's niece had travelled up from Bunbury to Perth and declared it would not be a good idea for such a young boy to be present at the service, so she kept him away.

'It affected Brad pretty badly,' said Nance. 'He thought the family just didn't want him to be there, although at the time the opposite was true. We just didn't want him to be even more upset than he was. We think probably that the death of his brother, that business with the funeral, the problems he'd had with the Aborigines in his younger days and the break up of his marriage all had some kind of effect on Brad. He kept it to himself, but it may have led to him heading out on the road, travelling around to wherever the next day took him.'

In his early teens, Brad started swimming classes, getting up at 5 am so his mother could drive him to the local pool where he showed great promise, so much so that he made it into the State squad. He also belonged to the local lifesavers, his burgeoning frame being found at many of Perth's popular beaches. Gary, meanwhile, had joined the army, where he served for three years. He had wanted to go to Vietnam, but instead was sent to Malaysia.

In time Colin and Nance used their money from Colin's engineering business to buy a service station in the coastal town of Busselton, 50 kilometres from Donnybrook, which they knew so well. There, Brad attended the local high school. Sometimes he would help his parents in the service station, where Nance took on the responsibility of the cooking. But times were hard, not helped by the fact that Nance had to travel to Perth for an ear operation, and in the end they sold out at a loss. With Gary away, Nance, Colin and Brad took up roots and moved into a caravan. Colin got a job as a fitter with a wheat company in Albany and Brad found work as a roustabout, rounding up cattle and shearing sheep, before getting employment as a boner at an abattoirs, where Nance also had a job inspecting the meat.

Tiring of that work, Brad Murdoch headed for South Australia, telling his parents he was going to seek his fortune. He was taken on in the Port Pirie steel foundry, processing metal and helping to brick the big chimney, one of the town's features. Then it was time to move on again, working on the railways for a while and taking a job after that with a Broken Hill earth-moving company.

'Brad once completely rebuilt a truck from the ground up, that was how clever he was with his hands,' Colin said as we sat around the loungeroom table. 'He had turned into a regular jack-of-all-trades. And remember, Nan,' he said, turning to his wife, 'how we all went off fruit picking, you, me and Brad? Where was it we went ...? All around Australia, really, but mainly we did all that grape picking in the Barossa Valley. They were good days, weren't they, Nan?

'He kept me going, you know, did Brad. When he was with the earth-moving firm their mechanic was done for drunken driving, so I took on the job at the age of 62, working with Brad. They were good days, too. Later Brad got a job driving trucks from Perth to Darwin and Gary got a driving job too and I went up on a separate trip with Gary to Darwin. Very big distances those, all through the outback, and I still wonder how Brad has been able to do it, time after time, up and back. He would have covered hundreds of thousands, probably millions of kilometres, because he also drove trucks filled with explosives from Wyndham to the diamond mines. And you know what people said about him? That he was a bit of a rough diamond himself but you could put your life in his hands. If he was your mate, he was your mate in the truest sense of the word.'

They knew their son carried guns but they said he had always had an interest in them and if they were ever fired they were fired at wild pigs. They didn't know if Brad was a good shot or not, but Colin said he certainly knew how to use his fists. Before his 21st birthday he fought in amateur fights in Adelaide and floored more than one opponent who fancied himself. 'If Brad wanted to put you down he could do it as easily as swatting a fly,' said Colin. 'He was, and still is, a very powerful man and you know that's got us thinking a lot about this business in Barrow Creek. If Brad had wanted to restrain anyone they wouldn't have got away, believe me.'

Had Brad lost his front teeth through boxing? 'Oh goodness, no,' said Nance. 'He lost them because he ate too many chocolates. He was a chocoholic.'

I touched on the subject of Brad Murdoch's marriage, although it was apparent that it was not a period his parents cared to remember. 'He'd been living with Diane for five years,' Nance ventured, 'and he was 26 when they got married. He could have had any woman because he was tall and handsome, but he settled on her and it was a big mistake.'

They had met through family contacts—Gary's wife and Diane's mother were sisters. It started to go wrong in the first couple of years, mainly through problems with Diane's mother. 'They had a son who would be in his mid-teens about now,' said Nance, 'but the boy never got to know his father. The marriage lasted no more than four years and Brad was gone when the boy was 18 months old. After she married a New Zealander Diane had four or five more kids.'

It was time to leave Nance and Colin Murdoch, an elderly couple worried desperately about the enormous case that had engulfed their younger living son. By then in jail in Darwin, he was able to ring them from time to time because he was still on remand awaiting a committal hearing, which would decide whether he should be sent for trial.

'He's very confident, you know,' said Colin. He staggered slightly as he stood up and reached for the table to steady himself. 'He told us before the Adelaide case that he didn't do what they were accusing him of and we believed him. The jury did, too. So he told us the truth with that and we believe him when he says he wasn't involved in any murder. Anyway, there are too many discrepancies for him to have done it.

'Even that business with the dog. You can't mistake a dalmation even by torchlight, so how did that girl get it so wrong? You can draw your own conclusions from that. Jack had huge feet, too, and he'd leave prints all over the place. I'd like someone to explain why nobody found any. Besides, we all know what Brad was carrying when he drove up north. That's pretty much an open secret. Doesn't make any sense at all, does it, for a man with all that stuff in the back of his bus to risk everything by trying to hold up a couple of tourists? If you were carrying marijuana in your car and also a heap of cash, would you risk getting caught trying to commit a crime? Brad's not that dumb.'

'He's got new teeth,' said Nance in a flash of humour as we said our good-byes at the door. 'He had them sent up from the jail in South Australia but he's having terrible trouble with them. He doesn't know how to use them. I wish I could go up and visit him but I don't have the strength for that. He knows we love him. And he still calls us mum and dad.'

X

Bradley Murdoch, prisoner number 39672, wrote a letter from his Adelaide jail cell to a friend. It revealed his love for things mechanical, but it also provided an insight into his world—a world of drugs, shady characters with bizarre nicknames and, according to his words, dirty cops. He referred to people who would 'muck around with DNA' to set others up. Murdoch wrote of a contact called Ferret who was allegedly involved in illegal bird smuggling and who, it was claimed, had a contact known as Birdman Bob. There was one person in authority who was involved in the racket and it was Murdoch's belief that if someone high up could be involved in bird smuggling they could also be prepared to set someone up for a crime.

Murdoch wrote about high-powered boats doing a big trade off the West Australian coast in crystal meth, speed, as well as heroin and cocaine. He wrote of a trawler that was deliberately sunk after travelling from South America. Several weeks later a man Murdoch knew, along with a gang, were loaded up with the same drugs from the boat. 'The stuff was everywhere,' Murdoch wrote.

But there was also a note of concern in his letter. He claimed that a former acquaintance had sent a friend around to a place where Murdoch had been staying to pick up cigarette butts. 'Now why would he want those?' he asked. 'More DNA perhaps?'

Murdoch also wrote about his ex-friend James Hepi, pointing out in his letter that when Hepi went to court on drug charges—a court that was closed—the only people present were Hepi and 'two black fellows'. Through a friend, Murdoch learned that it had been stated in court that Hepi had $800 000 in assets and could only prove how he had obtained about half of that amount. However, the judge, according to information

Murdoch received, had ignored the discrepancy because Hepi had been helpful to police 'for dobbing in a number of people'.

Towards the end of his rambling letter, Murdoch said he was 'getting a bit sick of thinking and writing about this shit. I know what has happened, I don't care what people say and write about me. My closest friends know and that is all I think about.'

He revealed he was concerned about Jack the dalmation. Jack had been seen with the mother and daughter who had brought the rape and kidnapping charges against him. Jack had also been seen running around Hepi's block of land 'so it won't be long before he will disappear. That dog was one of the pieces of evidence over that Alice stuff.'

Whether Jack the dog would have a role to play in Murdoch's defence when he appeared for his committal hearing and expected trial remained to be seen. But I would not have betted against it.

Chapter 14
The woman who waits

Jan Pitman sipped a soft drink in the Satay Club, a five minute walk from the Broome house that Brad Murdoch had shared with former friend James Hepi. She had known Murdoch since 1999, when they started chatting in this same leafy outdoor bar area. A former naval WRAN, with which she had served for 13 years on land bases, she was previously married but had been 'free' for 16 years.

'We were never allowed to go to sea as women while I was in the service,' said the mother of two who now worked in a bakery. 'The year I left was the year they allowed it to happen. I was sad to have missed out but that was the way it was. You just ride along.'

Which was what she was doing now, telling me that she would see out the tempestuous months, and perhaps years, that she knew lay ahead for the big man she had fallen in love with. 'I've told Brad I'll wait. If there is any justice in this world it won't be long because I know he didn't kill Peter Falconio. I know Brad too well for that. It's not in him to hold someone up and then shoot the man. That's not Brad.'

It was late in the afternoon as we talked, a quiet time in the bar, which has seen the world's most colourful strangers pass by. There have been druggies, menacing motorcycle gang members along with their girls, knockabout blokes waiting for a job to drop into their laps but content to drink a few beers in the meantime, singers, dancers, social climbers, beauties and beasts. Hearts were broken or mended in the Satay Club. Many said they hated the place, but they always came back.

Jan ended up visiting Brad at the house he shared with Hepi and she often stayed there. She saw their friends and associates come and go, saw how easy he was with them all. She fell in love with him, but Jan was to become one of the Satay Club's broken-hearted patrons when she learned that Brad was sleeping with another woman. She learned the woman was a drug addict and believed that Brad had simply got carried away with an easy lay. 'He admitted it to me, you know,' she said. 'I was glad he was honest with me about it, but then he was honest with me about every-thing. I knew it wouldn't last and of course it didn't. He told me eventually that he had got out of that relationship. He said: "I just couldn't hack it any more—she was always throwing up, for a start".'

She knew that Murdoch would be found not guilty of the rape charge in South Australia. There were rumours all around town that Hepi had put the mother and daughter up to screaming rape so the police would have a reason to pull Murdoch in. Jan pulled a sheet of paper from her bag. She had tried to remember Murdoch's movements around the time of the Falconio incident. She had gone right back to 12 June, a month before, when Murdoch was in Broome with Jack the dog and then he had headed off some time after 17 June. It was not until 29 July that she next saw him and by then people were whispering that he was the bloke involved.

'The mother and daughter have been looking after Jack,' said Jan. 'He wrote me a letter from jail asking how they could look after the pet dog of a man who was supposed to have raped them. He has been very calm about it, but you can imagine what he must be thinking deep down; that there's been dirty work afoot all the way through.'

Brad Murdoch's circle of friends were, not unnaturally, very protective of him in the months following his arrest and the aftermath of the Adelaide hearing when he had been formally charged with Falconio's murder. Quite simply they could not believe he had killed a tourist and tried to kidnap his girlfriend. They had heard the rumours before his arrest that he might be involved with Falconio's disappearance but on studying the information that had been fed to the public and comparing it all with Murdoch's appearance and that of his van, along with his general character, they were convinced he had been wrongly blamed.

At his home in Broome, Brett Duthie, who had employed Murdoch on a part-time basis at his engineering business, shook his head at suggestions the black cap the man at the Shell service station was wearing was identical to one issued by Duthie's company, as had been suggested in media reports. 'Don't worry, mate, I've had a very careful look at that photo, stared at it a million times, and I can assure you that it's not one of my caps. Yes, we had a cap with a logo on the front but none of ours would fit Brad's head because they were all too small. And unlike the cap worn by the man in the photo, ours doesn't have a logo on the back. I've travelled around with Brad and worked with him and he would wear a hat or a cap if he was out in the sun all day, but he'd never wear one in the car at night.'

Duthie had noticed another big discrepancy—he believed the vehicle in the Shell service station picture had six wheel studs, while Murdoch's vehicle had only five. Murdoch also never wore glasses to drive or walk around. And no matter what Joanne Lees had described, Duthie said that anyone trying to get from the cabin into the rear of Murdoch's vehicle would have to be better than Houdini, because there was no access.

Duthie, who was questioned by the police for three days about his friend, agreed Murdoch had changed the profile of his vehicle, fitting a new canopy on the back, but he had ordered all the materials for that work before the Barrow Creek incident. If anything, Murdoch was always 'mucking around' with his vehicles, rearranging the insides and working on the engines. His four-wheel drive was his home more than anything else and, like anyone living in a house, he liked to 'move the furniture around' from time to time. But he was also ready to drive off to any work assignment at the shortest notice. If someone on an outlying property wanted a fitter, Brad Murdoch was the man to go because he could sleep in the vehicle at the end of a good day's work.

Murdoch had told Duthie that he always intended to have new work done on the vehicle once he returned from down south because the old canopy would rattle to the point that it would drive a passenger insane. Before the Falconio incident, Duthie recalled, the canopy on the rear of the Toyota was a complicated affair with aluminium mesh rising up on each side towards the roof and a canvas cover over the top of the mesh. In order to open the side or the back of the canopy, it was necessary to first undo the canvas and roll it up. Next the sides of the tray around the edges of the base of the canopy had to be dropped down. Finally the aluminium sides or back of the vehicle could be raised. It was quite a procedure.

Murdoch planned to change the sides, replacing them with an aluminium mesh security screen that could be raised hydraulically. Duthie supplied Murdoch with a turbo charger, which the two of them fitted to his vehicle and he had invoices to show that that work was done as far back as 2000.

Brad Murdoch ordered all the parts for the new mesh sides before July 2001, Duthie recalled, and arranged with a local welding firm to do the work. But Duthie recalled he and the firm had a falling out for some reason, so Murdoch had collected all the aluminium materials and brought them around to his workshop. The parts remained there until, after his return to Broome following the Barrow Creek incident, Murdoch took the parts to Steve Galvin, of Galvin's Marine.

Duthie saw Murdoch on the morning of Monday 16 July—two days after the incident—when he and Hepi had called at the workshop to pick up heavy duty batteries, two for Hepi's 91–92 HJ75 vehicle and two for Murdoch's 98 HZJ-75 Toyota. Murdoch had telephoned on 10 July, although Duthie did not know from where, to order the batteries and when he turned up with Hepi he appeared normal and calm. But he later told Duthi that 'there's going to be a big load of shit happening and it's going to be a major set-up.'

Duthie sat with his wife in their kitchen and gazed at one of their photos of Murdoch, hair cut short, at a barbecue shortly before the Barrow Creek incident. 'One thing I told the cops was that Brad is a bleeder. He bleeds all over the place. If he got involved in any kind of scrap with Falconio or his girlfriend his own blood would be all over the road, believe me.'

At the boat workshop, Steve Galvin welcomed me into his huge shed. Yes, it was quite true that Brad Murdoch had arrived at his place with metal parts for the canopy that he had ordered long before. Murdoch had arrived at Galvin's place some time in August, about a month after the Barrow Creek incident. 'He told me that he had tried to get another welding company to do it but had become tired of waiting and had had a falling out with them. So I set to work, putting in a metal mesh and fitting an aluminium rear on the canopy. I think he might have gone somewhere else later to have a new canvas fitted over the back.

'He offered me $45 an hour and came in every day to watch me doing the work. He paid $900 all up and he even offered me a bit of dope. When the police came around here later to talk to me about him I was a little bit worried because I thought they had come to talk about the hash. I told them that Murdoch had brought the parts around and they had already been cut to shape somewhere else.'

X

Sweat poured off the face of Peter Jamieson as he crawled from under a truck in his workshop in the small desert town of Fitzroy Crossing, 300 kilometres east of Broome, a community which grew up in the late 1800s around a small inn and trade store where travellers about to cross the Fitzroy River stopped by. Its other historical claim to fame was its use as a base for the search for the Aboriginal outlaw Pigeon and his gang at the end of the last century. A former police tracker, Pigeon turned against authority when he shot a policeman at the lonely Lillimoorla police station and released all the prisoners. With his gang, made up of many of the released Aborigines, he went on a three-year spree of robbery before other trackers cornered him and killed him. During the dry season, it is a hot and dusty dot on the map and during the 'wet' the town is often cut off when the river floods.

On this day when Jamieson took me into his shed it was unbearably hot but he was anxious to sit in his sweat-stained shirt to talk about his mate Brad Murdoch because he was convinced it was not in him to kill someone in cold blood. 'I've always thought Brad would end up in hot water one way or another but not like this,' said the middle-aged former owner of the local petrol station. 'If he was shot in a bar-room brawl I wouldn't be surprised; if he was arrested for travelling with the kind of stuff in his van that would raise eyebrows I wouldn't be surprised; but killing someone, trying to kidnap someone, no way.'

Jamieson had seen Murdoch come through Fitzroy Crossing early on Monday morning—about 6 am he thought—after the Saturday night incident at Barrow Creek. Jack was with him, a fact later confirmed by Hepi who greeted his mate when he arrived at Broome later that morning.

It was 1040 kilometres from Alice Springs to the outskirts of Fitzroy Crossing along the Tanami Track and if that was Brad Murdoch in the Alice Springs truck stop he could easily have covered the distance in 28 hours. He could do it travelling at 40 kilometres per hour, although that was a taxing average to maintain on that bad road. 'But the question is, was it Brad in the truckstop?' asked Jamieson. 'Even if it was, why are there so many discrepancies about things surrounding his van?

'I've picked out a number of differences between his ute and the one on the photo. The service station ute had a heavy duty tow bar and Brad's didn't and also in the photo you can see tool boxes along the side of the vehicle, but Brad didn't have those. He kept everything inside the canopy because he'd had stuff stolen in the past.'

Jamieson raised the same question that other friends of Murdoch had raised—if he had been at Barrow Creek, why did he drive back to Alice Springs to get fuel when he was already a couple of hundred kilometres north? Murdoch had more than enough fuel to keep driving, for his vehicle had two normal tanks, giving him a travelling distance of 800 kilometres, plus a 60 litre container which would give him another 600 kilometres and there was also a long range tank that would take him a further 1000 kilometres.

'If Brad was at Barrow Creek—passing through the area but not involved in that Falconio incident—it meant that he had bypassed the Tanami Track, which is just north of Alice Springs, and was intending to go through to Broome on the Buchanan Highway, a long way to the north. Wouldn't he be playing with fire to drive south again with a body in the back of his vehicle, which is the only way that body could have disappeared?'

The softly spoken mechanic said that was one of the most questionable aspects of the murder charge. If Brad Murdoch had killed Peter Falconio, it was hardly likely he would have been able to hide the body between leaving Barrow Creek and turning up at the Shell truckstop, even if he had fled Barrow Creek shortly after the Falconio incident. Allowing for a couple of hours drive, he would have had about an hour in which to dispose of the body so well in the pitch darkness that no-one had ever been able to find it. And if he had not dumped the body somewhere, the obvious conclusion was that he still had the body in his vehicle when he pulled in at the truck-stop. 'It didn't look to me like the fellow in those video pictures had just murdered someone and had the body in the back,' said Jamieson.

'When he stopped by that morning here at my place, he had a smoke—he was a chain-smoker and used Gold Winfield—and a bit of a chat. There was nothing panicky about him. He groaned a bit about his bad back, a com-plaint from his truck driving days. He had to walk virtually sideways to get himself up into the truck and he also had a hernia, so that's something else that makes me wonder how he could have lifted Falconio up into his Toyota or even dragged him into a grave.'

Jamieson said it was no secret what Murdoch carried in his van on his runs through the outback. He estimated that on each trip he would be transporting thousands of dollars worth of marijuana, which would be distributed among the gangs and others in the Broome district. 'Do you really think he's going to risk a stupid hold-up or rape when he's carrying all that stuff in his vehicle?'

There was little doubt that Jamieson would do anything to help his mate, for that was the way it was with the 'old school' gang of outback men who had lived on the edge and with whom Murdoch had retained a friendship over the years. On one occasion, before the Barrow Creek incident, Murdoch arrived in Fitzroy Crossing with his mate Sherriff at about 3 pm in the afternoon. Murdoch asked Jamieson to look after a gun for him, withdrawing it from a canvas bag that was hidden inside the panel of the driver's door. 'Sure,' said Jamieson. No questions asked. That was the way it was.

X

In the weeks that followed Brad Murdoch's extradition to Darwin there was a flurry of activity by his defence team and by the police. The strongest element of the police case was the conclusion by their forensic team that DNA in a spot of blood on Joanne's T-shirt, when compared to a sample from Murdoch, meant he could not be excluded as the attacker.

On the defence side there would also be a battle over the reliability of DNA findings—and many questions about the statements provided by the chief prosecution witness, Joanne Lees. There was the dog and there was the evidence from a large number of people who had either travelled in Murdoch's van or worked on it who confirmed it was not possible to clamber from the front cabin into the rear.

Both sides knew that a bitter legal fight lay ahead—and that the outcome of the forthcoming trial, should Murdoch be found to have a case to answer at his committal, would have widespread implications for the backpacking industry. For if a jury ultimately found Bradley Murdoch had not murdered Peter Falconio, it could mean that the killer was still out there ... and might strike again.

Chapter 15
Drama at the committal

Joanne Lees disappeared from public view after her trip to Australia in early 2002 to participate in the filming of the British TV documentary which served to raise as many questions as provide answers about her Barrow Creek experience.

But in May 2004, Darwin was buzzing with anticipation. The mysterious Englishwoman—for that was the aura that had grown around her—had arrived in town to give evidence at Bradley John Murdoch's committal hearing. It would be the first time she would come face to face with the man accused of murdering her boyfriend and attempting to kidnap her. At least it was the first time in a court and time would tell whether it was the first time ever. Travelling with Peter Falconio's two brothers, Paul, 34, and Nicholas, 36, Joanne was whisked away by police to a private address to await her turn in the Darwin Supreme Court.

She also came to town with a secret that she realised would cause a sensation if it was uncovered.

First, there were the preliminaries—the outlining of the case against Murdoch by chief prosecutor Rex Wild. Courtroom six was crowded on the morning of Monday, 17 May 2004, as 45-year-old Murdoch, thickset, grey hair cropped short and wearing a blue shirt and light fawn trousers without a belt, was led into the glass-edged dock by prison officers. He sat to the right of Magistrate Alasdair McGregor and put on a pair of thin, gold-framed spectacles to gaze at a sheath of documents in his hand.

Mr Wild led the court through the alleged events ... the British couple travelling north from Alice Springs, a man in a white four-wheel drive truck signalling them to stop and talking to Peter Falconio, a bang, the man appearing at the driver's window with a long-barrelled silver pistol. He told how Joanne was handcuffed with black cable ties, had a sack pulled over her head and was forced into the front of the four-wheel drive. Then the sack was dislodged and she saw a dog on the front driver's seat. Mr Wild said she later described the dog as being medium sized 'it's a blue heeler, brown and white, shorthaired.'

This comment was at odds with the description she had given to police initially, when she had said the attacker's dog was red-coloured, a red heeler perhaps, with no trace of white. It was also at odds with what police artist David Stagg had learned from her—which was total confusion over the type of dog the man had. She had not been able to pinpoint his dog in a book of pictures of various breeds.

After trying to get out of the driver's door, which was blocked by the dog, Joanne, said Mr Wild, was forced into the back of the four-wheel drive by the man. He made no reference to her scrambling over the seats into the back. While in the rear, she shouted out, 'What do you want? Is it money? Is it the van? Just take it. Are you going to rape me?'

Murdoch was then said to have gone to the back of the vehicle and told her, 'Shut up and you won't get shot.'

As he walked away, she called out, 'Have you shot my boyfriend? Have you shot Pete?'

The defendant, said Mr Wild, responded, 'No.'

The prosecutor then told how she managed to slide out of the vehicle and hide in the roadside scrub.

Mr Wild said it would be argued that Murdoch tried to change his appearance and that of his truck shortly after the incident, including fitting new bullbars, a new rear canopy and repainting the chassis. 'It will be submitted that the defendant was trying to disguise the appearance of a guilty face and an incriminating vehicle.'

Paul Falconio, from New Mill, near Huddersfield, was called to support the prosecution claim that Peter was indeed dead. Paul said the family had not heard from him in the three years since the Barrow Creek incident, despite being in fortnightly contact with them previously during the nine months he had been travelling with Joanne. 'We even heard from him in Nepal,' he said. 'He always managed to get to a phone and let us know.'

On Tuesday 18 May, Joanne Lees stepped into the witness box. The courtroom was packed to hear the Englishwoman, dressed in a white blouse, black skirt and black low-heeled court shoes, with her black hair tied back in a ponytail, give her evidence. Now aged 30, she bit her lower lip as she glanced around the court, her eyes resting momentarily on Murdoch, for she knew this was not going to be easy—the eyes of the rest of the world, through the journalists crowded into the chamber, were on her.

Guided by Mr Wild, she described the tour of Australia she and her boyfriend had been on and how they had stopped at a truckstop to watch the sunset and smoke cannabis together.

'Pete rolled a joint and we smoked it. We chatted and watched the sunset. It was beautiful.'

Then, as they continued on their way north, they stopped at the suggestion of the man who had driven up beside them in a white four-wheel drive. As she revved the engine at the suggestion of Peter, who had got out to look at the exhaust with the stranger, she heard a bang 'like the sound of a vehicle backfiring ... the sound of a gunshot. I turned around to look through the window and I saw a man stood there with a gun. He was pointing it towards me. He opened the door and started coming into the van. He pushed me into the passenger seat. He asked me to turn the engine off. I tried but my hands were shaky, so he did it. He was to the side of me and beside me. He seemed to be all over me and around me.'

He ordered her to put her head on her knees and place her hands behind her back. 'I went to and then I tried to struggle and fight. He repeated the question again and pointed the gun to my head. I did what I was told and put my hands down behind my back.'

Her hands were tied together loosely and she was pushed from the van, injuring her knees. Then the attacker tried to tape her ankles together but she kicked and struggled with him. 'He hit me on the right side of my head. It stunned me,' she told the court.

She was dragged to her feet and frogmarched to the man's truck. After unsuccessfully trying to gag her mouth with tape—which ended up sticking to her hair—the man lifted up the canopy covering the back of his truck and pulled out a canvas sack, which he pulled over her head before bundling her into the front of his vehicle.

'I was shouting for Pete,' she recalled. 'I was shouting for help.'

'Did you ever see Peter again?' asked Mr Wild.

'No,' she said, choking with emotion. Murdoch barely looked up at her as she continued, his eyes on the documents on his lap.

As she was pushed into the van she was able to see the attacker's dog in the passenger seat. She could hear the gunman moving around outside. 'I was screaming and shouting. I asked him about what he wanted of me. Whether he wanted money. He came back and told me to be quiet and if I didn't he would shoot me. I was quiet for a moment and then I asked him if he was going to rape me and had he shot Pete. He came back and he said "No".'

She told the court that when the man moved away again she was able to slide out of the back of the truck. Her legs were free, so she was able to run into bushes by the side of the road, where she waited as the man searched for her by torchlight with his dog.

'I could hear him—the crunching of dried grass and branches under his feet. He came very near ... very close, a metre away. I wasn't even breathing.'

She had curled up as much as she could. The night was pitch black—no moon. Finally, she said, he gave up searching. She heard him dragging something across the gravel. Then she heard a vehicle, which she guessed was the Volkswagen, being driven off. Some 20 minutes later she heard another vehicle, possibly the gunman's, heading off in the opposite direction.

She waited for more than five hours before venturing from her hiding place to flag down help. During that time she managed to bring her hands from behind her back to her front and get a tube of lip gloss from her pocket, which she rubbed on the handcuffs in the hope this would help slip them off.

X

Finally, it was the turn of Murdoch's Adelaide lawyer, Grant Algie, to question Joanne. He went over her description of the night again and then began to look more at her personal life. He wanted to know how much she had been paid to talk to ITV about her ordeal. When Mr Wild objected, Mr Algie insisted the question was relevant 'because motive to perpetuate this story is relevant'. Joanne then confirmed she had been paid AUD$120 000 for an exclusive interview.

And what of her relationship with Peter Falconio, her boyfriend of six years? They got on very well, she said, and denied Mr Algie's suggestions they had a fight at a lodge in Alice Springs the night before he disappeared.

There came a week of legal delays before Joanne, who had received the highest security to keep her hidden from photographers who had tried in vain to find her, stepped back into the witness box. Mr Algie asked her if she had been concerned that police had become aware of emails from someone called Steph. She was asked who Steph was, to which she replied, 'I don't know.'

'Is not Steph the pseudonym ... adopted to write to you through the email by somebody called Nick?' asked Mr Algie.

'Yes.'

'Who is Nick?'

'A friend.'

'A friend from Sydney with whom you had a relationship?'

'No,' she replied.

The magistrate ruled that any further questions on the matter were irrelevant, but Mr Algie argued that his information about the alleged relationship might be highly relevant at the end of the day to the credibility of the witness.

Magistrate McGregor refused permission for Mr Algie to continue the line of questioning but the lawyer was able to ascertain more details about her email accounts, which she began clearing in Alice Springs in the week after 14 July—when she was still giving evidence to the police.

She admitted she had a 'second but not secret' email account and denied when questioned by Mr Algie that she was uneasy about a policewoman who stayed with her knowing about it. 'I was very scared and I was happy to have someone around,' she told the court. But she revealed she had deleted a number of emails from the accounts because they were full.

She was asked about a photograph of a man in the Shell service station and said he was 'similar to the man I described'. However, she had not recognised the man when first shown the photograph several weeks after the killing because it was 'much poorer quality'.

And what of drugs—had she taken drugs other than marijuana? 'There was one occasion when I had half an ecstasy tablet,' she admitted. Mr Algie wanted to know if Falconio had regular contact with dealers.

'Pete didn't have a dealer,' she said.

Why hadn't she told police about smoking marijuana? 'Because they didn't ask,' she said, adding, 'they would have found our marijuana in the van and would have asked if they wanted to.'

While that day had been sensational enough, there was more about her secret friend Nick to come when she stepped back into the witness box the following day. For she confessed that after the death of her boyfriend, she had begun making plans to meet Nick—with whom, it was revealed, she had been having a sexual relationship during the six months she had been in Sydney with Falconio.

Allowed to continue his questioning of Joanne's personal life, Mr Algie put to her: 'During the time in Sydney with Peter you had an affair, a sexual relationship, over a period of weeks, with Nick—yes or no?'

She paused briefly as the hushed court waited for her answer. Then she replied in a calm voice: 'I'm going to answer yes, but I would not class it as an affair or a relationship.'

Mr Algie had to argue for the right to continue his line of questioning, saying that the issue was critical to the case. 'The picture painted by this prosecution, and indeed this witness, is one of a harmonious, loving relationship. That's not necessarily the case and I should be permitted to explore it,' he said.

Magistrate McGregor told him he did not think it would get him very far but he would allow the personal questions. The court heard that Falconio and Joanne had planned to drive the Volkswagen around Australia before selling it in Brisbane and then flying to New Zealand. But Falconio later made plans to travel on his own to Papua New Guinea. Mr Algie wanted to know whether the change of plan was prompted by problems in their relationship. 'It was actually on 14 July, when you were in Alice Springs, that you went and booked and paid for a single air fare for yourself from Brisbane to Sydney, didn't you?' he asked.

'Pete and I booked the ticket together,' she said, describing it as 'a holiday within a holiday'.

Asked if she was going to Sydney to 'see Nick', she replied, 'No, he wasn't even in Australia.'

She admitted that after the incident at Barrow Creek on 14 July she was corresponding with Nick by email.

While she said she could not remember being questioned by two detectives about her plans to meet Nick in Berlin, she agreed that was the idea.

'Do you deny that you made arrangements to meet with Nick in Berlin?'

'I made the suggestion,' she replied.

'You were to meet in Berlin on the way home?'

'No.'

'You deny that?'

'Not on the way home. No. Maybe at a later date.'

Her evidence about the affair shocked Peter Falconio's brothers. They stared at her in disbelief as she made her confession.

There was another surprise to come and it concerned the dog that had accompanied Joanne's attacker. She told the court that it had been a white spotty dog, prompting Mr Algie to accuse her of changing her story to fit the police case.

'Who told you your dog didn't fit with the police case?' the defence lawyer asked her.

She said no-one had. But then she agreed that at some time in the previous two weeks while she had been in Darwin, the prosecutor had shown her pictures of a white spotty dog which, she said, appeared to have been more of a match to the dog she remembered.

Joanne left the witness box after a total of three gruelling days. Emotions among the public attending the court had rolled from sympathy to suspicion during her evidence. One fact could not be avoided—Joanne had cheated on her boyfriend and had lied to the court about her secret lover. She flew out of Darwin, her credibility in tatters.

But for the prosecution and Joanne herself, there was worse to come, and it came from the police. For when Superintendent Jeanette Kerr was called into the witness box, she revealed that there had been significant doubts about the story relayed to police by Joanne Lees. The policewoman conceded, under intense cross-examination, that there had been inconsistencies in the version of events given by the British woman. There had been doubts about the gun she had described, the vehicle allegedly involved in the attack, Joanne's physical state and the fact that no footprints of an attacker were found at the crime scene.

In an attempt to extract more details from Joanne, the court heard, police hypnotised her, but the session revealed inconsistencies, which prompted police to interview her again to clarify certain points. These included her description of the inside of the four-wheel drive belonging to the suspected gunman.

Nobody, said the police officer, had ever seen a vehicle with an interior similar to the one Joanne had described, which allowed access from the front cab to the rear trailer.

'Detectives had made extensive inquiries with panel beaters and mechanics but not a single vehicle matching that description could be located,' said Superintendent Kerr.

As for the gun, identified by Joanne as a revolver with a distinct marking on the side, the police officer said Joanne's description bore a striking similarity to a pattern on the door of the Volkwagen van. And what of the apparent lack of injuries on Miss Lees after the attack—were these concerns raised with the doctor who attended her at the time? Mr Algie wanted to know.

'Yes,' said Superintendent Kerr.

Doubts about Joanne's account did not stop there, the officer agreed, as Mr Algie asked about electrical tape, which was meant to have been bound around the Englishwoman's ankles.

'It was apparently only 70 centimetres, insufficient length to do so,' he suggested.

'I put that to her,' said Superintendent Kerr.

She had questioned Joanne about the five hours she had reportedly hidden in the bush. She was asked by Mr Algie, 'Did you tell her that police had obtained the opinion of Aboriginal trackers who said that nobody had stayed in that spot for anything like that length of time?'

'Yes,' said the policewoman.

'And was it of concern that the dog she described in the attacker's car was a dog of the same kind she'd seen at Barrow Creek a few hours later?'

'Yes,' said the officer, agreeing to a reference in court earlier that Joanne had identified a blue heeler dog at the Barrow Creek Hotel, where she had been taken by the two truck drivers who picked her up, as similar to the animal in the attacker's vehicle.

Superintendent Kerr revealed more concerns about Joanne's story. Officers were puzzled about a canvas bag that Miss Lees said her attacker had thrust over her head—for the description she gave was similar to a canvas mailbag she had seen at the Barrow Creek Hotel after the attack.

As she continued to be cross-examined, the policewoman confirmed that she had also raised concerns that Joanne's footprints were found at the scene but 'no others in pursuit'. She agreed with Mr Algie that aside from there being no footprints other than those of Joanne, there was no forensic evidence of a body having been dragged anywhere 'be it Mr Falconio or anyone else'. And there was concern that although Joanne said she had endured a bitterly cold night in the open, there was no sign of frostbite on her body. In all, said Superintendent Kerr, there were more than a dozen points in Joanne Lees' story that did not appear to make sense.

Yet police, if the DNA evidence could be substantiated, could show that Brad Murdoch had been in contact with the British woman. The prosecution sought to nail that point home by calling the Northern Territory Forensic scientist, Carmen Eckhoff, who told the court of finding a smudge of DNA on Joanne's T-shirt. The smudge appeared to have been from a weeping type of wound such as from a torn-back fingernail and the chances of that smear not being from Murdoch were at least 640 billion times to one.

His DNA could also not be excluded from two areas in the Volkswagen. She explained this by stating that DNA taken from the gearstick would match one in 678 individuals in the Northern Territory—and Murdoch could be included in that group. Further, she said she had obtained mixed results from the steering wheel but if the DNA profiles of Joanne and Falconio were excluded 'I would say that Bradley Murdoch could not be excluded as a possible contributor.' Yet she had found no DNA matching Murdoch's on the crude handcuffs used to restrain the Englishwoman. She said this could have been because the person who had made them was wearing gloves, but agreed with defence lawyer Mark Twiggs, assisting Grant Algie, that it was possible Murdoch had not handled them at all.

I watched as people I had spoken to long before the case stepped forward to give their evidence, either directly or by videolink ... Brett Duthie, Loi Odore, Steve Galvin. They repeated their stories: yes, Brad Murdoch had changed the profile of his Toyota; no, you cannot clamber from the front to the back; no he'd never had a red dog or even a grey cattle dog.

By the time Magistrate McGregor committed Murdoch for trial, an expected formality, the incident at Barrow Creek had become an even greater puzzle. The police had admitted to problems with Joanne Lees story—problems I had raised long before—yet there was allegedly DNA evidence that appeared to put him in contact with her.

Murdoch was a man who, according to the DNA, appeared to have been in the area of Barrow Creek on the night of the alleged murder, yet could not have been involved in the incident described by Joanne Lees if the shared concerns of Superintendent Kerr and myself were later acknowledged by a jury.

Bradley John Murdoch rose to his feet as Magistrate McGregor announced at the end of a hearing that had run for nearly five weeks that enough evidence had been presented to commit him for trial before a jury. Asked if he had anything to say, Murdoch replied in a strong voice, 'I am not guilty of any of these allegations, Your Honour.'

His defence team had elected not to call him as a witness during the committal, indicating they would call their own witnesses at the trial. While evidence during the committal had flowed backwards and forwards, the greatest sensation had not involved Murdoch at all.

It was the confession by Joanne Lees that she had been cheating on her boyfriend—and had lied to the court when she claimed she did not know who 'Steph' was. Her, or his, real identity as it transpired, was Nick, she had ultimately agreed. But who was Nick?

Within days he had been identified as a man from Britain, Nick Riley. It had not taken long for friends and associates to contact the newspapers to reveal his name. What they had to say was a further shock to those who had believed that Joanne was devoted to Peter Falconio. It transpired that she had allegedly been systematically cheating on him until just days before he disappeared. Even while living with Peter in Sydney, she would meet the former public schoolboy Nick Riley for weekly sex sessions, telling Falconio that she was gong out with a girlfriend, while in reality she was meeting Riley for sex.

But in a curious twist, it was claimed that she had even cheekily introduced her lover to her long-term boyfriend. Yet he had no knowledge of the lovers' Thursday night sex sessions that occurred for a month between May and June 2000—right up to the time they left on their outback excursion—at a private house in the bohemian Newtown district of Sydney.

They originally met while Riley was working at a coffee shop near the Dymocks bookshop where Joanne was employed. 'They enjoyed cappuccinos together a couple of times a day,' Mike Baskerville, manager of the coffee shop recalled, remembering that Joanne even introduced Riley to Falconio, although the latter would not have been aware of the secret trysts that had begun. 'Sometimes, Nick would join Peter and Joanne,' Mr Baskerville recalled. 'They used to go out drinking in the bars around town. Nick and Peter got on well. There was no tension between them.'

Things might have been different had Falconio been aware of what Joanne got up to on her Thursday nights away 'with a girlfriend'.

A friend of Riley's recalled: 'Joanne would turn up on a Thursday night. I remember it clearly because that was our weekly night at the pub. She was bright and friendly, happy to talk to people without being overly loud. She didn't seem to be a big party girl, but then she was with a crowd who didn't know her very well. It was a small group of friends, probably not more than eight. Most of us knew Joanne had a longtime boyfriend but you never ask about these things and you don't cast judgements. Joanne certainly seemed to like Nick. I wouldn't say they were all over each other, but they certainly seemed comfortable in each other's company and she always stayed the night in an upstairs bedroom at the front of the house. Nick had been in Sydney for eight or nine months and had established a reputation as a young man who liked a beer, pretty women and a good time.'

People who knew them started to come forward, although they kept their identities to themselves. One young woman who had coffee with Riley and Joanne in a popular coffee shop in the main shopping area of King Street recalled, 'They were right on top of each other—really close, holding hands, and it was pretty obvious they were more than just good friends. Some of us who knew Nick fairly well wondered if it was going to last because he didn't miss an opportunity with any girl. But in time you could tell that Joanne had really affected him. He seemed to be quite smitten with her. I didn't know she already had a boyfriend. You'd never have guessed it the way she was behaving with Nick. I got the impression this was something that was going to last for a very long time.'

Another former friend told *The Sydney Morning Herald,* 'Nick was a smart guy, but probably partied a bit much. He wanted to be known as a lad. He worked in a few different jobs, in finance and IT, as I remember. The only thing I noticed was that he seemed to try and cover his obvious public school background. It was a bit grating at times because he would put on a Cockney accent that didn't sound real. But he was a nice sort of guy.'

A photograph of Riley, taken in June 2001 sitting in Kelly's Hotel, an Irish pub in Newtown, with a beer in front of him, was flashed across the world. Within weeks of it being taken, both he and Joanne had set off on their separate travels, but it was clear they intended to meet up again later—Joanne had already admitted that in court. In any case, she kept in touch with him by email, unaware that the day would come when her secret correspondence would be revealed to the world.

With the revelations about the emails, Joanne Lees had generated more fascinating questions about herself. Under different circumstances her plight would have brought nothing but sympathy but her courtroom confession caused deep distress to the Falconio family. Whether her motive in initially denying the affair was to spare the family further hurt is a question only she could answer. And it remained unanswered. Her stepfather,

Vincent James, attempted to defend her, accusing lawyers of trying to blacken her name but his words seemed frail against the chorus of shocked gossip.

In the two Newtown pubs where Joanne and Riley drank with friends during their nights out—Kelly's Bar and the Cooper's Arms—drinkers tend to defend her attempts to cover up the affair. Even the most righteous of people would lie when it came to sexual indiscretions, most agreed. 'Hey, look at President Clinton's grilling over his fling with Monica Lewinksi,' said one woman. 'He was the most powerful man on earth yet he stared blatantly into the camera and lied to the whole world. Let's not attack Joanne Lees for fibbing about once-a-week sex with a bloke on the side.'

Even so, Joanne's attempts to deceive the court earned her few friends and such was the reaction that Britain's *Sunday Telegraph* observed, 'One might think that it is she who is on trial and not the drifter Bradley Murdoch.' Even in her adopted community in the south of England there was little sympathy for her, according to the local newspaper, the *Brighton Argus*. 'The feeling here is there's something a bit fishy about her,' said a senior editorial member. In her hometown of Huddersfield, too, there were contrasting feelings about her. 'It's a mixture of support, distrust and voyeuristic curiosity,' remarked news editor Andrew Baldwin. 'A lot of people still think that she did it.'

But Joanne's stepfather ignored the public attacks as his town recovered from the shock of her affair with Nick Riley. He said her indiscretions amounted to nothing more than human foibles. 'It happened to Beckham, it happened to Princess Diana. She is human, like anybody else,' he said.

Joanne had, of course, always portrayed her relationship with Falconio as loving and there were many photographs of them together to support the bond. Why, they had even talked about marriage. But now it must be wondered what secret thoughts were going through her mind as she posed for a photo of herself and Falconio in the Volkswagen before they set out from Sydney. As she sat on the top of Uluru with Falconio, was she wondering where Riley was? Was she thinking about an email she might send off to him from Alice Springs?

Her private thoughts remained just that—private. For in the three years since Falconio vanished, she kept her head down, living in anonymity in

Hove and working for a charity helping children with learning difficulties. She moved into the Hove address, a short distance from the apartment she had shared with Falconio in March 2004 and gave out her phone number to only her closest friends. A neighbour at a former address remarked, 'She seemed like a lost soul. She was very private.'

British newspapers tried to learn more about the woman who had become such a mystery figure. It seemed that everyone who had met her remembered her for something—she was offhand, she was cold, she was lost ... A source at Granada TV, from which she had collected the AUD$120 000 for an interview, recalled, 'It was a strange interview. She seemed almost cold as she spoke about events on the day Peter Falconio died. When the interview was over, she stood up and said "Right, are we done? Can I go home now?" '

When she travelled to Australia as part of the interview, she upset Les Pilton and his partner Helen Jones, who had cared for her on the night of the incident and had continued to check on her welfare. They were still running the Barrow Creek Hotel but were disappointed to hear she had not bothered to contact them. 'Les and Helen were pretty upset she didn't even say hello,' said a barmaid. 'After all they had done for her that night and in the days following, she didn't even care to pick up the phone and see how they were. That just makes you sick.'

Chapter 16

A chat with the accused

You could pick him a mile off, a burly figure with heavily tattooed arms sitting at a table in the visitor's courtyard of the Berrimah Jail. Other prisoners, mostly Aborigines, were talking to relatives around similar tables, the tops of which were etched with indigenous paintings of animals and insects. Dressed in an orange T-shirt, blue shorts and thongs, he grinned as I approached and stood up to shake hands, his frame towering over my six foot one inches. Two prison officers watched carefully at the exchange.

For a man facing life imprisonment should he be convicted, Bradley John Murdoch seemed remarkably calm. He explained he could not talk in detail about his upcoming trial—but then decided he wanted to talk about the DNA, which he believed the whole case hinged on. 'DNA,' he said, intertwining his big fingers, 'can be a very difficult area. Get it wrong and it can send innocent people to jail for life, or free people who should not be free. It also works the other way, too, freeing the innocent and sending the guilty away. It works all ways, but everybody knows that that van Joanne and Falconio were driving had all manner of people in it and that's where the confusion will arise in this case. They'd picked up a couple of German tourists at King's Canyon and don't forget it was also in a workshop in Alice Springs.'

But what of that smudge on Joanne's T-shirt? He smacked at air. 'A smudge—it could have come from anywhere. It's a crowded world out there, people are bumping up against each other all the time. Your own DNA will be on a thousand people—doesn't mean to say you've assaulted them does it? You can rip a nail back, which I've heard the forensic woman suggest in court might have left the weeping, bloody, smear on Joanne's T-shirt, and then you brush up against someone somewhere. It's easily done. Unless of course it's been planted there.'

Other visitors were arriving to speak to inmates, most of them Aborigines. I wondered what Murdoch, given his past experiences with them, was thinking, but I later learned that he had made a number of friends among the imprisoned indigenous people and had even helped advise them with their cases.

'Let me tell you this now, mate,' he said. 'The truth will come out one day and in the meantime I just have to be patient. I'm feeling very good about it and it won't be very long before everyone hears why. I've got a very good lawyer and he isn't letting anything slip by. There are so many elements to all of this and when the time comes, you'll see that everything falls in my favour.

'For example, I can tell you now that she got those scrapes on her knee when she fell over as she was running after the truck which she had waved down. And look at the positioning of where she was. There's been various versions about where the truck that picked her up came to a stop, but we've been working hard on this because it's very important. What we've now concluded from what the truckies have told the police is that the pool of blood at the roadside was right beside the place they'd pulled up. That means Joanne must have run out onto the road much further up, allowing for that big truck to pull up. How come she said she had run straight into the scrub after the incident—if she'd run straight out again the truck she waved down would be more than 100 metres down the road by the time it stopped. If she were further up the road when she ran out, it would have put her in about the position where the Volkswagen was found hidden. So you have to wonder what Joanne was doing up there beside the kombi. Did she drive it in there? There's all these little things, but they add up to a lot of questions about what she's been saying.'

I was struck by his reference to Joanne, the primary witness whose testimony could help send him away for the rest of his life. There was no 'that woman' or 'Lees'. It was soft ... Joanne. Joanne says this; Joanne says that.

I asked him what he thought had happened out there in the cold darkness of the highway running north from Barrow Creek, if in fact he was not involved. He smiled. 'As wild as it sounds, I think, and I can only think this because I don't know, that Peter Falconio has a part to play in his ultimate fate, whatever that was. That amount of blood was nothing—what was it, less than half a litre? Bloody hell, I've had more than that taken out of me at one time. It's not for me to say what he may or may not have done but what I will say is that it's not hard to take your own blood out and store it.'

A preposterous suggestion? 'Nothing's preposterous in this day and age,' he replied. 'Peter Falconio must have known about Joanne's affair. If he didn't, he'd have to be pretty naive. He couldn't dump her if he knew because if he wanted to just clear off for whatever reason he would still need her to help him with a cover story. This will all come out one day. Anyway, what was all that "holiday within a holiday" stuff all about? Bit of a coincidence, too, isn't it, that this incident should have occurred on the same day that she'd bought a ticket to go back to Sydney with?

'I've heard the forensic scientist say that it may be my DNA on the steering wheel and gear stick. May be. Take note of that. Yet she found nothing on those cable-tie handcuffs. She suggested it could have been because I was wearing gloves. Now, if that was me out there, would I have been so stupid as to wear gloves when picking up the handcuffs and then taken them off to drive the Volkswagen? And if she maintains I was wearing gloves to pick up the handcuffs, how could I have left a smudge of my blood on Joanne's T-shirt? They can't have it both ways.'

I told Murdoch that his friends had insisted during my prolonged investigations into the affair that it was impossible for anyone to pass from the cabin of his Toyota to the rear without, of course, getting out and climbing in through the back or the sides, if the winged mesh was already raised. 'That's quite true,' he said. 'Everybody knows that. Even the cops know that. At the back of the cabin, there's a tiny window, but it's sealed. Okay, you might just be able to squeeze through if the window was removed but it would be a damn tight fit. But the window wasn't out and Joanne wouldn't have got through there anyway because it would be too small. In any case, wouldn't she have remembered trying to squeeze through a tiny space like that?

'To make a hole big enough to climb into the back, you would need to cut away the metal beneath the window, and then the whole vehicle would collapse in on itself because that part—the metal struts in the lower part of the rear of the cab—is like a retaining wall in a building.'

The prison officers had lost interest in us as we continued our conversation. They were now chatting among themselves as Brad Murdoch turned his thoughts to the claim that he had shot Falconio.

'If he was killed there at such close range, where is the gunshot residue? The scientists would have found it on the back of the Volkswagen. Why didn't Joanne smell gun smoke if I had supposedly shoved a gun in her face moments later? I want to know where the drag marks are, showing that I hauled Falconio into my four-wheel drive, because that's the only way he could have been removed from there if I had shot him. But do you think I would risk carrying a dead body away in my vehicle?'

Murdoch readily admitted he carried guns. 'Of course I was tooled up. The business I was in, and I think everyone knows about that, was very dangerous. I'm not in the (motorcycle) gangs any more and don't have their protection. I was on my own. It was generally known that I was carrying marijuana and cash—large sums of cash. I would always carry a big amount with me because if someone I was dealing with said they had a few extra kilos of marijuana I would need to be ready to pay for it.

'I was very, very careful wherever I went—there could be no risks of any kind. In a bag I carried with me everywhere was a bug detector. If I went into a building and someone was trying to record my conversation the detector would start screaming. That was how careful I was.'

He talked about his friends in the feared gangs, the Gypsy Jokers, the Coffin Cheaters. Many of them were reluctant to answer police requests to talk about him or answer directives to go to court. Rules were rules in his game, he conceded, and one of them was you never went into the witness box.

'You know, they say that people I know would tell all kinds of lies to protect me, yet on the other hand look at the deceptive picture that's been painted from Joanne's side. People have talked of a wonderful loving couple, yet all the time she's been having a fling with some bloke on the side.'

There was one question that had to be asked. It was pointless in asking him directly if he had indeed killed Peter Falconio because his answer would be obvious—but if Falconio did not die on that outback road, how did he get away?

'Perhaps he was never there in the first place,' said Murdoch. 'There are lots of ways of getting away from the area. There's a way through Oodnadatta that he could have gone. And we all know that it's dead easy to get a new identity. How do we know that he didn't have all this set up even before he arrived in Australia? I know for a fact that there are lots of recluses in Europe that you can buy an identity from. They have one or two "spare" identities they are willing to sell. You can change your appearance to fit that identity and off you go. If he's not still in Australia he would have found a way out—it's not that hard if you have the paperwork and if you don't you can still get away and start a new life somewhere.'

I left Bradley John Murdoch to return to his cell. He had been given access to a computer on which he was going through all the evidence that the prosecution were using against him. I watched him stride away with an escort at his side. The door clanged shut behind him.

Now there was only the waiting for the trial.

As the months rolled by rumours and theories, some wild, came my way. It was Brad Murdoch but he was wearing a wig. Joanne and Falconio had indeed been followed by a white van, but it was driven by an accomplice who drove him away after faking a crime scene with his previously drawn blood. The British couple had fled Alice Springs late in the day because they had picked up marijuana from Murdoch and had fled without paying him, resulting in him giving chase. Murdoch knew them before the incident, meeting up in one of the caravan parks along the way, and had even helped fix a problem in their kombi. Joanne killed Falconio before they even reached Barrow Creek, then gave a description of Murdoch as the killer because she had seen him on the road earlier. Murdoch did kill Falconio during a drug argument, then, threatening Joanne that he would implicate her in the death, told her to make up a story about hiding in the bushes for hours, giving him time to get away. She had made up her story on the run and, not aware that the cabins of Toyota utes were sealed, used the inside of her own VW—which was not sealed—to mistakenly describe her attacker's vehicle. Things she had seen such as the scrolling on the door handle of the VW and the mailbag in the Barrow Creek hotel were used in descriptions of her attacker's gun and the bag he threw over her head.

One persistent opinion was that Murdoch could not have killed Falconio under circumstances described by Joanne. Many discussing the bizarre saga across the world agreed it would be impossible for Falconio to have been killed and hidden so efficiently in the time frame that his body could never be found. If he had been shot then his killer would have had little time to find a good hiding place in the dark, knowing that police would soon be looking for him. To hide a body so that it could never be found, by trackers, police, hawks, flies, took a lot of planning—and Murdoch would not have had the time.

And back in England there were former workmates who had known Falconio who were troubled by one very important question. Was it not an incredible coincidence that a man who had shown such an interest in the way people faked their deaths overseas should himself totally vanish in circumstances that have raised numerous questions? Of all the thousands of British backpackers in Australia at the time, why, of all people was it Falconio who had disappeared, in the dark, in the middle of nowhere, with only his girlfriend as a witness?

As the weeks rolled by towards the start of Bradley Murdoch's trial I found myself questioning what I had established as I travelled around Australia talking to his family and friends. So much pointed against Joanne Lees' account. Had I got it all wrong? Had I misheard comments, misinterpreted what people had said, unfairly drawn conclusions because Joanne had behaved in a way people had not expected? Were the police holding back some damning information that would blow all of Bradley Murdoch's defence out of the water—and certainly out of court.

Had Joanne really told the police that she scrambled over the four-wheel drive's seats into the back? Had she really told them from the beginning that the dog was a cattle dog, possibly a red heeler—certainly an animal that bore no resemblance to a dalmation with its unmistakable spots. Had I made some terrible mistakes?

I went back through my notebooks, right back to the early days of the attack and the hunt for the gunman. There were notes from the police press conferences, the scribbled shorthand referring to a red dog and an escape through the back of the gunman's van and, of course, all the newspaper stories. Still, I wished I had more, something concrete that would set my mind at rest and convince me that I had been on the right track all along. Rex Wild, the prosecutor at the committal hearing, had changed all that I believed I had established. He had talked around the way Joanne had found herself in the back of the assailant's van and had spoken of a blue heeler, brown and white, short-haired.

I found one of my old laptop computers, went through all its files, and there, in glorious colour, was a photo that left me in no doubt that what Joanne had been saying in more recent times clashed with her earlier information. I was looking at a picture I had taken in November 2001. It showed Superintendent Kate Vanderlaan, in charge of the Alice Springs investigations into Falconio's disappearance, posing in front of a whiteboard in the operations room, to which I had been given access.

Although she was standing in front of some of the information on the whiteboard, enough was visible to set my mind at rest. There were identikit images of a POI—person of interest—and a description of a white male, aged between 40 and 45 years, possibly older, with dark hair and grey streaks. The hair was straight and shoulder length. He had a droopy moustache, tapering below the corner of the mouth, a long, thin face and was of medium build.

In a column next to this description were details provided by Joanne of the POI's clothing—a dark baseball cap with a yellow motif, a black and white check, long-sleeve shirt and a dark T-shirt and heavy jeans. Partially hidden by Superintendent Vanderlaan were descriptions of the dog, but enough was visible to confirm that Joanne had not mentioned a dalmation, or anything like it. The words that could be seen revealed a description of a cattle dog ... a heeler of some kind.

Further along the whiteboard were more details that have continued to cast doubt on Joanne's story. Under the heading 'Possible Vehicle', were the words 'Cabin to Tray Access, light in colour, polished bullbar'.

Cabin to Tray Access. They were damning words.

Chapter 17
THE TRIAL

Week One

Joanne Lees flew into Darwin, from Britain, at 4.10 on the morning of Friday 14 October for what the local newspaper, the Northern Territory News, described as 'the most talked about trial in the Territory since the Chamberlain case'. She was a woman transformed. In contrast to diving and ducking from photographers during the committal hearing, she walked with her head held high through the airport terminal, dressed in a beige sleeveless knit top, jeans and gold sandals, her dark hair tinted brown and tumbling down over her shoulders. It was a movie star entrance as cameras flashed and passengers turned to stare at the glamorous woman whose face, to some, seemed vaguely familiar.

Three days earlier Peter Falconio's younger brother, Nick, and his parents, Joan and Luciano, had touched down in Darwin. Peter's older brother, Paul, arrived early on Sunday morning, the day before the trial. The stage was set.

Darwin, sweltering under stifling humidity ahead of the rainy season, was abuzz. As the local paper said, there had been nothing like this since Lindy Chamberlain stood accused of murdering her baby Azaria in the Territory's supreme court. Of course, it was not Joanne who was on trial, although many people were asking what, if any secrets, she had. Would she reveal them at last under cross-examination by the defence as the case against Bradley John Murdoch, now 47, progressed? Certainly there were many questions that needed to be answered and perhaps, finally, they would come as the trial proceeded in Court No. 6 under the jurisdiction of the Territory's Chief Justice, Brian Martin.

There were three questions that would now, surely, be answered once and for all. Did Brad Murdoch kill Peter Falconio? Did Joanne provide an accurate description of everything that occurred that night as the couple headed north up the Stuart Highway? Did Peter Falconio even die?

I had carried out my own lengthy research and found holes in aspects of Joanne's story, areas of doubt that the police, carrying out parallel inquiries to my own, had also uncovered. Would those holes now be sealed with explanations from the witness box, particularly from Joanne herself? The mystery of how she was able to get into the back of Murdoch's van—assuming he was there that night—had remained unanswered. Would she, or one of the prosecution or defence witnesses, finally provide us with a definitive explanation?

It was the Territory's Director of Public Prosecutions, Rex Wild, QC, who, as in the committal hearing nearly 18 months earlier, opened the case against Murdoch after the jury of six men and six women were empanelled. Dressed in a blue shirt and beige trousers, Murdoch pleaded not guilty to murdering Peter Falconio and not guilty to assaulting Joanne and depriving her of her liberty, and then sat in the glass-enclosed dock to listen to Mr Wild outlining the case against him. At the back of the court were Joan Falconio and Nick, waiting for Luciano to be called as the first witnesses to say the family had not heard from Peter since the Barrow Creek affair. Sitting not far away from the Falconios was Murdoch's faithful girlfriend, Jan Pitman, dressed in a bright yellow dress and clutching a handbag with a large photo of a Dalmatian embossed on it. Few realised the significance.

Mr Wild outlined the Barrow Creek story almost in verbal note form… 'puts the sack on her head, she's still struggling, the sack comes off, she's forced into the front of his vehicle…she is then forced into the back of the vehicle…' So there was that description of Joanne ending up in the rear of the vehicle, but with no explanation how it was actually accomplished.

The prosecutor left the jury in no doubt what Murdoch was up to as he travelled through outback Australia. He had gone into business with James Hepi to transport marijuana from South Australia to Broome, where it was sold. He preferred to avoid contact with the police when he was carrying cannabis and did not use credit cards. There was nothing new generally in what Mr Wild had to tell the court—until he came to the question of DNA.

Then came a bombshell new claim. Mr Wild revealed what, on the face of it, sounded like damning evidence against the defence. He claimed that, not only was Murdoch's DNA found on Joanne's T-shirt, but that a specialised technique by Dr Jonathan Whitaker from England had found a match with Murdoch's DNA on the gear stick of the campervan. Significantly, he added, Dr Whitaker had found a Murdoch DNA match on the inside of the layers of tape that made up the crude pair of handcuffs that bound Joanne.

Turning to face the jury Wild said: 'Now you might think there can be a casual contact between me and you in the street and somewhere or other I brush into you and I've got a hang-nail and a bit of blood and I put some blood on your back. But how did it get deep in here?' he asked in relation to the handcuff tape.

It was a powerful opening for the prosecution—and then it was Joanne's turn. She strode into the witness box, an air of confidence about her, dressed formally in a white shirt, black skirt and black high heeled court shoes. Her hair was tied back and anyone who didn't know her could have mistaken her for a personal assistant or even a legal secretary. Before she was led through the story of her ordeal, there was one matter the prosecution clearly wanted to deal with almost immediately and set it to one side: Joanne's affair with Nick Reilly. Yes, she said, while living in Sydney with Peter she had a 'particular friend' called Nick, whom she had met through colleagues at the bookshop where she was working.

'He was a good friend and we became close and we were intimate at one time,' she said, her eyes on the jury.

'Was Peter aware of the way that relationship went?' asked Mr Wild.

'No,' she replied. 'We were friends and we overstepped the boundary of friendship, but it ended and later we became friends again.'

The affair did not interfere with her relationship with Peter, she added.

Meanwhile in Britain, journalists were searching for Nick Reilly. Having established that his name was spelled differently from the initial 'Riley', they had tracked him down to a house in North London. Now aged 31, he refused to answer questions about his affair with Joanne and made it known through friends that he had been 'severely embarrassed' that his name had emerged in court. 'As far as he's concerned, he had absolutely nothing to do with what happened and he wasn't even on the same continent when the murder took place,' said one of his friends.

'He was appalled when lawyers introduced his name and used him as a stick to try and damage Joanne's credibility. He would never want to talk about his relationship with her. It barely lasted a month, after all.'

Having swiftly dealt with the infidelity, Mr Wild led Joanne through the story of her night on the Stuart Highway. The jury hung on every word as she told of her fear of rape from the the gunman who stopped her and her boyfriend and manacled her hands. 'I was so frightened. I was more scared of being raped than I was of dying and being shot by the man,' she said. Several times during her testimony she choked on her words and had to stop on two occasions to brush away her tears.

When asked if she recognised the man she said tricked her and Falconio into stopping their kombi, she glared across the courtroom at Murdoch.

'Do you see that man here today?' asked Mr Wild.

'Yes,' she said, 'I'm looking at him.' She stared at the accused man for several seconds, while Murdoch shook his head, indicating she was mistaken. She then appeared to mouth something at him, but her words could not be determined.

She described in detail her ordeal of having a gun pointed at her head and being bound by the gunman. It was only when Chief Justice Martin asked how she felt emotionally during the events that night that she found difficulty in finding her words through her tears.

'The jury has not had the experience of being stopped in the middle of the night on a dark road in the middle of the outback,' said the judge, asking her to tell the jury how she felt. What was she thinking when the gun was pointed at her?

'I kept thinking, "this isn't happening to me",' said Joanne. '"I can't believe this is happening." I felt alone, I kept shouting for Peter. I thought I was going to die.'

After being bound by the gunman, Jonne said she was led, following a violent struggle, to his vehicle, parked behind the VW, and pushed into the front cabin, through the passenger door. She tried to escape through the driver's door but the man's dog was in the way. 'Somehow he pushed me into the rear of his vehicle. I thought I got there from the cabin, maybe over some seats in the back,' she said, although she admitted later she was not sure if she had ended up in the back of the vehicle by being pushed through the canvas-covered side.

'You say you are not sure if you went around the side?' asked the judge.

In answer to the judge, Joanne said that what had caused her to doubt her initial statement—about how she got into the rear—was the fact that her own vehicle, the kombi, had front to rear access and she may have confused the two.

'I presumed that's how I got there. But as I had time to reflect after my initial statement I remember landing in the rear of this vehicle on my stomach and side. It is possible he may have pushed me through the side of the canvas.'

There was still no clear answer as to how she gained access to the back and there were questions about the way she had identified Murdoch that may have been noted by the jury. Joanne agreed that when she first saw the video picture of the man in the truck stop in Alice Springs she had dismissed him as being her attacker because she thought he was too old, but she now told the court 'it was the man who attacked me.' She had changed her mind because the police had shown her a better quality picture. She also picked Murdoch's picture from a group of 10 photos she was shown at a Sussex police station in England on 18 November, 2002—after she had earlier seen a photo of the suspected gunman on a BBC website.

Now it was the turn of Murdoch's lawyer Grant Algie, looking like a character from a Western movie with his shoulder-length wavy hair, to question Miss Lees. He started softly, asking her to describe the bullbars on the front of the gunman's vehicle before leading her on to the moment when she heard a bang—after Peter had climbed from the kombi to join the other man at the rear.

Then the man had appeared at the driver's door, climbing inside and putting a gun to her temple.

'Did you feel heat coming from the barrel of the gun?'

'No.'

'Smell gunpowder, anything like that?'

'No.'

Mr Algie pressed her on numerous details—was the gunman kneeling on the seat, did he put a knee in her back when he was restraining her with the handcuffs, did she fight him, how did she get injuries on her elbows if she had fallen from the kombi onto the ground face down?

There were moments, incidents, she could not remember or could not be sure about, but there were others she recalled clearly—how she reached up to try to grab her assailants testicles as he sat on her back beside the campervan and attempted to put tape around her ankles.

Was she satisfied with the picture put out publicly profiling the man who had attacked her—a man with long hair? No, said Lees she was not because she wasn't sure about his hair as he was wearing a cap, 'and I wasn't given as much time (with the artist) as I would have liked to have had'.

'Did you go back to the police and suggest alterations?' asked Mr Algie.

'I wasn't given the opportunity.'

Mr Algie continued. As the gunman led her to his four-wheel drive, did she look to see if Peter was between the two vehicles? 'No', said Lees, she had not 'because the man had his hand on my neck. He was slightly posi-tioned behind me, but turning his body, and I was looking where he was leading me, where we were walking to.'

Mr Algie pressed her further. 'You had heard a bang and seen a man with a gun and then the incident of the man on the ground'—a reference to the struggle she had after being dragged, or falling, from the kombi with the man sitting on her while trying to tie her ankles. 'You must have been concerned about Peter.'

'Yes.'

'You had last seen him behind the kombi, you believed looking or listening to the exhaust. And now you were being taken past the rear of the kombi towards the four-wheel drive where the lights of the vehicle are on...'

'... possibly they are on,' she interjected.

'Why didn't you glance to see if Peter was okay?'

'I was concerned for my own life.'

After the man had put a canvas bag over her head, she screamed and said she couldn't breathe and he had to loosen it, but she could not recall how it came off. She was pushed in backwards into the cabin of the man's four-wheel drive. There was a dog on the driver's seat and she ended up shoulder-to-shoulder with it. She was still screaming out, distressed and frenzied.

Now Mr Algie brought Joanne to the question that had puzzled Murdoch's friends—how she got into the back from a cabin that was sealed. The defence barrister reminded her that she had told the police she had been pushed from the cabin into the back area through a space between the two front seats. He wanted to know why she now doubted that claim.

The police, she explained, had told her that there was no such vehicle with front to rear access 'that put doubt in my mind. All I know is that I got from the front to the back quite easily and I did not walk around the vehicle. It is possible the point where he took the canvas bag from (under a side flap of the rear canvas) is also the possibility of how I got in.'

'Do you have any recollection at all of getting back out of the cabin of the vehicle?'

'No.'

'Do you have any recollection at all of climbing or being put into the back of the vehicle over the tray?'

'No.'

'Is it the case that your recollection is that you were pushed through a space between the seats?'

'I don't recollect it now. I just got from the front to the rear, not by my own steam. I was put there forcibly by the man.'

Mr Algie insisted on exploring this more, questioning Joanne about an interview she had with the police in which they had also asked her if she was sure she went from the front to the back, over the seats. The police had asked her to think hard 'about that bit. Concentrate.' Her answer then was still: 'Between the seats.'

She was asked about the driver who turned up at the Barrow Creek hotel the morning after the attack—the man I spoke to, Chris Malouf, who had camped near Barrow Creek. Despite him and pub owner, Les Pilton, both telling me she had carefully inspected Malouf and his vehicle, she told the court it 'all happened very quickly. It was a quick glance.'

Malouf was not named in court, but Mr Algie asked if she had rejected him as her attacker because:

1. There was no access from the front to the rear of his vehicle. To which she replied: 'I don't recall giving those reasons. All I remember is that it wasn't the man's vehicle and it wasn't the man who attacked me that night. I wanted to get inside (the hotel) and get on with my statement to find the man who attacked me.'
2. There was no bed: 'I don't remember saying that.'
3. The canopy of the man's vehicle was a darker colour, possibly black: 'I don't remember saying that.'

Mr Algie questioned Joanne at length about her descriptions of the vehicle and how those descriptions related to drawings that were made public. Her session with the artist was in the order of six hours, but in many of her answers to Mr Algie, she said that if there were discrepancies they were the fault of the artist. She claimed that the artist had told her at times that, 'it might have been like this, it must have been like that' and had made his own input into the drawings.

'The canopy appears rounded,' said Mr Algie, referring to one drawing. 'Was that provided by you?'

'No.'

'Can you explain how it came about it was drawn as it is?'

'No.'

'Did you tell (the artist) Mr Stagg that you felt around that circular shape in the back of the vehicle?'

'No.'

'And describe to him an inner circular shape?'

'No.'

'Did you tell Mr Stagg that you managed to bring your hands behind you when you were in the back?'

'No.'

'And it was then that you were able to feel the angle of the circular shape?'

'No.'

Mr Algie appeared to be getting nowhere with that line of questioning. Joanne gave the jury the final word on when she manoeuvred her hands to the front of her body—it was when she was in the bush.

The Englishwoman then told how after picking up a couple of Canadian hitchhikers near Uluru, the VW had developed a fault with the steering rod. She could not confirm Mr Algie's suggestion that the problem had been repaired with cable ties, although she said it was possible Falconio had cable ties in the vehicle.

In Alice Springs Falconio had gone to an accountant's where he had learned the bad news that he was not going to get a tax rebate and had heard that it was possible he who might owe money.

Now, for the first time, Mr Algie introduced a totally new scenario—the possibility that Joanne, Falconio and Murdoch had crossed paths at a fast food outlet in Alice Springs. He asked Joanne if she had seen Mr Murdoch in the Red Rooster, to which she said she had not—'why would I?' She did not recall bumping into or coming close to anybody or anyone speaking to her. Did she and Falconio go to a Repco car parts shop, across the road from the take-away premises? No they had not.

The defence barrister suggested to her that she and Falconio had left Alice Springs to travel north between 2pm and 2.30pm, judging by a phone call he said she had made to a friend, Amanda, in Sydney telling her she had been to the Camel Cup. Joanne said she couldn't remember telling Amanda that. This contrasted to the prosecution case that the couple had left Alice Springs some two hours later, at 4.30pm.

Mr Algie suggested it was more likely they had left at 2.30pm, because there was a receipt showing they had purchased petrol in Ti Tree at 6.21pm.

Based on an average travelling time in the VW of 55-58kph over the 197kms from Alice Springs, that would fit in with them leaving at 2.30pm.

The lawyer asked if after leaving Alice Springs they had stopped at the Aileron Road House, before Ti Tree. Joanne said they had not.

Shortly after lunch on the fourth day of the trial Joanne sat on the floor in front of the jury, her hands secured behind her back by a necktie. She had offered to show the court how easily it was to bring her hands to her front, even if her wrists were closer together than they were in the crude handcuffs. Despite Mr Algie's objections, the judge directed that the demonstration should go ahead. An inch or so separated Joanne's wrists and, lifting her bottom briefly off the ground, she completed the manoeuvre in one to two seconds. It was an impressive performance.

Back in the witness box and under questioning by Mr Algie, she was asked about a roadside fire she had referred to several times in the past. She could not say whether it was closer to Barrow Creek or Ti Tree, or whether it was a grass fire or a bush, but the blaze appeared to have been deliberately lit and far enough onto the road to cause Peter to manoeuvre the VW around it. Peter had suggested stopping to put it out but she had told him 'No, it might be a trap.' She offered no explanation to the court why she had thought that.

There was only one big proposition that the defence lawyer wanted to put to Joanne at the end of her three days of testimony: that Murdoch was not the man she had described, that he was not her attacker.

'At the end of the day,' she said, the defiance unmistakable in her voice, 'I was there. I know what happened...'

Her testimony had clearly impressed the Falconio family. Observers at the committal hearing and during the early days of the trial had noticed the chill between Joanne and the Falconios from the moment she had been forced to admit her infidelity nearly 18 months earlier. But now as she stepped from the court at the end of her evidence, she was flanked on either side by Peter's brothers Paul and Nick. A crowd of photographers fired away. There was no doubt this was a carefully stage-managed exit for the cameras, a show of unity.

And the next day, at the end of the first week of the trial, Joanne stood on the steps of the court and kissed Joan and Luciano on the cheek. It appeared a rift had been healed. But for all of them there were many weeks ahead and perhaps many new questions about the events at Barrow Creek.

Week Two

As the first week of the trial had proceeded, it was clear that the defence team was determined to show that aspects of Joanne's story were not credible. In the second week, as the first of the police witnesses began to take the stand, there were allegations of bungling and even more serious concerns: the alleged planting of evidence.

Joanne had stated clearly that she and Falconio had not stopped at the Aileron roadhouse as they travelled north from Alice Springs, but two witnesses called by the prosecution insisted in court that they had seen the English couple there. Although their descriptions of the couple were at odds with one another, Michael Oatley and Greg Dick said they had seen two young travellers arrive in an orange and white kombi, one even recalling a white pop-up roof. They could not be definite about the time, but they placed the couple's arrival between 3pm and 4.30. As the roadhouse is some 130km north of Alice Springs, their arrival—if indeed the couple was Joanne and Falconio—would have made it impossible for them to have left Alice Springs at about 4.30pm, as Joanne had claimed. The two men from the roadhouse had left a lingering impression in the court, Mr Oatley saying he was '90 per cent sure' that the couple he saw were the same as the two shown to him in photographs by police. And Mr Dick commented that although he 'didn't perve' on the woman that hard, 'I would say it was definitely them, otherwise they have a good set of twins in Australia.'

Joanne and the Falconio family were sitting in court when police played a 30-minute video of the Barrow Creek scene, shot the day after the incident. The camera, held by a crime scene officer from Alice Springs, focused on the bloodstain on the road before following a rough trail through the undergrowth, past head-high bushes and through knee-deep grass to the abandoned orange and white VW kombi. Slowly the camera circled the vehicle, peered in through the passenger's side window and moved on to pick up a scrolling pattern, painted on each side of the vehicle. For Mrs Joan Falconio, the camera's return to the bloodstain was too much to bear and she stumbled from the court in despair.

Mr Falconio, a small grey-haired man with a strong Italian accent despite the years he has lived in Britain, remained in his seat, although it was not difficult to imagine the torment he was going through. My mind went back to Colin Murdoch, Bradley Murdoch's father, who had passed away earlier that year, just a few months after I had last sat with him and his wife in their West Australian home. Two fathers—one grieving for a lost son, the other uncertain what would happen to his as he faced a murder charge—both gentle men whose worlds had collapsed as a result of the incident at Barrow Creek. Colin Murdoch would not survive long enough to find out the result of his son's trial. I could still remember his slight stagger as he rose to say goodbye to me. For Mr Falconio however, the anxiety was destined to go on and on…

It was such a tiny piece of physical evidence, but the issue of a lip balm container placed two crime scene officers under penetrating questions from Grant Algie. Joanne had told police that while hiding under a bush from the gunman she had reached into her shorts' pocket and removed a tube of lip balm and had then rubbed the waxy substance on her wrists in the hope of slipping her hands through the cable-tie handcuffs. She had failed to free herself of her bonds that way and had also been unable to chew through the tape that made up the restraints, spitting bits of tape onto the ground.

Senior Constable Ian Spilsbury recalled being asked to return to Barrow Creek the day after the video was shot at the scene because the lid of a lip balm container had been found. On his arrival, accompanied by Senior Constable Tim Sandry, he took close-up photographs of the lip balm lid, lying in situ under the bush where they suspected Joanne had hidden. Three months later, in October 2001, other officers found the main container of the lip balm, containing the waxy balm itself, under the same bush. This appeared to be absolute confirmation that this was the bush under which Joanne had hidden and helped to support her story of the events of that night in July.

Mr Algie, however, was having nothing of it. He wanted to know why Senior Constable Spilsbury, taking close-up photographs of such a tiny item as the lip balm lid on his first visit to the bush, had failed to notice the rest of the container.

'Certainly we looked under the tree,' said the police officer. 'If we'd seen the lip gloss we would have collected it.'

'Is that because there wasn't a lip gloss there?' asked Mr Algie.

'I don't know,' replied Senior Constable Spilsbury.

Later the officer was asked if he knew whether 'someone' had put the lip balm container and a piece of tape, which Joanne said she had chewed from the crude restraints, under the tree. It was as good as asking if it had been planted there. Senior Constable Spilsbury replied: 'No.'

Asked why he had failed to look around for the rest of the lip balm container when he had photographed the lid, Senior Constable Spilsbury said he assumed that other officers would carry out a detailed search, but they probably thought that he had searched the area. He admitted that it was a breakdown in communications.

While this questioning was continuing, my mind went back to the searches made by the Aboriginal trackers on the afternoon following the incident. The police had taken at least one of them to the place where Joanne said she had hidden and they'd had a good look around themselves. They hadn't seen any lip balm, but perhaps, I considered, the police had taken them to the wrong place. Learning how thoroughly they had looked at the scene, including examining blades of grass, it seemed curious that they had not discovered the lip balm lid or the main container.

As the case neared the end of the second week, Chief Justice Martin told the jury that there was a 'very relevant matter' for them to consider. He reminded them that Joanne had seen a photograph of the alleged murderer on a BBC news website in October 2002 while she was in Sicily—shortly before she returned to England and formally identified her attacker from photographs police showed to her.

The judge told the jury they should read the BBC article, which was printed out for them, when they considered the reliability of Joanne's identification of her attacker.

The defence's own attack on the police witnesses turned to the question of contamination of evidence. Prosecutor Rex Wild, QC, had already told the court that the inner layers of the handcuffs had contained DNA that matched Murdoch's but the defence were about to show how that could have come about.

After Murdoch had been arrested, Senior Constable Sandry was asked to fly with the handcuffs to Adelaide, South Australia on October 8, 2002. He placed them in two paper bags, to avoid spoiling any DNA evidence, and stored them on a shelf in an exhibits room at police headquarters. He put them there, he told the jury, because he knew he would be dealing with items seized from Murdoch's South Australian property and he wanted to keep the restraints away from all the other items.

'I knew I would come in contact with Mr Murdoch's possessions and there was the possibility of contaminating those cuffs,' said Senior Constable Sandry. They were left on the shelf, about three metres from where Murdoch's other possessions were stored, for three days.

From Mr Algie's questioning, it appeared that another officer from the Northern Territory, Superintendent Colleen Gwynne, had taken the hand-cuffs to the prison where Murdoch was being held. Senior Constable Sandry said that when she asked for the handcuffs he had not asked her what she planned to do with them.

'Did you impress on her the need to avoid contamination?' asked Mr Algie.

'I made her aware of contamination issues, but I didn't sit down and talk to her.'

'You didn't know she was going to go to the prison to see Mr Murdoch and take the cable ties with her?'

'No.'

The crime scene officer said the handcuffs were not DNA tested until three years after Mr Falconio was allegedly murdered. He had examined them shortly after the Englishman's disappearance, but he did not dismantle them until May 2004. His hours in the witness box led to a further revelation that when he was examining a piece of duct tape from among Murdoch's seized property, the tape was placed on a laboratory bench about 1.5cm from the handcuffs. This led to spectators in the court wondering if the items were that close they could have actually touched, spreading Murdoch's DNA which may have been on the tape to the handcuffs.

Senior Constable Spilsbury admitted that the cable-ties-and-tape handcuffs were an 'an important piece of evidence', yet he conceded a log book from the Northern Territory police forensic biology section may not have recorded every time he or another person examined the restraints.

The logbook also recorded that he had examined the restraints for two days in February 2002—when, in fact, he said he did not work on them.

He also agreed with Mr Algie that there appeared to be no entries in the logbook about who had come into contact with the handcuffs after October 2002. It is known that the handcuffs were sent to the UK for testing 18 months later and Mr Algie wanted to know why there were no further entries in the log book. 'Is the reason there is no entry because from a forensic science point of view the cable ties were no longer of biological importance?' he asked.

Chief Justice Martin intervened before the police officer could answer, saying he was not going to allow the question, but told Mr Algie, 'It is a very good point you have made to the jury.'

Week three

Mr Algie, the longhaired lawyer variously described as 'the third Bee Gee' and 'a southern gentleman', was aware that the prosecution would be calling witnesses to reveal scientific findings. He would need to continue making 'good points' to the jury as he faced up to a challenging third week of the trial.

He knew the prosecution would allegedly place his client at the scene—and in the kombi itself. Crucially, there would be a British expert who would—in his opinion—add support to Rex Wild's opening statement that Murdoch's DNA had not only been found in the vehicle, but deep within the layers of tape that made up the handcuffs.

First, however, the court heard grim evidence from a witness who was not even there—at least not in person. Forensic pathologist Dr Noel

Woodford, who has dealt with scores of gunshot-wound victims, appeared on a video link-up from Melbourne. He gave his expert opinion on what may have happened to Peter Falconio if he had been shot in the head and explained why there would be no evidence—such as bone fragments or brain matter—at the Barrow Creek scene.

Based on Joanne's recollection of seeing a revolver in her assailant's hands, Dr Woodford said that if a .22 had been used to kill Mr Falconio, the bullet would not necessarily have exited from his head—if that indeed was where he had been shot. He explained that a .22 bullet had a comparatively low velocity and rather than going straight through the victim's head would 'ricochet around the inside of the skull.' It would not necessarily even pass through the body if Mr Falconio were shot there. If the bullet entered his chest it would lose a lot of velocity if it hit a rib, the breastbone or the spine, where it might finally lodge.

Asked by the prosecutor about the flow of blood, resulting in the roadside bloodstain, Dr Woodford said the heart of someone shot in the head might keep beating, resulting in blood flowing from the entrance wound or from the nose, for instance.

The focus shifted to the police superintendent who took the manacles to Yatala prison, Colleen Gwynn. She insisted that the only reason she had done so was to have them on hand should Murdoch have agreed to a formal interview. They were kept on a side table, still within a paper bag, away from the prisoner when he entered a room at the jail and the bag was never opened.

'During the time you had these manacles with you, to and from Yatala, did you or any other officer in your presence interfere with them at all?' Mr Algie asked.

'No,' Gwynn replied.

'You did not contaminate them in any way with any other item?'

'No.'

'Put DNA on them?'

'No.'

'But you could have, couldn't you?'

She agreed that was always a possibility 'but I never did that.'

At that moment Murdoch shook his head and laughed silently.

Then it was the turn of forensic scientist Carmen Eckhoff, the woman called in to examine the campervan and the scene at Barrow Creek while the police interviewed Joanne in Alice Springs. Miss Eckhoff was in the witness box for the best part of three days, under intense questioning by both the prosecution and the defence. Yes, she agreed, the laboratory where Joanne's clothing and the cable-tie handcuffs were stored did have its shortcomings until the staff were able to move into new premises three months later. Important evidence was even kept in a freezer in a hallway, prompting her to concede that 'you had to be careful carrying samples in what was a public hallway.'

After describing her searches for blood and DNA on the road and in the campervan, Miss Eckhoff came under questioning from Mr Algie about possible contamination. She admitted that when she tested some sections of the handcuffs in May 2004—three years after the Barrow Creek incident—two of the samples returned no result, while a third sample returned a mixed DNA profile which included a positive match with laboratory director Dr Peter Thatcher and a profile from an unknown second contributor. Any testing at the laboratory was done with gloves, she said, but admitted it was possible that the director touched the restraints when not wearing any.

'How did that happen?' Mr Algie wanted to know.

'You'll have to ask him,' she said. 'I wasn't there when he was handling (the restraints). He has handled it on several occasions and he can say what happened. It could be that he handled it without gloves. There are a number of reasons.'

Was she concerned about the handcuffs being taken from her laboratory to South Australia? 'Yes,' she told the court, she was.

'Did you protest about the proposal they should be taken to Adelaide?' asked the defence barrister.

Miss Eckhoff replied: 'I was unhappy about them leaving my possession if the forensic examination may not have been complete. I made that known to Dr Thatcher.'

In fact, she added, she suggested that instead of the original item being taken to South Australia, a mock-up or a photograph could be taken instead. She had also made her feelings known to Superintendent Gwynn.

The scientist was questioned on how easy it would be to transfer DNA from one object to another, such as lifting a sample from a glass or bottle or even a cigarette butt and contaminating another object with it. She agreed it could be done 'if one was so inclined.'

Mr Algie suggested that once the handcuffs were out of her control there was very little she could do and that when they were returned to her no-one was going to tell her, 'I put Bradley Murdoch's DNA on them.'

If there was one witness many in the court were intrigued to hear from it was the much-touted Dr Jonathan Whitaker, who, it was rumoured, would present evidence that would be devastating for the defence. A tall slim man with a broad northern English accent, he had arrived in Darwin from his laboratory in Wetherby, Yorkshire, with files bulging with statistics. He used a unique system to search for DNA on exhibits when routine tests failed to produce any conclusive results. Simply put, Dr Whitaker's low copy number technique amplified weak DNA to give him a probability, or even a confirmation, of who had touched a particular object.

As the prosecution were preparing to call Dr Whitaker, the judge turned and told the jury that in relation to the kombi's gearstick, they had already heard evidence that it was not the whole of DNA which is examined, unlike having fingerprint evidence where it could be said a particular person was clearly identified. This particular DNA swab from the gearstick was very partial and at a very low level. It was a piece of circumstantial evidence, but as far as the tests went, the accused could not be excluded, the Chief Justice told the six men and six women of the jury.

Dr Whitaker spent several minutes agreeing with senior counsel Anthony Elliott as he outlined the scientist's long list of credentials, which included giving evidence in a large number of courts around the world. A Bachelor of Science in genetics, he was the co-author of scientific papers and he provided training to other forensic scientists. His laboratory, Forensic Science Service, was once part of the Home Office in the UK. For the past 14 years it had worked as an independent entity and could be called upon to carry out scientific interpretations for anyone. The DNA sites he and his colleagues examined were copied many times by a process of amplification, which produced numbers, making up a DNA profile.

The difference between Whitaker's method and routine DNA testing was a result that was more robust and reliable because the examinations were carried out in duplicate, Elliott explained.

So the stage was set to hear what Dr Whitaker had to say about swabs from the VW's steering wheel, the knob of the gearstick and a loop from the homemade handcuffs. It was not long before the court found that the whispers about his allegedly finding evidence of Bradley Murdoch being in the van and making the handcuffs were true. Dr Whitaker explained that his tests led him to conclude that the accused man had touched the gearstick and the handcuffs.

According to Dr Whitaker the likelihood of the DNA profile found on the gearstick not being that of Murdoch was 1 in 19 000. In respect to the electrical tape used to make the handcuffs, he said he had found DNA that was 100 million times more likely to be Murdoch's than anyone else's.

During a robust exchange with Mr Algie, Dr Whitaker defended his methods and at one point, when Mr Algie suggested he had mistaken one element of the DNA reading for another, declared, 'I am the expert.'

The British scientist's evidence was often complex, the jury hearing scientific descriptions of genetic make-up such as alleles, bands and stutters, as well as being shown graphs and documents filled with numbers.

Using words that anyone in the court could clearly follow he agreed with the prosecution barrister that his technique of amplifying low DNA traces had led him to conclude that Murdoch had touched the gearstick in the campervan and had constructed the homemade handcuffs from tape and cable-ties. As for the steering wheel, the swab he examined left him with a DNA mixture that had originated from at least three people. It was a type of mixture that did not have a major or minor contributor but he said he could not exclude Peter Falconio, Joanne Lees or Bradley Murdoch.

When examining a sample taken from the knob of the gearstick, he said there was evidence of two people touching it. He had been given DNA samples from Peter Falconio and from Bradely Murdoch, taken after his arrest in South Australia. Aside from Mr Falconio's DNA on the gearstick he found a 'foreign' band, which compared with Murdoch's.

'Could these results exclude Mr Murdoch as being the donor?' Dr Whitaker was asked.

'No.'

It was then time for the scientist to explain his findings on one of the central loops from the handcuffs. He recalled taking a sample from beneath two layers of tape and while doing this his expectation would be that he would find DNA from Miss Lees and from the person who had made the restraints.

He found a 'minor' match with Miss Lees and there was a second 'substantial' major DNA profile.

'Whose profile did that match in the areas where you got a result?' asked Mr Elliott.

'That profile matched Mr Murdoch,' replied Dr Whitaker.

The scientist agreed with Mr Algie that his laboratory in Wetherby was the only institution in the world that carried out his low copy number technique. But he said it had been recognised in a number of countries that the method had an 'absolute value'.

'Well, the FBI won't use it, will they?' asked Murdoch's lawyer.

'No, but I don't think that is significant,' replied Dr Whitaker.

During a heated question and answer session, Mr Algie suggested to Dr Whitaker that one concern the FBI had with the low copy number technique was that by amplifying the samples it also amplified any contamination on those samples.

The lawyer also said that another concern of the FBI was that any casual contact between a person and the victim before an alleged crime could leave a DNA trace that could be detected by the method used by Dr Whitaker. It was clearly a reference to Mr Algie's hint earlier in the trial that Murdoch may have bumped into Joanne Lees in the Red Rooster fast food outlet in Alice Springs—a suggestion she had denied.

Week Four

After a week of DNA evidence suggesting that Bradley Murdoch was involved in the Barrow Creek incident, the prosecution team were ready to enhance their case by calling the mechanic's former drug-running partner, James Hepi.

The burly 38-year-old Maori ambled through the courtroom to the witness box under the glare of the accused man, who was sitting in the dock a short distance away. The look that Mr Hepi—confident almost to the point of being cocky—returned left no doubt that there was no love lost between the two.

Admitting that he had once been a drug runner, carrying marijuana between Broome and South Australia, Mr Hepi's testimony did not vary greatly from what he had said about Murdoch at the committal hearing. It was the first time the jury had heard his account. Would the way this self-assured witness—with his own dark past—behaved as he gave his evidence have any influence on the six men and six women in the jury box?

Mr Hepi told the jury that he and Murdoch would take turns to make the 6000km drug-running round trip, transporting 4.5kg to 9kg of cannabis and taking different routes to avoid police. Sometimes they travelled across the Nullarbor Plain and through Perth, but their favoured route was through Alice Springs and then along the Tanami Track. They would take amphetamines to stay awake. Murdoch travelled the most kilometres—usually alone—with his dog Jack on the passenger seat beside him. By January 2001 both men had completed 'at least four trips' each.

Mr Hepi claimed that after Murdoch had finished a run in July 2001 he'd cut his hair, his 'mo' was shorter and he had put his four-wheel drive in for repairs, dramatically changing its appearance.

His partner's behaviour, said Mr Hepi, was 'scattered' because 'he'd been on the gear'—meaning amphetamines—'for four or five days, racing around the country.' Later, said the New Zealander, 'the moustache came off completely'.

Not long after Mr Falconio disappeared, he said, people around town were talking and Murdoch had said 'No, it wasn't me.'

Hepi added: 'Later on he offered up that the photo taken in the roadhouse was himself, that he had to be there.' The jury was then shown the security video from the Shell truck stop, taken a few hours after the Barrow Creek incident, 300kms away. The man seen buying ice and fuel, according to Mr Hepi, was Bradley Murdoch. 'There's a certain way in which Bradley walks: the way he was wearing the hat to disguise his face.'

Mr Hepi was then asked about the time he had seen Murdoch working in a shed on the South Australian property. He had been 'playing with zip ties,' he claimed. 'He was making manacles. He was making handcuffs with heavy duty zip ties, taped together. I don't know where Brad put them. They may have been the pair that were used, I don't know.'

Murdoch stared grimly, mouthing silently at his former friend as Hepi told of the conversation they had had about hiding a body: 'What would you do in the middle of the desert? Where would you put a body?'

The witness said he that had told Murdoch: 'Well, I don't need to, I run drugs, not kill people.' He claimed that Murdoch told him that hiding a body in a spoon drain was a fairly good place. The digging was easy because the drains were regularly worked over by machinery.

Despite their earlier friendship, they had a bitter falling out at a pub in Perth in late 2001 over a drug deal that had gone wrong. 'Drugs and money from one job never turned up,' Mr Hepi recalled. He claimed that Murdoch told him he had trouble crossing the border because police were 'looking for the Territory murderer'.

At that moment Murdoch shook his head animatedly and muttered what many in the court believed was 'You're a f—king liar.'

James Hepi turned to him and startled the jury as he yelled across the court: 'F—k you!'

'That's enough,' interrupted the judge. 'Enough.'

Mr Algie had attacked Mr Hepi's evidence at the committal hearing and he was not going to allow the former drug dealer to walk away lightly this time either. He asked whether it would be wrong to suggest he had been lying, fabricating and exaggerating his evidence.

'Yes, it would be wrong,' Mr Hepi replied, although he conceded that giving evidence to police had provided him with a 'get out of jail card' from drug offences involving 4.5kg of marijuana that he had faced in 2002.

'Would it be wrong to suggest you might be doing that in order to save your skin?' asked the defence lawyer.

'My skin is already saved mate,' the witness replied, turning his gaze towards Murdoch. 'I'm sitting here, he's sitting there,' (in the dock).

Then it was the turn of one of Murdoch's former lovers, Beverley Allan, 42, to take her place in the witness box. She told the jury that when Murdoch returned to Broome from a trip in July 2001 he appeared to be 'strung out', saying it had not been a good trip. There had been a few dramas and he'd suspected someone was following him. He had to 'deal with them'. She said she hadn't asked him what he meant by that.

Giving a new piece of evidence, Miss Allan said that in August that year Murdoch pointed out a photograph on the front page of a newspaper showing the man at the truck stop and his vehicle. 'He said it couldn't have been him because he was actually towing a camper trailer at that time. He told me that it wasn't him on the front of the paper.'

She told the court that she was still fairly convinced it was him in the picture because of the man's posture. 'When you know somebody, you know someone,' she said.

Mr Algie wanted to ask her about her reference to Murdoch being strung out. Wouldn't he be stressed, worried about police possibly busting him on the trip?

'I guess what they were doing was a stressful little business, wasn't it?' she agreed.

He also asked her about Murdoch's hair. 'He never had shoulder-length or long hair, did he?' the lawyer asked.

'No,' said Miss Allan.

He also asked, 'had he regularly changed his facial hair?'

'No, not in the time I knew him.'

Occasionally, and particularly during the evidence of Mr Hepi, details of the accused man's life slipped out from witnesses that the judge believed could place an unfair picture of Murdoch in the minds of the jury.

On three occasions he had to ask the jury to remain impartial and objective and not judge Murdoch's character from evidence about his alleged involvement with drugs, guns and an earlier matter, where he was acquitted.

Week Five

'Impossible!'

Bradley Murdoch's angry voice filled the courtroom for the first time as he denied involvement in the murder and disappearance of Peter Falconio.

His words were in a phone conversation secretly taped by police as he spoke to his parents and friends from prison between 2002 and 2003 after his arrest. In November 2002, he told his parents, Nance and Colin Murdoch, he could not be the man involved because he was in Western Australia less than 24 hours after the Briton vanished.

'If I was supposed to have done it from 11 o'clock to 12 o'clock, 20 hours later I have done 1700 kilometres through some of the roughest bloody dirt in Australia,' he argued. 'Impossible.'

In another phone discussion with his parents, Murdoch turned his anger on his former drug-running partner, James Hepi, accusing him of helping police to set him up for the crime. The authorities, he said, were trying to build a case up against him with lies. 'They've got a sample of this DNA,' he told his parents. 'But they are now trying to construct this case against me because nothing else adds up. This James Hepi has planted my DNA.'

He was aware of the allegations that he'd tried to disguise the look of his ute by changing the canopy after he arrived back in Broome from his trip down south, but he told his parents he'd already bought the aluminium a month before the Englishman disappeared.

'I was already building a new canopy before all this went on,' he said, admitting to his parents, however, that a 'hard, long battle' lay ahead. He was innocent, he told them. 'I don't care what happens. My close, immediate friends and my family and the rest of it know.'

The secrct tapes were played after the court heard from David Stagg, the art teacher called in by police to draw pictures of the gunman and his van, as described by Joanne. Admitting that he was 'no expert' at sketching guns, he recanted the evidence he had given at the committal hearing when he had testified Joanne had told him she moved her bound hands from behind her to her front while she was in the gunman's vehicle.

'I think I made a mistake there and I got that confused,' he said.

The trial had now reached its approximate halfway stage and as the prosecution witnesses came and went throughout the fifth week I was struck by how much the original story had changed ...

Joanne had been adamant from the outset that she had been thrust into the cab of the gunman's vehicle and had then been able to make her escape by squirming over the seats into the rear, before dropping out onto the road. She had since admitted she was not sure how she got into the rear, suggesting the gunman may have forced her in through the side of the vehicle. It was a vital part of her story that I had questioned very early on. Even at this stage of the trial, how she got into the back remained a mystery.

Then there was the dog. Subtly, as Joanne's story had been repeated over the months and then the years, the dog travelling with the gunman had changed from a red heeler type of animal, to one marked with grey patches and finally into a dog that had virtually morphed into Jack the Dalmatian. The description the jury heard was nothing like the original picture described by Joanne.

My reflections on the changes were brought on by the testimony of the artist, David Stagg, who had once so clearly repeated how Joanne had struggled in the ute to bring her hands to her front so that she could then reach up and feel the square shape of the canvas canopy.

Another change from the original picture came with the testimony of shoe impression examiner Paul Sheldon. At the very beginning of the investigation, police had called a press conference to tell of two footprints that had been found in the bush and both had matched Joanne's sandals. Now, however, Mr Sheldon was telling a different story. He had been able to identify four footprints, but only one was good enough to be analysed. He tried finding a match with Joanne's sandals and with shoes seized from Murdoch after his arrest, including work boots, ugg boots and moccasin slippers. None of the soles matched the footprint, but, he added, the size of the footprint matched that of shoes worn by Murdoch.

While the existence of the video footage of the man in the truck stop was not available immediately after the Barrow Creek incident, Mr David Ringrose, a Federal Police technical investigator—who has since carefully studied the blurry frames—told the court that he estimated the man seen entering the shop was 191cm tall, but possibly between 185cm and 196.5cm. Murdoch is 196cm, yet according to police at the time of the incident Joanne had described her attacker as being of medium height and build. Even taking Mr Ringrose's lowest estimate, the gunman appeared to have 'grown' since her original description, based on an average male height of 177.8cm.

On one of my visits to Broome in the wake of Murdoch's arrest, I had established—long before the jury heard Murdoch's taped comments about purchasing new parts for his ute—that he had ordered the materials before the Barrow Creek incident with the intention of upgrading the vehicle. I wondered whether the jury would be influenced by that information and whether mistakes by police in their investigation would also have a bearing on the decision they would ultimately have to make on Murdoch's guilt or innocence. The jury would not be aware of all the subtle, and sometimes major, differences that had arisen since Joanne told her original story but they would have heard the defence's criticism of the investigation, including the revelation that a cigarette butt found at the Barrow Creek scene had been carelessly tossed there by a police officer. There had also been the moment when a police officer was seen touching the kombi's steering wheel with his bare hands shortly after it had been removed to Alice Springs from Barrow Creek.

The judge advised the jury that it was 'quite proper' for them to take into account criticisms of the police work.

At the end of the fifth week of the trial, Justice Martin told the jurors it may be 'very relevant' for them to consider the failings of police to find key evidence, citing the time when they had not discovered the lip balm container and two pieces of tape in the bushes as one example of a legitimate area for defence lawyers to explore.

Turning to the six men and six women on the jury, the judge told them, 'You will appreciate from the cross-examination that there have been criticisms of the police investigation. It is quite proper for you to take into account those criticisms. There may be other areas that counsel will point to in due course.'

Week Six

The prosecution revealed that they were nearing the end of their witnesses, to which the defence came out fighting. They suggested that in the estimated two weeks of the trial to run they were going to attack every aspect of the Crown case.

In a dramatic new development at the end of the sixth week, Grant Algie asked police directly—and for the first time—whether they had planted DNA evidence to bring about an arrest. Police had already been asked before, of course, whether a lip balm container had been 'put' under the bush where Joanne said she had hidden from her attacker. The questions to Detective Sergeant David Chalker, however, marked the first time police had been asked outright about a corrupt act involving DNA.

'Did you put Mr Murdoch's DNA on the handcuffs?' Mr Algie asked after the court heard that Detective Chalker had accompanied Superintendent Colleen Gwynn to Yatala Prison in 2002 in the hope of interviewing Murdoch.

The detective replied: 'I really find that offensive and no, I would not.'

He also denied 'having a peek' inside the bag, saying he did not even have a quick look out of curiosity. The handcuffs were left on a bench in a room at the prison when Murdoch was brought in. The detective admitted that the arrested man's lawyer was not present at the time.

Statements were presented, and evidence heard, from men who had worked with Murdoch, travelled with him, or who had carried out changes to his vehicle after the Barrow Creek incident. Filling station attendants Melissa Kendall and Rob Brown added a curious twist to the evidence when they repeated what they had told the committal hearing. They were certain 'Peter Falconio' had walked into their Bourke premises a week after he disappeared.

The trial, was beginning to have a 'winding up' feel. Even some members of the public admitted that. There was a great deal of speculation during the lunch break and at the end of the week's events, whether the defence would call Bradley Murdoch to the witness box. Apart from denying his guilt—and a few swear words hurled at James Hepi—he had not spoken throughout the committal hearing or the trial.

Grant Algie gave nothing away. All would be revealed in the coming week. Whether there would be a 'surprise' recall—as was being suggested—would also be revealed. In any case, within about a fortnight, the world would know whether Bradley John Murdoch was going to spend the rest of his life in prison or was going to walk from the Darwin court a free man.

Week Seven

'Where did you bury the body?'

For a moment, Bradley Murdoch was stunned by the question from the Crown Prosecutor who launched into his cross examination after the defence called the mechanic into the witness box. Before Murdoch could reply, Grant Algie objected to the question on the grounds that it implied 'a fact that is simply not true.'

Mr Wild was not to be deterred and asked Murdoch if he had ever talked about burying bodies.

'No, I didn't,' came the reply.

'You buried Peter Falconio, didn't you?'

'No, I did not.'

Murdoch could not explain how his DNA matched the small bloodstain found on Joanne's T-shirt. 'I don't know whether I crossed her path or not,' he said, although he had earlier told the court that he had visited the same Alice Springs Red Rooster restaurant that Joanne and Falconio had called into on 14 July, 2001.

Grant Algie had decided, after a week-end of careful deliberation, to call Murdoch into the box. He calculated that it was as much his demeanour as his answers, and the facts the jury had before them, that would help them make up their minds about his guilt or innocence. Now the court was to hear his alibi for the first time. It could hardly have been more simple. Flanked by two security guards and dressed in a blue shirt and cream pants, he told how he had left Alice Springs at 3.30 pm and taken the Tanami Track more than three hours before the Barrow Creek incident.

Further, there were fundamental differences between his four-wheel drive and the vehicle in the security camera footage. His own truck had a different bull bar and he was even towing a trailer at the time he passed through Alice Springs. In addition, vehicle seen at the truck stop had a different exhaust pipe, mudguards and a side fuel tank, which his did not.

He was, he said, hundreds of kilometres away in a remote Aboriginal settlement, Yuendumu, 600kms west of Alice Springs, at the time of the incident. The track was rough, but he was not in a rush to get back to Broome.

'I'm not in a hurry, you're doing the Tommy tourist thing, you just wander along and everything in the back stays in the same position. It doesn't get broken and you know you're going to get out the other side of the Tanami.'

Nevertheless, Mr Algie had to put the question directly to his client: 'Did you have anything to do with the alleged disappearance of Peter Falconio?'

'No I didn't,' Murdoch replied firmly.

He was calm, confident even, as he turned frequently to the jury to give his answers.

Slowly, the events of that day in July, as they related to him, unravelled. He camped outside Alice Springs and drove into the town at about 10.30am. He spent part of the day in 'the Alice' buying food and petrol but he did not visit the Shell truck stop. In fact, he said, he had filled up with fuel about 11 hours earlier at a BP garage. He knew it wasn't him in the footage 'because I wasn't there.'

He stopped at a Red Rooster outlet to buy a chicken burger and a box of nuggets for Jack the dog. At 1.15 pm he went to a Repco motor accessories' shop where he bought two fuel containers, which was verified in court by an employee of the shop, who remembered the tall, taciturn customer. He bought some groceries and turned onto the Tanami track at about 3.30pm.

His visit to Alice Springs was among a number of journeys he regularly made as part of a drug run from South Australia to Broome. On this occasion he had nine kilograms of cannabis hidden in a secret compartment inside a long-range fuel tank. As a result, he said, he drove to avoid unwanted attention.

Denying that he owned a silver-barrelled, 'western-style' revolver of a type Joanne described as having been pointed at her, he agreed he had carried two guns—a 357 colt 'Dirty Harry' weapon and a black 38 palm-sized Beretta—in case anyone tried to rob him.

'There was other people doing it' (running drugs). 'Other people know what you're up to, so as a protectant.'

As he was giving his evidence, Joanne—who had been absent from the court at the start of his testimony—entered and stared hard at the big man in the witness box. She walked a few more steps then stopped and glared at him again. Murdoch appeared not to notice her.

'Yes,' he agreed, he used cable ties in the course of his work and they were the sort that had been used to bind Joanne's wrists, but, he added, 'There's not a workshop around that doesn't work with cable ties.'

He loved playing around with vehicles, which was why he changed the look of his four-wheel drive. 'Some people call it an obsession. You could call it a hobby,' he told the jury.

Despite speculation that Murdoch would be giving evidence for at least two days, his testimony was over on the first day. It was obvious that—if he had simply passed through Alice Springs and had taken the Tanami Track—there was nothing he could say about the Barrow Creek incident.

Now that he had been called however, he was open to attack by Mr Wild. First, there was that dramatic opening question by the prosecution about where Murdoch had buried the body. A further robust interrogation of the defendant followed. Mr Wild accused him of panicking and wrapping Falconio's head in a denim jacket he stole from the kombi so that he would avoid spilling the victim's blood when he loaded the body into his truck.

'You're a fastidious man, aren't you, Mr Murdoch?' asked Mr Wild.

'I'm a bit meticulous,' came the reply.

'You didn't want any blood in your vehicle. You used a denim jacket to wrap his head in.'

'No I didn't. I never had Peter Falconio in my vehicle.'

Mr Rice asked if Murdoch could offer any explanation for his DNA being found on Joanne's T-shirt and inside the cable ties. 'No,' said Murdoch, he could not.

'I suggest you pulled over the kombi and met the driver at the back.'

'No.'

'You shot him in the head. You threatened and assaulted Joanne Lees at that time.'

'No.'

'You forced her out on to the gravel on the side of the road, having tied her hands up with manacles. That's how your DNA was found deep inside those handcuffs.'

'No.'

'Despite forcing her into your vehicle, she managed to escape.'

'No.'

'You had to move the body on the roadway.'

'No.'

'That you didn't look for her very long because you were panicking.'

'No.'

'That you fled to Alice Springs to fill your car up.'

'No I didn't.'

'You deny you were at the truck stop. Is that because it puts you in the frame for this murder?'

'No, I was not at the truck stop.'

It was not an easy day for Murdoch as Mr Wild fired accusation after accusation at him.

The defendant was shown a recording of the truck-stop video and he admitted that many of his friends—even his father—claimed that it looked like him.

'There was a general conversation by people who said, "That looks like you, Brad", but I knew it wasn't me. End of subject.'

Mr Wild explained that the driver in the video even bought the same kind of items that Murdoch would purchase on his drug runs, including bottled water and a carton of iced coffee.

'I would never buy just one iced coffee and I don't believe in bottled water. I had plenty of my own in the vehicle,' argued the man in the witness box.

Murdoch's strong Australian accent filled the courtroom as he vigorously disagreed with prosecution claims that he could have 'easily' completed the drive from Alice Springs to Broome if he had left around 1am on the Saturday night of the attack. He could have been in Broome by 4 am on the Monday.

The accused man's testimony completed, Mr Algie called an Adelaide University professor, anatomist Maciej Henneberg, to tell the court that the man in the truck-stop video was not Bradley Murdoch. Comparing facial characteristics and body, Professor Henneberg said the head of the man in the video was larger than Murdoch's. He claimed that the man's body build, size and stature were also different to the accused.

A second facial expert, Professor Gale Spring from Melbourne, said the truck-stop images were of such poor quality and so small that they could not be analysed. It was not possible, said the professor, to even determine if a dark area under the man's nose was a moustache or sunken dentures.

Doubts were cast too, on the reliability of the British technique that claimed to find samples of Murdoch's DNA on the gearstick of the kombi and inside the cable-ties. Dr Katrin Both from the Forensic Science Centre in Adelaide said she had concerns about the British method. 'It was', she said, 'dangerous and unreliable'. She agreed that the FBI did not use it.

The final witness had been called. Eighty people gave evidence for the Crown, while the defence had called just five. Close to 350 exhibits were tendered. Soon the defence and prosecution would make their final speeches and the judge would sum up one of the more dramatic cases in Australian legal history.

I still had a mystery to solve: the ants and the blood. The Aboriginal trackers had wondered why there were no ants on the bloodstain at the roadside. 'Against all insect behaviour', they thought.

As the trial neared its end, Rob Brown—one of the trackers summoned to Barrow Creek in the daylight hours after the attack and who now lives in the Tennant Creek district—remained disturbed about what they believed were discrepancies at the scene. He and his fellow trackers, he said, remained baffled by the lack of clues offered up by the blood.

'I can't explain the ants,' he said. 'None of us can. We also cannot understand why we could not find any smudging on the edges of that pool of blood. You move a body away from blood there is going to be a smudge.

Why didn't anybody call us to the court to ask our opinion? We would have told them that we didn't like the look of that blood.'

A leading Aboriginal in Tennant Creek, David Curtis, who is Rob's uncle, also queried the bloodstain when I contacted him. 'I've done a lot of hunting and I know that if you pick up a dead roo or any kind of animal in the first hour or so, there's going to be a drop of blood pooling into the main area,' he said.

'If, as they say in the court, Falconio's head was wrapped up to stop the blood flowing, you're still going to get a smudge or a smear. You can't help it. And in the dark, with a man supposedly bleeding all over the place… well, Rob, me and the others we still wonder about it.'

Week Eight
The Defence sums up

The good news, Grant Algie said—as he rose and turned to face the jury on the morning of Monday 5 December 2005—was that his job was almost over. What he had to do now was assist the six men and six women of the jury to decide how they might reach a verdict.

'It is not an easy job,' he said, 'to sit in judgement of another individual charged with very serious offences.'

Bradley Murdoch had to be presumed innocent unless they, the jury, decided otherwise. The onus of proof remained at all times with the prosecution. Not only was an accused person under no obligation to prove anything, there was also the standard of proof: proof beyond all reasonable doubt.

Brad Murdoch should not be found guilty unless there was proof beyond all reasonable doubt. Innocent people had been found guilty in the past, he said.

So where should the jury start? 'One place,' he suggested, 'was that place 10kms north of Barrow Creek.' There was a limit to how much he could help the jury on that because, he said, 'Brad Murdoch wasn't there.'

Along with the absence of any blood spatter on the back of the campervan, Mr Algie suggested that the bloodstain on the side of the road could be a concern for the jury. 'Why wasn't there some sort of blood trail, or a dragging through the blood pool?' He said that while experts had told the court how there might be no blood spatter—and how a low-calibre bullet could bounce around inside a skull without causing any bone or brain matter to exit—the absence of spatter was another feature that didn't add up.

Mr Algie turned to three scuffmarks or impressions in the scrub. 'They might be footprints,' he said, 'but they were not the footprints of Joanne Lees.' Apparently they were not left by any of the eight pairs of shoes that police had seized from Murdoch. 'So who left them there, these three footprints?'

Continuing to cast doubt on the prosecution's case, he turned to what he said was a major feature the jury might think was a 'little odd': the fact that there was no body. The jury would be tempted to think that this was because the 'bad guy' had taken it away and buried it, but this was worthy of more analysis.

He presented the simplified scene: the British couple driving north of Barrow Creek when an unknown bad guy pulled them over. He didn't know them. It was completely random, unrelated to anything and—for reasons that were hard to understand—the bad guy shot Falconio at the side of the road. After trying to restrain Miss Lees, she escaped and the bad guy couldn't find her.

'So, you have the unknown, unrelated bad guy 10kms north of Barrow Creek. You have a dead man and you have the eyewitness hiding in the bush, who can't be found. You just go, don't you? You just get in the four-wheel drive and go. Why would you pick up a dead body, complete with blood presumably and put it in your car? Why would you do that? You'd have to be nuts. There is absolutely no rational explanation.

Whoever drove off with the body would have to expect there would be a significant and reasonable likelihood that the eyewitness was going to run onto the road, stop the first vehicle and raise the alarm.

How could it be expected that Miss Lees would wait for so many hours?

Was there something strange about the manacles?

Would not a perpetrator simply grab cable ties and go zip! What was the point of making handcuffs with three loops in the middle? Could it be that it allowed ease of movement of the arms from the front to the back? And why?'

'Look too,' Mr Algie urged the jury, 'at the injuries to Miss Lees' elbows. How could that have occurred when she was lying face down after the attack with her hands secured behind her? As the perpetrator was leading Miss Lees to the four-wheel drive—which had its lights on—she said she failed to see the body of Peter Falconio. The Crown case and her evidence is that he was shot at the back of the kombi, in front of the four-wheel drive. Surely she was bound to see where Peter was.'

Now it was the turn of Jack the dog to become part of Mr Algie's closing address. 'Have you ever heard of such a dog? It is sitting there in the car, not barking or sniffing but staring straight ahead. This is when a stranger is being pushed into the vehicle. This dog doesn't do anything. I struggle with an explanation for that, and, members of the jury, perhaps there are such dogs: guide dogs or such that sit quietly looking towards the front.'

If the gunman had taken the dog with him when he looked for the Englishwoman, why, he wondered, hadn't the dog found her? 'Dogs are good at finding people,' he said.

There were other issues he urged the jury to look at, such as the evidence of the schoolteacher, David Stagg. He told the court that he was mistaken when he initially stated Miss Lees had brought her hands from behind her to her front when she was in the gunman's vehicle. 'Do you think he might have just got it wrong when he gave evidence or do you think he is a man who is not entirely clear and has retracted and changed his story?'

What did the jury make of the evidence of the two Aborigines, Pamela Brown and Jasper Haines, who saw a white vehicle heading north? If it was the bad guy's vehicle, with the body of Falconio in it, 'where does that leave you with the orange kombi still on the side of the road?'

Who then drove it from the side of the road into the bush if the perpetrator had already driven off in his four-wheel drive? 'Is that not just a little curious?'

Continuing his line of 'unusual features' in the prosecution case, Mr Algie reminded the jury that the Crown would ask them to find that the prosecution had proved a case of murder when there was no body. They might think it likely that Falconio's body would have been found by now. The lawyer presented them with a time line that, he said, gave the bad guy very little time to bury the body, if indeed it was the perpetrator in the Shell truck-stop video. Assuming the Barrow Creek incident occurred between 8pm and 8.30pm, it would at best be around 9pm or 9.30pm before the bad guy left Barrow Creek and drove the 300kms to the Alice Springs truck stop, arriving at about 12.30am. That gave him three hours to drive that 300kms, but he also had to bury the body.

'If he has only half an hour spare, if he choses to drive off the Stuart Highway as you might think he would logically do, how much time does he have? Fifteen minutes, perhaps, to bury the body? The point I make to you is that—when you look at it—there is very little opportunity to get rid of the body too far away from the Stuart Highway for it to be found. Then there is the extensive line-searching by the police, line-searching hundreds of metres on either side of the Stuart Highway. They even found the remains of a kangaroo 53kms north. If there was a body it would have likely been found.'

He referred to birds of prey being attracted to a body and it was here that I too was reminded of the Aboriginal trackers who first arrived on the scene. Circling hawks would have been their clue to a body lying somewhere in the bush.

Mr Algie addressed the possibility of Falconio's body being in the four-wheel drive when it was parked at the truck stop, if that was indeed the gunman's vehicle. 'How,' he asked, 'could the man at the truck stop have any confidence that the alarm had not already been raised?' There was even a police car on night patrol there. 'The absence of a body is a legitimate concern when you are asked to consider a case of murder,' said the lawyer.

He was so worried about features of the bloodstain that he raised it again, reminding the jury that there were no drag marks in the pool, no blood trails, no blood spatter, despite Miss Lees saying she heard dragging noises while she was in the bushes.

There were also the claims by the couple from Bourke, Melissa Kendall and Robert Brown, who said they had seen a man who looked just like Peter Falconio. Miss Kendall, said the lawyer, was so obviously troubled by what she saw that she reported it to the police. 'Some people do disappear themselves for reasons best known to them,' he said. 'Sometimes they turn up later. Sometimes they don't.'

Why had the bad guy driven off with the body? 'There is no reason why Peter Falconio's body was in the four-wheel drive when it left Barrow Creek. There is no reason why the bad guy would take the body. Unless he (Falconio) wasn't dead,' Mr Algie said to the jury.

If the jury decided that Falconio was killed at Barrow Creek, the next question was: who did it? Was there any evidence that the man in the truck stop was the same man at Barrow Creek? The man at the truck stop could have come from anywhere and he was certainly not Brad Murdoch, said Mr Algie. It was known that Murdoch had gone to the Red Rooster shop—also visited by Miss Lees and Falconio—and there was a very real chance that his DNA could have been deposited on the back of her T-shirt without anybody knowing about it. A secondary transfer, perhaps? He had done some work on his vehicle, cut himself and left a small amount of blood on a doorframe or seat in the Red Rooster. 'How easily could that have happened?'

Mr Algie cast several doubts on the prosecution case. Miss Lees identified Murdoch in an official photo file after first seeing his image as a suspect on a BBC website. There would be a degree of suggestibility that would most likely displace any actual memory she had, he said. Prosecution experts, he said, could also get it wrong and he singled out the English scientist Dr Jonathan Whitaker, who said he had found traces of Murdoch's DNA inside the home-made handcuffs and on the kombi's gearstick swab. 'It may be that you take the view that experts telling us colonials that that is the way it is, because they say it is, is unsatisfactory.'

Contamination of the DNA samples was a serious concern, Mr Algie asserted. What confidence could anyone have in a laboratory that ended up with its director's DNA all over the handcuffs? How did Murdoch's DNA get inside the handcuffs? Mr Algie suggested they had been tampered with by police and reminded the jury of the 'extraordinary and unbelievable' journey the restraints had made to Yatala prison, where Murdoch was being held. Would police have contaminated them intentionally? 'There were four years before they were sent to England. It is possible police, or some-body who had access to these items, could have fitted them up.

The jury should not forget, either, he said, the events of some 20 years ago when experts gave evidence of foetal blood inside a car. He was, of course, referring to the Azaria Chamberlain case. The experts' opinions led to a conviction for murder. 'They were the experts, but they got it wrong.'

Referring to the 'extraordinary tale' of the lip balm lid, he found it almost embarrassing to suggest that two crime scene officers, having found the lid, would not search for the container. 'Of course they did!' Did someone plant the container later to make Miss Lees' story a 'nice neat picture'?

Mr Algie then declared that, 'It wasn't Murdoch at the truck stop because there were identifiable features of his vehicle that were different.' A glaring disparity was that there was no camper trailer in the video pictures. Murdoch, he said, had a trailer and he was not the sort of person who would leave it unguarded at the side of the road somewhere. Perhaps, he suggested, there had been 'movement away' from the initial description of the man at Barrow Creek. Even the prosecution now gave the notion that the gunman's vehicle did not have front to rear access and the canopy had changed to the colour green because Murdoch's was green.

Jack the dog came up again. Overlooking changes in Miss Lees' original description of a man with a brown dog, Mr Algie nevertheless told the jury that, after she had looked at the 'dogalog', police were looking for a man with an animal similar to a blue heeler.

'Bradley Murdoch has a dalmation. You can duck and weave as much as you like—a bit of kelpie or a bit of cattle dog—but to the casual observer that dog is a dalmation. His four-wheel drive didn't have front to rear access and his dog is a dalmation.' Bradley Murdoch did not have long hair either.

It was now Tuesday, 6 December. Mr Algie had one more thing to say before he concluded his address to the jury: a verdict of not guilty did not mean that Peter Falconio was alive or that Joanne Lees was a liar or that nothing happened at Barrow Creek. 'It could simply mean that something happened at Barrow Creek but we are not sure what it was...'

One thing was certain: no matter what the jury's decision, the puzzle of the speck of DNA on Joanne's T-shirt would linger. Why so little when she had described a violent struggle in her attacker's attempts to abduct her? Had he suddenly decided to pull on gloves? Why no flakes of skin or hair from the man? Why no DNA on the outer parts of the handcuffs or the tape around her ankles, yet there were those traces on the gearstick? Was he yanking his gloves off and on?

The Prosecution sums up

'He wasn't happy. He was strung out, very stressed. It hadn't been a good trip—a few dramas—he suspected that someone had been following him. He had taken a different route, he said, to go around roadblocks. What were the dramas? Who had been following him. What did he have to deal with?'

Those were the opening remarks of the Director of Public Prosecutions, Mr Rex Wild. As with Mr Algie before him, this was his last chance to convince the jury that his case, for the Crown, was the stronger.

'While Mr Algie had made a very fine speech,' said Mr Wild, he suggested that the jury might find it difficult to be confronted with allegations of police corruption and talk of conspiracies.

He referred to 'the most powerful piece of evidence against Bradley Murdoch', the DNA on Miss Lees' T-shirt. Three days after the Barrow Creek incident forensic scientists had extracted the DNA but there was no suspect to match it against. That was the case for at least 12 months. 'Who,' he asked, 'were the police trying to "fit up" between July 2001 and August 2002?'

Eager to quash the defence's allegations of evidence being planted, he said it was nonsense to suggest someone had put the lip balm container under the bush. If the police planted evidence, why not put Murdoch's DNA everywhere? There was not 'one tittle' of evidence to support corruption or conspiracies.

'I've heard it said many times that this is the Falconio mystery. There is no mystery. Peter Falconio died, the body was hidden, Joanne Lees was threatened, attacked, handcuffed by restraints, which were meticulously put together by someone with a great deal of time and patience.' Mr Wild continued, 'She was thrown out of the vehicle, hit the ground, punched and manhandled, then she escaped. You might guess what would have happened if she had not escaped. She would not have walked free.'

He added that the jury might think that the man who cleaned up the scene, who put the soil on the blood and moved the body was a meticulous man. Where was Peter Falconio? There had been a thorough search for the body. 'You know how remote central Australia is. It is not difficult to hide a body. One day it will be found. It might take some time,' he declared.

On hearing this, the Englishman's elderly parents, Luciano and Joan, who were sitting in the back of court began to weep. Their distress did not diminish as Mr Wild continued to tell the jury that on 14 July 2001, Peter Falconio had everything to live for: travelling on the trip of a lifetime with his partner, watching a beautiful sunset and looking forward to celebrating Joanne's birthday in Fiji. After the attack Miss Lees, hiding in the bushes, called out to Falconio in her anguish but he couldn't come. 'He has not disappeared himself,' said Mr Wild. 'He has been disappeared by Bradley John Murdoch.'

'Joanne,' he said using her Christian name, 'told the truth about a terrifying experience, even though the defence had suggested that—as there was no body—perhaps she knew more than she had told the court.'

The prosecutor indicated that she was extremely tired and stressed in the many hours after the event. There were reasons why she had, for example, expressed some doubts about how she had got from the front to the back of the gunman's vehicle.

'She is entitled to have some doubt. The fact is that this whole episode is one that none of us have confronted in our lives,' Mr Wild continued. She was in a state of emergency, fighting for her life and the jury should make 'proper allowances' for discrepancies in her testimony. She was not taking notes.

He reminded the jury of the story—as it had been relayed numerous times before—turning to the perpetrator, who he said had to be Bradley Murdoch. 'He carried guns as part of his "business", he had a four-wheel drive and there was plenty of time for him to get from Barrow Creek to Alice Springs to fill up his vehicle before taking the Tanami Track.'

He raised doubts about 'sightings' of the British couple at the Aileron roadhouse and in Bourke, pointing to discrepancies in the descriptions given by witnesses. As for Jack the dog, he said it was not a pure bred dalmation, neither was it a 'mad barking dog'. 'He's a good dog. People like Jack. The way he behaved in the front seat is how he would behave.'

People driving up the Stuart Highway did not all have dogs, did not all have guns, did not all have four-wheel drives, did not all walk with a slight stoop—as had been testified about Murdoch's gait. These matches were all part of the circumstantial case.

His voice dropping almost to a whisper at times as he leaned towards the jury, like a man holding a conversation with friends, Mr Wild said: 'There are a lot of coincidences there for you to consider and the Crown submission to you is that they are not coincidences. They are part of the circumstantial case, circumstances you can use in relation to Bradley Murdoch, finding he was the man.'

'The difficulty for Murdoch,' he maintained, was this: 'how did his DNA get onto Miss Lees' T-shirt? That DNA was damning evidence. It really is the lynchpin in this case.'

A man assaulted Joanne Lees, wrestled with her, was into her back, was all over her. Her head was down between her knees and he was trying to put the handcuffs on her. The same applied when she was walked along the bitumen towards his vehicle with her hands behind her, his hands on her neck, forcing her into the vehicle. It gave that man the opportunity to plant blood from a scratch on her.

'You can have a little bit of doubt about this or that, but this (the DNA) makes all those doubts no point, because it ties this man to this woman on this day. What the data says is that the DNA that Bradley Murdoch has matches exactly the DNA which is found in the blood smear on Joanne's T-shirt. We have an exact match. You have been told what that means. It is an astronomical figure.'

There was also DNA on the kombi's gear stick, although it was a 'mixed bag' and the percentages were not so great. There was also the DNA, matching Murdoch's, deep inside the manacles: 'exactly where you would have expected the maker of the cable ties to leave his DNA.' He added, 'It doesn't fly through the air, this DNA. It is not a miraculous thing that flies around the skies. It has to be transferred in a very positive way.'

The defence said there was a very real possibility that any blood could have been transferred at the Red Rooster in Alice Springs or Ti Tree, that it could have been accidentally deposited without anyone knowing about it.

'The Crown says that is the most remote possibility. You might think we are wrong, but there has been no suggestion that they were there together or that she bumped into a wall or chair where he was. He says he was there at 10.30am. There are no receipts, only cash. This is a time carefully selected, you might think, to cover the whole day that she might have been there.'

'Any part of the DNA evidence might be capable of explanation,' said Mr Wild, but the strength of the three pieces of DNA—on the T-shirt, the gearstick and the handcuffs—came not from looking at them alone but together. 'Look at it all together and it becomes a collective, powerful, *powerful* piece of evidence.'

Now he was ready to bring all his arguments on the DNA together. If Murdoch was completely innocent, it would be an unfortunate series of events if his blood got onto a wall or chair at the Red Rooster and happened to become smudged onto the back of the T-shirt of the young woman. A young woman who just happened, later that day, to find herself in the back of a four-wheel drive belonging to a man who happened to look like Murdoch and who had a dog. The attacker, Mr Wild continued with his proposition, left no DNA on her but Murdoch, who accidentally left his DNA in Alice Springs earlier, did leave a sample. 'How unfortunate,' said Mr Wild, the sarcasm ringing in his voice. He was not finished.

He asked the jury to ask themselves how, somehow or other, some other person, perhaps the person who was responsible for the attack, deposited DNA matching Murdoch's on the gearstick and then drove off. 'How unlucky would he be in these two sets of circumstances?' There was more, a third circumstance. In the most remarkable of coincidences, that same DNA turns up deep inside the cable ties.

'You are asked to conclude that all that came about by innocent means, that Mr Murdoch is in no way connected to the crime. The combination of those three things makes a powerful case. All of this, ladies and gentlemen, all of his DNA is on top of an identification of this man by Joanne Lees, the vehicle he has, the gun he has...'

The Prosecutor was ready now to move into the closing part of his speech, words he hoped would convince the jury to send Bradley Murdoch to jail, for perhaps the rest of his life.

He returned to the hours after the attack, when there was a gunman on the loose in the Northern Territory. Police were looking for him. It was a massive undertaking with roadblocks set up. This man had to be found. He had killed somebody. A woman had been tied up and managed to escape, but this man was out in the bush somewhere and the police feared that they might be too late to catch him. They had lost four or five hours already by the time the brave woman went out onto the road. The best the police could do was put up roadblocks on the arterial roads. By the time they were set up it was daylight and the man was long gone.

'You would think that, if this is the action of a crazed gunman, he would be found pretty quickly, but this man is not a crazed gunman,' asserted Mr Wild. 'This man is cunning, alert, a practised driver, fit, awake with speed, able to move quickly and get away. He is a fastidious man, as you know, and he is concerned to clear that scene as best as he can, as quickly as he can. He tries to hide the blood, moves the body to a safe place, a place where it has not been found since. The possibilities of the police getting him are pretty slim.'

Here Mr Wild paused dramatically to reach back and tap his black gown at a point behind his shoulder. 'Except,' he said, 'for the DNA on the T-shirt.'

What though, was the motive? The court had not heard Mr Wild's thoughts on this. When they came, they were not defined. The Crown could not tell the jury exactly why the English couple were attacked, he said, except that it had to be premeditated because the handcuffs were pre-made some time before. He raised the possibility that—based on a conversation Murdoch had with Bev Allan, his girlfriend of the time—he may have thought someone who was after his marijuana was following him and he had to deal with it.

There was another possibility: he had decided to attack who he thought was a single woman travelling on her own, after seeing her driving the kombi earlier while Peter Falconio slept in the back.

'Murder by its nature happens in the pitch black of night. There is no-one there to see it. The man who shot Peter Falconio,' he said, 'must have intended to either kill him or do him grievous harm. Put all the circumstances together and the Crown submission is that while you or Joanne Lees did not see it happen, you can use the circumstances to find Bradley Murdoch guilty of murder.'

Before he sat down, Mr Wild looked carefully at the jury—as if as an afterthought—and asked: 'What type of person would manufacture those handcuffs, try to hide the blood, clean up the scene, try to prevent blood going into his car—perhaps using Joanne Lees' jacket—and dispose of the body in such a way that it would not be found for a long time? He would be a meticulous, perhaps obsessive person. Someone just like Bradley Murdoch.'

The Chief Justice directs the jury

At last the Prosecutor sat down and Chief Justice Brian Martin began giving his directions to the jury in a case that was every bit as sensational as the death of Azaria Chamberlain.

It was to be a very detailed summing up, examining the central points of both the prosecution and the defence. He would turn to a matter raised by the prosecution, refer to the submissions by the defence and put to the jury what they might care to consider.

Had the prosecution proved this point? Did the defence have a good argument against it? That was how he proceeded throughout his address, constantly making it clear to the jury that each claim by either Mr Wild or Mr Algie was, ultimately, 'a matter for you'.

In the early stages of his summing up, Justice Martin was forced to pause as the missing Englishman's mother abruptly rose from her seat and hurried from the court with her ears covered. The dramatic interruption came as the judge referred to evidence that had been presented about the effects of a gunshot wound to the head—how a bullet could bounce around inside the skull without necessarily causing an exit wound.

Noticing the disturbance at the rear of the court—where Mrs Falconio had been sitting with her family—Justice Martin stopped and allowed the distressed mother to leave. Turning to the jury, he said they may have seen members of Peter Falconio's family leaving the courtroom from time to time. 'This evidence is distressing for someone in the position of Mrs Falconio,' he said. 'You must put aside an emotion that you see in other people or that you might feel and decide these questions purely objectively and not be influenced by those emotions.'

'The evidence of Joanne Lees,' the Chief Justice said, 'was the critical link. It comes down to whether you accept the evidence of Miss Lees without a reasonable doubt.' He warned the jury that they should approach the identification of her attacker as Murdoch with caution, because she had first seen his photo in a news story on the Internet.

As another example of the care they had to take, he cited the evidence of James Hepi, saying it would be 'dangerous' to rely on what he had said because he was 'not a person of integrity or good character'. He had a motive to implicate Murdoch because they had fallen out and Hepi believed Murdoch had 'dobbed him in' to the police. In addition, Hepi had said he would seek a reward for giving police information about Murdoch if the accused man was convicted.

It was Tuesday morning, 13 December, before Justice Martin reached the closing stages of his fourth day of summing up. He urged the jury to put aside 'flamboyant suggestions' by the defence counsel, who had said the court did not need experts from the mother country to 'teach us colonials a thing or two.' Justice Martin added, 'Please put aside the hyperbole and concentrate on the evidence before you.'

He examined in detail the evidence of the DNA, raising a number of questions about how it could have been left on the T-shirt, inside the cable-ties and on the kombi's gear stick. The defence had raised the possibility of it being left accidentally in the Red Rooster shop. The prosecution had said this was nonsense. While the defence had also suggested that the DNA might have been planted on the cable-ties, the judge reminded the jury of the Crown's proposal that it would have been very unfortunate if Murdoch's DNA had been accidentally left on a seat, smudged onto the T-shirt and then Miss Lees was attacked by someone else who did not leave his DNA on her or on the gearstick.

While he had examined each DNA item separately, Justice Martin stressed that the jury should consider the impact of the evidence in its entirety. It was a point he had made, and would make again, during his summing up.

At 12.50pm on Tuesday, the jury left the court to consider their verdict.

What was the mood of the public and the media as they filed from the court building? Most tended to agree that the verdict would go against Bradley Murdoch, although some suggested that—while he would be found guilty of assaulting Joanne—he would be found not guilty of murdering Falconio. Nobody had seen him do it. Not even Joanne.

Murdoch's faithful girlfriend, Jan Pitman had remained in court throughout each day of the evidence. Now she wandered through the Darwin mall in a red blouse, her face glum. She was not feeling good about the forthcoming verdict. 'The jury are dealing with a man's life here and what they've heard is a load of bullshit,' she said, fighting her emotions. 'It's just bullshit.'

The Verdict

The jury returned at 5.15pm, after four and a half hour's deliberation, to ask for clarification on a verdict of guilty without a body. It appeared from the question that they were asking themselves if they could reach such a verdict. This was seen as a clue to which way the result was going to go. Justice Martin told them that the absence of a body was not a bar to a guilty verdict of murder.

The jury retired again and the anxious waiting began for friends and relatives on both sides of the drama.

At 8.45pm, Justice Martin reconvened the court. In the jury's absence he suggested that—since they had been deliberating for eight hours—he was happy for them to retire for the night.

When the jury came back into the court—and Justice Martin was in the process of suggesting they could stop for the evening if they wished—a bailiff of the court approached and told him they had, in fact, reached a verdict on all three counts: murder, assaulting Joanne Lees and depriving her of her liberty.

In front of a packed court—there was standing room only at the back of the room—Justice Martin asked the foreman, if they were unanimously agreed on a verdict?

'Yes we are,' said the foreman.

The charges were read out again for everyone to hear...

On count one: that near Barrow Creek in the Northern Territory of Australia, Bradley John Murdoch murdered Peter Falconio...

'Guilty or not guilty?' asked the Chief Justice.

The juror's voice came back strongly: 'Guilty.'

It seemed that the result of the other charges was academic. Even as guilty verdicts for the other charges followed, Joanne leaned forward and put her head in her hands as if in gratitude. Mr Falconio's brother, Paul, put his arm around her shoulder while his parents, Joan and Luciano, turned to grip her hands in a gesture of support. They also shook hands with their sons Paul and Nick.

Murdoch, wearing a blue shirt and beige trousers, sat without emotion. He had not even been asked to stand when the verdict, which Justice Martin said he entirely agreed with, was announced. It was as if he expected the Chief Justice's next words: 'You have been found guilty by a jury of the crime of murder. There is only one judgement that is practised by the law in the Northern Territory and that is imprisonment for life.'

Before he was led away from the court for the last time Bradley John Murdoch looked across to Jan Pitman and just shrugged his shoulders.

Outside the court Grant Algie made it clear that he was disappointed at the result and planned an appeal.

They stepped out from the court later under the glare of television lights and camera flashes: Joanne Lees in the centre, flanked by the two Falconio brothers and Peter's parents. They offered their thanks to all who had supported them, but there was one request Joanne wanted to make... to the convicted man himself.

'I would like Bradley John Murdoch to seriously consider telling me, Joan and Luciano and Pete's brothers what he has done with Pete,' she said.

It was the conclusion, she added, of an intense period of distress for her and the Falconio family that would enable them to take another step in the grieving process for Pete.

Upstairs, near Court Number 6 where the man she had waited for so long was being led away for life, Jan Pitman wept in a corner...

On the Stuart Highway north of Barrow Creek, the stain that was Peter Falconio's blood has faded. The Aboriginal trackers, however, whose ancient skills were not called into evidence, still ask how a body was removed without drag marks or any kind of blood trail. The mystery endures.